THE RISING

The Complete Story
of Easter Week

BY

DESMOND RYAN

GOLDEN EAGLE BOOKS LIMITED
STANDARD HOUSE, DUBLIN

First Published, Easter, 1949
Second Edition, October, 1949

PRINTED IN IRELAND
BY CAHILL & CO., LTD., PARKGATE PRINTING WORKS, DUBLIN
FOR GOLDEN EAGLE BOOKS, LTD., STANDARD HOUSE, DUBLIN

N
W
E
S
Archbishop's Palace
Croydon Park
Mountjoy Prison
Ballybough Bridge
Annesley Bridge
Rotunda Hospital
Parnell Monument
Amiens St. Station
Pro-Cathedral
Nelson's Pillar
General Post Office
Liberty Hall
Custom House
North Wall Station
Tivoli
Kelly's Corner
River Liffey
Fire Brigade Station
Bank of Ireland
Telephone Company
City Hall
Trinity College
Westland Row Railway Stn
Ringsend
Dublin Castle
Mansion House
Shelbourne Hotel
Merrion Square
Boland's Mill
College of Surgeons
St. Stephens Green
Clanwilliam Place
School House
Irishtown
Childrens Hospital
Haddington Road
Beggars Bush Barracks
Harcourt St Railway Station
City of Dublin Hospital
Alderman Kelly's Shop
Carrisbrooke House
Trinity College Botanic Gardens
Davys Public House
Portobello Bridge
Portobello Barracks
Ballsbridge
Royal Dublin Society Bld
Whitworth Road
Clonliffe Road
Royal Canal
Mater Hospital
Great Northern Railway
Fairview Strand
Philipsburg Avenue
Drumcondra Road
Grace Park Road
Dorset Street
River Dodder
Dublin & South Eastern Rly.
Clyde Road
Dublin South Eastern Railway

THE RISING

Contents

		PAGE
I.	THE ROAD TO INSURRECTION	1
II.	GERMAN AID AND THE INSURRECTION	14
III.	CASEMENT IN GERMANY	30
IV.	THE KIDNAPPING OF JAMES CONNOLLY	47
V.	A MOST OPPORTUNE DOCUMENT	64
VI.	EASTER EVE	76
VII.	WHY THE ARMS LANDING FAILED	101
VIII.	THE CITIZEN ARMY FIRES THE FIRST SHOT	115
IX.	AT THE GENERAL POST OFFICE	124
X.	AT THE MENDICITY INSTITUTION	155
XI.	MACDONAGH AND MACBRIDE AT JACOBS	164
XII.	CEANNT AND BRUGHA AT THE SOUTH DUBLIN UNION	172
XIII.	DE VALERA AT BOLAND'S MILLS	187
XIV.	MOUNT STREET BRIDGE : " THEY SHALL NOT PASS"	193
XV.	EDWARD DALY TAKES THE FOUR COURTS	203
XVI.	THE BATTLE OF ASHBOURNE	218
XVII.	THE RISING IN THE COUNTRY	228
XVIII.	PEARSE ORDERS THE SURRENDER	251

APPENDICES

		PAGE
I.	PEARSE'S COURT-MARTIAL AND LAST SPEECH	258
II.	THREE SPEECHES OF CONNOLLY	261
III.	THE EXECUTIONS	263
IV.	VOLUNTEERS AND CITIZEN ARMY MEN KILLED DURING THE RISING	265
V.	THE POSITION IN THE WEST	265
VI.	THE RISING AND ULSTER	267
VII.	THE CONNOLLY KIDNAPPING	268

INDEX 269

CHAPTER I

THE Supreme Council of the Irish Republican Brotherhood held a meeting in the middle of August just after the outbreak of the war between the Allied and the Central Powers and decided to organise an insurrection in Ireland before the war ended. And within two years they organised an insurrection that changed the history of Ireland. Their leaders were then unknown, their organisation numbered no more than two thousand men, and even a year later, the strength of the open armed movement of the Irish Volunteers which they had originally inspired, and whose higher ranks they controlled, numbered no more than 18,000 throughout the country.

Insurrection in 1914 was a dead word so far as Ireland was concerned. Robert Emmet had tried it in 1803, Smith O'Brien, Mitchel and Meagher in 1848, the Fenians in 1867 and all had failed. There was a popular flourish of the constitutionalist orators of the day about the short way in which a British Government could deal with any nonsense like that, one battleship in Galway, one in Dublin, two shells from their guns that would meet in Athlone, and grind all tinpike men to powder. Even war on the grand scale was regarded as unlikely in an enlightened age. Yet in 1914 war broke out and lasted four years, and for a week the insurrection of Nineteen Sixteen flamed up in the midst of it all.

Then the road to the Rising was plainly seen. The British Government set up a Royal Commission of Inquiry. During the sessions the name of John Devoy of the Clan na Gael in America was mentioned, and a learned judge asked, and could get no definite answer: "Is that the same old Fenian who created so much trouble during the Land League in the 'eighties?" Mr. Augustine Birrell, Chief Secretary for Ireland, gave an eloquent explanation which began: "The spirit of what to-day is called

Sinn Féinism is mainly composed of the old hatred and distrust of the British connection, always noticeable in all classes and in all places, varying in degree and finding different ways of expression, but always *there,* as the background of Irish politics and character." He explained in answer to a question that Sinn Féinism was not an excuse to dodge the war: "No—Sinn Féinism is spread all over the place. ' Leave us alone ' that is what they call it. They are sick of Parliamentary Parties. They say: ' Leave us alone. We are tired of all this talk. We shall never be happy unless we are allowed to develop ourselves in our own way.' "

For two reasons the question was an unnecessary one. The seven signatories of the Republican Proclamation had been executed. An inevitable rope was hanging over Roger Casement's head. Dublin's centre lay in ruins from British artillery and six days' fighting. So there was no relevance in discussing people who dodged wars. Very soon a ballad was to be heard, some lines of which ran:

> *Right proudly high over Dublin Town they hung out the Flag of War,*
> *'Twas better to die 'neath an Irish sky than at Suvla or Sud-El-Bar. . . .*

Then Mr. Birrell in his own way had mapped out the road to the Rising, though he had said before in the House of Commons that above all things the Irish people must not be misled into confusing that road with the fine roads Robert Emmet, William Smith O'Brien, the Fenians had trod in the bad times gone by. Yet his map of the 1916 road was a very fair one in its way, stages, place names and general route, even if some details were blurred, more omitted, and colour lacking generally:

"This dislike, hatred, disloyalty (so unintelligible to so many Englishmen) is hard to define but easy to discern, though incapable of exact measurement from year to year. You may assume it is always there and always dangerous. Reasons are often given for its persistency despite of efforts to obliterate it. Had Catholic Emancipation accompanied the Act of Union, had Land Tenure Reform been ante-dated half a century, had the Protestant Church of Ireland been disestablished a little more to please the Irish people, and not so much to gratify the British Noncomformist, had the university question been earlier settled, it is possible though not obvious, that this spirit of Sinn Féinism might by now have been exorcised. It had in point of fact been immensely weakened and restricted, and out of many Irish breasts it may perhaps have been removed altogether.

"The last twenty years have worked transformation. The face of the country is changed. . . . And yet despite all these things, and in face of prosperity among the farmers, cottages for the labourers, and control over her most important affairs, no close observer of Ireland as a whole, during the last two years or so could fail to notice that this Sinn Féin spirit was increasing. For a number of years the Home Rule controversy, which seemed at last to be on its way to a Parliamentary solution, absorbed most of the energies of active politicians, whilst those who were out of real sympathy with a movement which seemed to them limited and unromantic, were content to allow the controversy to be conducted in Parliament by able leaders and to run its course, whilst they stayed at home and attended to or at least supported the Gaelic League and other kindred and influential societies. This period was also marked by a genuine literary Irish Revival in prose, poetry and the drama which has produced remarkable books and plays and a school of acting, all characterised by originality and independence of thought and expression, quite divorced from any political Party, and all tending towards, and feeding latent desires for, some kind of separate Irish national existence. It was a curious situation to watch, but there was nothing in it suggestive of revolt or rebellion except in the realm of thought.

"Indeed it was quite the other way. The Abbey Theatre made merciless fun of mad political enterprises, and lashed with savage satire some historical aspects of the Irish Revolutionary. I was often amazed at the literary detachment and courage of the playwright, the relentless audacity of the actors and actresses, and the patience and comprehension of the audience. This new critical tone and temper, penetrating everything and influencing many minds in all ranks, while having its disintegrating effects upon old-fashioned political beliefs and worn-out controversial phrases, was the deadly foe of that wild sentimental passion which has once more led too many brave young fellows to a certain doom in the belief that any revolution in Ireland is better than none. A little more time, and but for the outbreak of the war, this new critical temper, would, in my belief, have finally prevailed, not, indeed, to destroy national sentiment (for that is immortal) but to kill by ridicule insensate revolt. But this was not to be."[1]

(On the very eve of the Rising, some of the brave young fellows in the last issue of a most seditious fly-sheet, *The Spark,* had summed up Mr. Birrell himself with not unkindly insight, even if a hint was dropped that James Connolly's rifles waiting for the impetuous General Friend's raiders down in Liberty Hall had deepened Mr. Birrell's political insight to the point of restraining the General even as his troops had assembled for the march, an insight that was absent when the Dublin police broke loose in 1913 and James Connolly had no guns, and, at the best, paving stones: "Augustine was no reactionary backwoodsman. Genial and kindly he bowled over the Unionist questioner with his flippancy. The fatherly care of the leader of our race worked Gus, unser Gus, into the mystic movement of the Celtic heart. And he waxed fat thereat, beaming all the time the satisfied smile of the protuberant waistcoat. Kindly, lovable, too flippant to be serious, unser Gus was the man to mollify the wild Celt, to lead him from his devious ways to paths of peace and Imperialism, to bridge the gulf, to make the British democracy to realise that the Celt, inscrutable, was not a bad fellow, if properly handled.")[2]

Then Mr. Birrell marshalled a small army of "contributory causes," and grave enough these were: "First, growing doubts about the actual advent of Home Rule . . . even with Home Rule on the Statute Book, the chance of its ever becoming *a fact* was so uncertain, the outstanding difficulty about Ulster was so obvious, and the details of the measure itself were so unattractive and difficult to transmute into telling platform phrases, that *Home Rule* as an emotional flag fell out of daily use in current Irish life." Thus, second, "other men, other thoughts, other methods, before somewhat harshly snubbed," came to the front; third, the Ulster Rebellion, gun-running at Larne, the Provisional Government, and its members, its plan of warfare in Belfast, its armed Volunteers, and public drillings, and the other "pomp and circumstance" of Revolution, had the most prodigious effect on disloyalists *elsewhere.* There was no anger with the Ulster

---

[1] Royal Commission on the Rebellion in Ireland, Minutes of Evidence. Pp. 20-26 (H.M. Stationery Office, London, 1916).

[2] Quoted, *Banba,* Dublin, April, 1922, "A Retrospect", M. J. Lennon.

Rebels: Catholic Ireland was very proud of them: "What they are allowed to do, we can do." So Mr. Birrell saying this needed no elaboration forbore to dwell on the Irish Volunteers, their foundation in November, 1913, the landing of arms at Howth in July, the clash of the Volunteers with the British troops, and the Bachelor's Walk shootings of civilians the same evening, less than a thousand rifles in all from Erskine Childers' yacht; somewhat of a contrast to the landing of 35,000 rifles at Larne three months before where the only casualty had been an aged coastguard who died of excitement. Contributory cause four was very serious:

"Then came the war on the 4th August, 1914. This was the moment of the greatest risk. Nobody could foretell what would happen in Ireland or what her attitude would be. It might easily have demanded 60,000 soldiers to keep her down. Mr. Redmond's spontaneous, patriotic, courageous, but British speech, was a bold stroke, and bravely has it succeeded. One hundred and fifty thousand Irish Volunteer soldiers are fighting, as Irish soldiers know how to fight, on the side of Great Britain. To me it is marvellous. But there were in Ireland men and women who thought that Mr. Redmond had thrown away a great opportunity and that he should have struck a bargain with the Crown ere he consented to become a recruiting officer for it. These men were in a small minority. Ireland preserved an unbroken front with the rest of the United Kingdom and the Empire, and this she did to the bitter disappointment of Germany. But the minority were still there, and were shortly to increase in numbers. Fifth: The Coalition Government with Sir Edward Carson in it! . . . This step seemed to make an end of Home Rule and strengthened the Sinn Féiners enormously all over the country."

This statement of Mr. Birrell ended with the last lap of the road to insurrection:

"Sixth: The prolongation of the war and its dubious end: Irish criticism of the war and its chances were not of the optimistic cast that prevail in Great Britain. Every event and result was put in the balance and weighed. The excitement was immense. So long as the war lasted, and it soon became obvious that it might last for years, there were not wholly unreasonable expectations of a German landing or landings in Ireland, and of partial risings in different parts of the country, which, if timed so as to synchronise with a German bombardment of the English coasts, and hosts of Zeppelins flying over the North of England and the Midlands, would be quite enough; so it might well be thought by an Irish Revolutionist to secure a fair chance of an immediate Irish success, which, were Germany ultimately victorious, could not but greatly damage British authority and rule in the future. German assistance was at the bottom of the outbreak. To this in Dublin was added the hoarded passions of the labour disputes and Bachelor's Walk."

The last sentence was very true; the penultimate sentence was plausible when the words were read, but, as will appear, very wide of the truth.

The men who planned the Rising were the members of the Military Council of the Irish Republican Brotherhood, Thomas J. Clarke, Seán MacDermott, Thomas MacDonagh, Patrick Henry Pearse, Eamonn Ceannt, James Connolly, Joseph Plunkett.

All these men stood for the policy of insurrection. They had come together by different paths. Tom Clarke had been sentenced to penal servitude for life in 1883, when he was twenty-five years old, for his part in the dynamite campaign sponsored by the Clan na Gael in the 'eighties, or rather a section of the Clan. He was a close friend of John Devoy, whom the judge remembered as having caused so much trouble about the same time in the Land League, the most famous of the Fenians, who was to be the link through his friendship with Clarke between the Military Council and the Irish-American Clan na Gael. After fifteen years in prison, with his fellow prisoners losing their reason or their lives through the vindictive régime, Tom Clarke was released, and went to the United States, from which he returned to Ireland in 1907. Years of exile and years of prison alike deepened his one constant and life-long purpose, an armed attempt to overthrow British rule in Ireland and establish a Republic. He was allied with a group of young men, including Bulmer Hobson, Dr. Patrick MacCartan, and Seán MacDermott, who had joined and pressed a more active policy on the semi-moribund Irish Republican Brotherhood, and eventually displaced the older leaders. Tom Clarke set up a tobacconist's and newsagency in Parnell Street which was very closely watched by Dublin Castle. The Secretary of the Post Office in Ireland, giving evidence before the 1916 Commission on the loyalty of Civil Servants, and precautions against disloyalty to the British Government, said that lists of dangerous, potentially

dangerous, and probably negligible persons, had been prepared, and
" it seemed safe to classify as dangerous those who were credibly
reported to be in more than occasional or chance communication
with some one or some of the small group of persons known in
Dublin to be dangerously seditious, *e.g.*, T. J. Clarke." Lord
Wimborne, when he was drawing up a list of persons for deportation, " unless they behave themselves," in March, 1916, forgot
some names for a moment but remembered in particular those of
Connolly and Clarke, who a month later gave him the greatest
surprise of his career.   Tom Clarke was an unassuming and kindly
man, although he had spent so many years in jail, been wrecked
on an iceberg on his first journey from the United States, known
privation and heartache after his release.   He wrote one book,
Glimpses of an Irish Felon's Prison Life, an unforgettable chronicle
of his prison life, and the lives of his fellow Fenians fighting for
life and sanity in a living hell.   The worst that his critics ever
said of him was that he was rigid and uncompromising and with
but one idea in his mind.   Where political principle was in question he could be relentless, bitter, and even unjust, though always
open and direct, as when he clashed with a colleague on an issue
of tactics, and asked him point-blank: " How much did the
Redmondites pay you?"   This was when his colleague had sided
with the majority which accepted the Redmond ultimatum for
control over the Irish Volunteer movement in 1914.   Though
they had long been friends he never spoke to Bulmer Hobson and
Casement after they had supported, for tactical reasons, acquiescence in the same Redmondite move.   He approved of those who
opposed the admission of Patrick Pearse into the Irish Republican
Brotherhood (because Pearse, also for tactical reasons, had spoken on
a Home Rule platform with Devlin and Redmond in 1912 and
advocated accepting the Irish Council Bill in 1907) until he had
a personal interview with Pearse, cross-examined him, and relented
somewhat.   Finally, Clarke was carried away by Pearse's power
as an orator and admitted: " By God! I never thought there was
such stuff in Pearse!"
     One story depicts him during the surrender in 1916 threaten-
ing to shoot himself, and then pocketing his revolver with the
words: " No, I will not give the British the excuse to say that I
am afraid of them.   They can do the shooting."   Tom Clarke's
colleagues asked him to sign the Republican Proclamation first,

and this mark of respect is said to have pleased but surprised him.[3]

Seán MacDermott, Tom Clarke's closest friend, was the second signatory of the Proclamation, a County Leitrim man, son of a small farmer, thirty-two years of age at his death. He became one of the most influential and tireless organisers of Sinn Féin and the I.R.B. A curious early training schooled him for such a task. He emigrated to Glasgow at the age of fifteen and became in turn a gardener, a tram conductor, and a barman. Still a barman, he returned to Ireland, and pulled pints for the citizens of Belfast. From these early experiences Seán MacDermott learned tact, silence, and the timely choice between persuasion and force. In exile he became more and more conscious of his nationality, and on his return political activity attracted him more and more. He began by a short but final flirtation with Home Rule constitutionalism and anti-Orangeism. He joined the Ancient Order of Hibernians, the constitutionalist counterblast to the Orange Order. He was twenty-one, and soon came under the influence of the Republican movement known as the Dungannon Club, founded by Denis MacCullough and Bulmer Hobson. In 1906 he joined the secret Irish Republican Brotherhood, and a year later was the ally of Tom Clarke, Hobson, MacCartan, and the younger men who were conducting a revolutionary overhaul of the I.R.B.

The Constitution of the Irish Republican Brotherhood declared, in accordance with the Fenian tradition of Stephens and O'Mahony, its purpose to be " the overthrowing of British power in Ireland and establishing an independent Republic." The Supreme Council (which consisted of eleven members, seven from the four provinces of Ireland and England and Scotland with power to co-opt four) was regarded " in fact as well as right the sole Government of the Irish Republic " until the recovery of the national territory, and the establishment of a permanent Government. A further clause declared that the objects of the I.R.B. in time of peace would be confined to moral influences while preparing Ireland for the task of recovering her independence by force of arms, and that " the I.R.B. shall await the decision of the Irish nation as expressed by

---

[3] The best account of Tom Clarke is his own *Glimpses of an Irish Felon's Prison Life*, which originally appeared in the I.R.B. monthly, *Irish Freedom*, 1912-13. It was published, with an introduction by P. S. O'Hegarty, as a book in 1922. There is a chapter on Tom Clarke by his friend, James Reidy, in *The Irish Rebellion of 1916 and Its Martyrs*, ed. Maurice Joy (New York, 1916). The only biography is by Louis N. Le Roux, *Tom Clarke and the Irish Freedom Movement* (Dublin, 1936).

a majority of the Irish people as to the fit hour of inaugurating a war against England, and shall, pending such an emergency, lend its support to every movement calculated to advance the cause of Irish independence, consistently with the preservation of its own integrity."[4] This clause was adopted following controversies arising out of the 1867 Rising.

The organisation of the I.R.B. was in Circles, each with a Centre, Secretary and Treasurer, District Centres and County Centres. The Supreme Council was elected by representatives of these District and County Centres. A committee of five from County or District Centres in each of the divisions elected the members of the S.C. for their respective divisions under a strict pledge of secrecy. The Executive of the I.R.B. consisted of the President, Secretary and Treasurer of the S.C.

Seán MacDermot became one of the best-known organisers of the secret organisation, and of Sinn Féin clubs, when the Dungannon Club was formally merged with Griffith's National Council into one united *Sinn Féin* association under the name Sinn Féin. He was widely recognised by the police, open and secret, to be a most dangerous and seditious person, who toured the entire country on foot, bicycle and car from 1907 to 1911. He was also manager of *Irish Freedom*. In 1912 he was struck down by infantile paralysis, and he walked thereafter with a limp, but as determined and as fanatical as ever, if a humorous and earnest man deserves such an adjective. By 1913 when the Irish Volunteers were afoot all the wires of his organisation were in his hands. He was a member of the Supreme Council for Leinster, and Tom Clarke's closest confidant, almost his only one, with the exception of the old Fenian fellow-prisoner of Clarke, John Daly of Limerick, to whose niece Tom Clarke was married. Like a thin thread through all the secret revolutionary history of the time, and through the open one runs the main record of MacDermott's activity, scrawled in many a policeman's notebook: " John MacDermott visited the town and addressed a meeting "——and wherever this happened,

---

[4] Statement to the writer by a former member of the S.C. of the I.R.B. Several versions of the Constitution of the I.R.B. have been circulated. One given in Pollard, *Secret Societies of Ireland*, as dating from 1914 is substantially the same as one quoted in part—or rather the Rules of Procedure quoted by Pollard—by Davitt and Devoy as genuine in 1880. The writer's informant stated that the version quoted above was that in force from 1873 until the insurrection when it was again revised. It was shorter but did not differ except in certain details from that given by Pollard, and often reprinted by others.

soon the I.R.B., the Gaelic League, the Sinn Féin Club, the Volunteers grew live and militant, and many a fighter for Irish freedom took the first step on a long and adventurous road. For an anti-recruiting speech in County Galway in 1915 Seán MacDermott was given three months' imprisonment. Liam Mellows, who was with him, said afterwards that MacDermott had no intention of indulging in such fireworks until the slavish pro-British attitude of the audience suddenly infuriated MacDermott who threw discretion to the winds, and singed the very ears of the note-taking police with such sedition that he was arrested promptly. Mellows saw an expression of horror on his face as they were together in the barracks. MacDermott confided to Mellows in a whisper that he had forgotten that he had some most incriminating documents on him.   He smuggled them to Mellows under the noses of the R.I.C., and Mellows took them away safely. He was a man of handsome presence and many moods. During the insurrection he strode with his limp and all right into the middle of the looters and harangued them with a fury that shook them.   In his last hours he jested about the very same looters, especially an old woman who had stolen a chest of tea, which was stolen from her in turn, and the old woman went round the streets denouncing the robbers who " took a poor old woman's little pinch of tea."   In the controversies which preceded Easter Week, an angry colleague stormed at him, saying : " When this is over, I'll have the life of some of you fellows, and your Military Council."   " Don't worry," said MacDermott with a smile, " none of us will survive!"

Clarke and MacDermott in 1914 were, as Secretary and Treasurer of the Supreme Council automatically two-thirds of the Executive, which consisted of three members, the third being the Chairman of the S.C. Hence, their power in that organisation was very great, quite apart from the powerful union of a single-minded idealist and an organiser whose personal influence reached every county in Ireland within the narrow compass of his own revolutionary organisation. Yet in themselves, even in the favourable circumstances of 1914, they could not have initiated a nation-wide revolution without the aid of two other members of the Military Council, both of whom had been critical of, if not hostile, for most of their lives to the I.R.B. itself, and who were regarded with deep suspicion by the purists and Old Guard of the same I.R.B.

These two men were Patrick Pearse and James Connolly.

Without them it is very doubtful whether there would have been an insurrection at all, and without them most certainly, the insurrection in defeat would not have made so terrific and revolutionary an impact on the popular imagination. Pearse had travelled the road to insurrection through his Gaelic idealism. He had been the educationalist of the Gaelic League. He became the orator of the Irish Volunteer movement, an orator of ultimate revolution, and his power of gripping the rank and file of the Volunteers was due to his mastery of language, his sincerity, his personality, his fire. He joined the I.R.B. in 1913, five months before the Irish Volunteers began. Until then he had been very critical of secret organisation, and that secret organisation in particular. He regarded himself, with some justice, as a more dangerous revolutionary than most other men in Ireland, inside or out of any organisation. What he really sought, as his writings are evidence, was an armed, popular and disciplined movement with a more persuasive popular propaganda than that prevailing in the somewhat arid and circumscribed circles of both Sinn Féin and the I.R.B. What he really wanted he found, like his friend and colleague, Thomas MacDonagh in the Irish Volunteer movement. Pearse had the power of the enkindling word. He could persuade, convince, inspire.

James Connolly was the greatest brain in the Labour movement, a student of revolutions all his life for an ulterior motive: he wanted nothing more in heaven and on earth than a social and political revolution in Ireland. He was at home in a library or on a barricade. He was the master of any crowd he addressed from the first minute through the sincerity and conviction behind his words. Off the platform his words were few, and few, if any, really knew him well.

Thomas MacDonagh was a scholar, a poet who wrote hundreds of lines every day, a University lecturer, a wit and a talker. Like Pearse and Ceannt he came to insurrection along the Gaelic road although there were many other roads further afield that he had rambled along. His friend, Joseph Plunkett was a poet and a mystic. At the first meeting of the Military Council, he produced a plan of the insurrection on which he had worked for years. James Connolly who had studied many revolutions, highly approved of Plunkett's plans, and together they worked on and perfected the first draft.

In July, 1914, Roger Casement was in the United States on a mission for the Irish Volunteers: speaking for them and collecting funds. When the war broke out Casement went to Germany. Among his activities there which had not succeeded too well was his Irish Brigade of Irish prisoners of war which he recruited on the express condition that they should be used only for an expedition to aid Irish freedom in their own country. Casement secured a clear and definite pledge that these men should never be used for any ulterior and exclusively German purpose. Roger Casement was then a man broken in health and racked in mind after two strenuous and unselfish campaigns to expose the horrifying persecution and brutal exploitation of the native rubber workers in the Congo and Putumayo. His reports had caused an international sensation. They were a chronicle of inhuman cruelty and terrible deeds which the famous war correspondent, Henry Nevinson— who knew all the horrors of every war for a generation—said were enough to turn the brain of any man who had lived through them. Then he began his last and greatest crusade, the crusade nearest to his heart: to raise the " Irish question " from a mere political debate on to an international plane. All through his life, Roger Casement had given generously out of his small means to assist the Irish-Ireland movement, its struggling journals, the Gaelic League, the impoverished people of the Irish-speaking west, Pearse's school, and finally the Irish Volunteers. In his heart, he was always a strong Irish nationalist, a separatist, a friend of complete Irish independence. Then, in the United States, in 1914, in spite even of the arguments of the Irish-American Clan na Gael leaders, he threw all his ease and honours and his career to the winds by his mission to Germany. He sent an appeal for help in his work of organising his Irish Brigade, he wanted a capable military man to come and help him in its organisation because he had found it a task beyond his unaided efforts when ill-health, the indifference of the Irish prisoners of war, and the scepticism of the Germans combined against him. Tom Clarke in Dublin on receiving this appeal through John Devoy decided that Robert Monteith was the very man, and Monteith agreed very enthusiastically with him.

Robert Monteith had been a soldier in the British Army, and saw service in India, South Africa, and China. He had just missed the Boxer Rising but he had had many adventures elsewhere. In the Boer War the sight of burning farms and concentration camps had made him an anti-imperialist, and turned him into a fierce nationalist. He learned many lessons in the art of guerrilla warfare. When the Irish Volunteers began Monteith was employed in the Ordnance Department at Islandbridge, Dublin. He was already closely in touch with the leaders of the Irish-Ireland movement, and his sympathies with the Labour movement of the time had brought him the friendship of such men as Larkin and Connolly. In particular, Monteith knew Tom Clarke and through him learned some time before the Volunteers were started that the movement was under way and agreed to be one of their military instructors. Within a year, he was out of a job, and under sentence of deportation from the British Government. He was ordered out of Dublin, and conducted a regular organising tour of the Volunteer organisation in the South. Few men knew so well the strength and weakness of the Volunteers of that time. Finally, when Tom Clarke interviewed him in Limerick, he agreed to go, and after many adventures en route which can be read best in his own *Casement's Last Adventure,* he arrived in Germany in the autumn of 1915.

CHAPTER II

ALTHOUGH the arrangements for the landing of arms from a German arms ship were an important part of the Rising, and the failure to carry through this arms-landing as originally planned was the principal cause of the collapse of the Military Council's plans, the part played by Germany in arming and encouraging the revolt was actually small and negligible. From the first, the I.R.B. leaders and the German military and naval chiefs were agreed on one thing: both were prepared to use the other in so far as it suited their purpose, and no further. The I.R.B. leaders looked with disfavour on a German invasion, and limited their demands to the German Government to arms, artillery, and at the most a small number of German officers to act as instructors to the insurgent forces. Casement's calculations based on an insurrection backed by an expeditionary force of 50,000 German invaders left them cold, partly because it seemed too fantastic, partly because they preferred to do their own fighting without any risk of substituting one master for another. Connolly detested the German Government as much as he detested the British, no matter what disingenuous flavour he gave to his propaganda when it suited the need of the hour, and as the war progressed his scepticism as to German intentions to aid Irish revolution deepened.

Roger Casement and Lenin, after the insurrection summed up matters succinctly. " I must state categorically," said Roger Casement from the dock, " that the rebellion was not made in Germany; that it was not directed from Germany; that it was not inspired from Germany; and that not one penny of German gold went to finance it." About the same time Lenin in his defence of the 1916 insurrection wrote: " The General Staffs in the present war assiduously strive to utilise all national and revolutionary movements in the camp of the enemy; the Germans utilise the Irish rebellion, the French utilise the Czech movement, etc. From their standpoint they are acting quite properly. They would not be treating a serious war seriously if they did not take advantage of the least weakness of the enemy, if they did not seize advantage of every opportunity that offered, the more so that it is impossible to know beforehand at what moment, where and with what force a powder magazine will explode."[1] In the same autumn of 1916, Joseph Pilsudski was seriously considering plans for withdrawing his Polish legion from the side of the Central Powers because as the translator of his memoirs puts it, he " had entered the war to fight against Russia, whom he considered the principal enemy of Poland, not as a defender of the interests of Austria or Germany: the one cause he recognised was that of his own nation." The exasperated Germans locked him up in the fortress of Magdeburg and made him a General: " to my great astonishment, and treated one may say, with the respect due to that rank."[2]

The Military Council learned from Joseph Plunkett on his return from Berlin in the autumn of 1915 that the Germans had no intention of sending arms, artillery or officers; that they considered a German expedition to Ireland on any large scale as impossible; that the only possible aid they proposed to send the Irish would be arms captured during the war. It was evident that the Germans had been disappointed by the participation of so many Irishmen in the war on the Allied side, by the failure of the Irish to rise in revolt earlier in the war, and by the lack of progress of the Casement propaganda among captured Irish soldiers to join his Irish Brigade. The actual help sent by Germany in 1916 on the *Aud* arms ship was 20,000 captured Russian rifles, some million rounds of ammunition, ten machine-guns, and some fire bombs; a smaller and less fortunate cargo than that landed for the Ulster Volunteers at Larne and Bangor two years before: 47,000 rifles and 3,000,000 rounds of ammunition purchased at Hamburg with good Tory gold and run through the Kiel Canal with the benevolence of the German Government. It is quite clear that powerful sections of the German Government and people were sceptical of and even hostile to the Irish expedition of 1916, and as an imperialist power with subject nationalities, this was understandable.

In the Irish camp there were also hesitations and misgivings. It was the national tradition to applaud the enemy of England, and

---

[1] See, *The Forged Casement Diaries*, Maloney, p. 12; *Lenin on Britain*, Marxist-Leninist Library, Vol. 18, p. 168.

[2] *Joseph Pilsudski.* Tr. by D. R. Gillie (London, 1931) p. 349, 354.

it was the Republican and separatist tradition from the days of Tone to look for Irish freedom from England's enemies in time of war. In this spirit, Pearse and Clarke looked to the European war as Ireland's opportunity. In such a situation, James Connolly, generally bitterly critical of former Irish nationalist pro-Russian and pro-German campaigns, sided with them. He used almost the same words that Lenin used in the defence of 1916 before noted. Lenin argued that a blow in Ireland against the British Empire had " a hundred times more political significance than a blow of equal weight would have in Asia and in Africa." In the *Workers' Republic,* Connolly wrote in January, 1916, that Ireland was in the position of a child that might stick a pin in a giant's heart; in such a strong tactical position that a defeat of England in India, Egypt, the Balkans or Flanders would not be so dangerous to the British Empire as the conflict of armed forces in Ireland; that the place for Ireland's battle was in Ireland, and the time for that battle was in a great European conflict alone. Across Connolly's headquarters at Liberty Hall a slogan streamed defiantly: " We serve neither King nor Kaiser, but Ireland." In private, he growled into the ears of Pearse and Clarke: " The Germans are as bad as the British. Do the job yourselves!" He had from the beginning no very firm confidence in any German benevolence towards Irish independence although he was perfectly ready to use whatever military aid came from any quarter. The very week the war broke out, he wrote in the *Irish Worker* a concise formulation of his views of the policy to be adopted: if a German army landed in Ireland, and gave adequate guarantees for Irish independence, then the Irish people would be perfectly justified in supporting that army. As the war progressed Connolly became more and more sceptical of German interest in Ireland. To the arguments of Casement retailed to him by Eoin MacNeill and others that no rising in Ireland was practicable until Germany could send a force of 50,000 men—the minimum in the Casement view for a successful uprising—Connolly retorted, when he bothered to retort, that a force of 10,000 or 5,000 would be very effective, if the Germans had any serious intention of aiding Irish freedom.

Monteith, who had gone to Germany to act as Casement's lieutenant in 1915, had a similar mood of scepticism as he drew near the Irish coast in 1916. He had repeatedly and in vain suggested to the German naval authorities that submarines might be used for gun-running; he was enlightened when a quartermaster on the submarine asked him: "Why don't you run arms to Ireland as we did to Senussi? We had special submarines for the purpose." German apologists later protested that Germany was poor in submarines in 1916, and that they were generous in giving one to Casement at all in the circumstances. Cynics have retorted that they were willing to risk a submarine at any rate to get rid of the persistent Casement. Certainly, the story of German attempts to arm Irish discontent shows that the Germans, much to their disadvantage, missed the significance of the Irish opportunity so clearly expressed by Connolly and Lenin. The bland and simple British were not quite so obtuse, as will soon appear.

The most tragic figure in the German-Irish negotiations was Roger Casement, and he is all too clearly seen in his mistakes and in his virtues through the eyes of his implacable critic, John Devoy, who had his doubts of Dublin's wisdom, was at loggerheads from the first with Casement, and who had no illusions whatever about the Germans or reproaches or accusations of bad faith against them after the event. When the Dublin leaders decided to strike in what seemed to Devoy an unfavourable war situation in February, 1916, he at once conceded their right, as the men on the spot, to decide, transmitted their request for arms to Berlin, and pressed Germany with all the patience and pertinacity a lifetime of conspiracy had taught him to send the most effective aid possible. Long before that, he had made up his mind that Casement—as his most constant Irish correspondent Tom Clarke, and Patrick Pearse also believed—was temperamentally unfitted to negotiate with the Germans, and this belief was confirmed by Casement's conduct there. He was angered by Casement's over-confidence in Christensen, his Norwegian servant whom he met casually in New York on the eve of his departure to Berlin; his handling of the scheme to organise an Irish Brigade from Irish prisoners of war; his independence of Clan na Gael counsels and direction. In a confidential letter in July, 1916, to Laurence de Lacy, an Irish Volunteer officer then in exile in America, Devoy accused Casement of being responsible for ruining the Rising:

"From our experience of a year of his utter impracticability—he had been assuring us, till we were sick, that 'there was no hope for the poor old woman' until the next war—we sent with the first

B

note from home that we transmitted to Berlin a request that R. *be asked to remain there,* 'to take care of Irish interests'. We knew that he would meddle in his honest but visionary way to such an extent as to spoil things, but we did not dream that he would ruin everything as he has done. He took no notice whatever of decisions or instructions, but without quarrelling, pursued his own dreams. The last letter I got from him, written last December, said that the only hope now of making a demonstration that would impress the world was to send the ' Brigade ' to Egypt. *To impress the world by sending sixty men to a place where they could do nothing.* We told him nearly a year before that we would not consent to this, but he took no notice. He was obsessed with the idea that he was a wonderful leader and that nothing could be done without him. His letters always kept me awake on the night of the day I got them. Miss R. says he told Duffy that the Germans treated us shamefully and that he had hard work to get the few arms that were on that ship; that they were no good, etc. Well, they were good enough for the Russians to overrun East Prussia with and to drive the Austrians across the Carpathians, and if our fellows got them they'd be able to shoot a good many Englishmen with them. It is not true that the Germans treated us badly; they did everything we asked, but they were weary of his impracticable dreams and told us to deal directly with them *here.* . . . He told Duffy he wanted to be landed in Galway, to go to Dublin and lay the situation before them—that is, to tell them that Germany was not sincere, etc., and then if they decided to fight that *he would go out and die with them.* Every note he struck was one of despair. And he told everything to every fellow who called on him. Christensen, who ' saved ' him, is one of the worst crooks I ever met, and was in the pay of the English all along. He, Casement, was warned of that from Ireland and the first thing he did was to tell the fellow himself and give him the name of the man who had warned him. Christensen was going over from here to testify against him—and incidentally to give away all our secrets that he had got from Roger, but *we kept him here.*"[3]

---

[3] Quoted, *Documents Relative to Sinn Féin Movement,* pp. 19-20. Devoy referred to this letter, *Gaelic American,* September 27, 1924. On its publication after the raid on de Lacy's home in California, Christensen, Devoy stated, protested to Joseph McGarrity against the charges but admitted he had worked for U.S. Secret Service; "That was the last I ever heard of him." *See also* Devoy, *Recollections,* p. 397.

Whatever the justice in Devoy's criticisms of Casement's manner of carrying out his mission in Germany and his actions on the eve of the Rising, Casement certainly was the man more than any other who had first in the years before the war raised the question of negotiations between the German Government from a vague slogan to actuality.   In doing this, he was not moved particularly by any sympathy with Germany or German aims.   Of German life and conditions he knew little—he had made only one short visit to the country in May, 1912—while of the German language he knew less; nor did he act under the inspiration of the Irish Republican Brotherhood or of the Clan na Gael.   It would be nearer the truth to say that he presented both these organisations with the first clear and public formulation of a German-Irish understanding in the case of war.   He expressed his aim in this briefly: to raise the Irish question from a mere issue in British party politics to an international one.

In July, 1913, as he retired from the British diplomatic service on pension, his health shattered by his experiences in his campaigns to expose the atrocious conditions under which the natives in the Belgian Congo and the Putumayo suffered, Casement opened his last campaign for the freedom of Ireland.   Over the pseudonym " Shan Van Vocht " he wrote his reply to Conan Doyle: " Ireland, Germany and the Next War."   Conan Doyle in an article in the *Fortnightly Review* in February argued that Ireland must stand by Great Britain in the approaching war; that she stood or fell politically and economically with the fortunes of the British Empire; that the British Fleet was Ireland's one shield.   Casement's reply appeared in the *Irish Review,* then edited by Padraic Colum, who later commented that this article was the first serious statement of an Irish nationalist policy for the coming war.[4]   Casement's article had been inspired by the belief his contacts with diplomatic circles had given him that a European war would break out not later than 1915; he was also angered by the Tory-Carsonite armed campaign against Home Rule, and the British defeat of his plans in February, 1914, to make Queenstown (Cobh) a port of call for German liners.

The *Irish Review* article, as well it might because of its clear arguments and evident knowledge of the situation, created much

---

[4] " The Career of Roger Casement ", Padraic Colum, *Dublin Magazine,* Oct.-Dec., 1931.

interest. It was quoted in the London *Times* and the German Press alike, and was duly noted by the German General Staff. Casement exacted a pledge of secrecy about the authorship of the article from Padraic Colum, and taxed Colum shortly afterwards with breaking this pledge. Colum then had to inform Casement that " the fault was his own if people knew that he had written the article, that a lady to whom he had made the disclosure was talking freely about it." Though critical of Casement's ability as a conspirator, Colum thought this new foreign policy was admirable although in his opinion Casement's judgment as to how to carry the policy into effect was very poor.

The central argument of Casement's *Irish Review* article was that the annexation of Ireland by Germany, if England were over-thrown in a European war, was not probable, and that " an Ireland already severed by a sea held by German warships, and temporarily occupied by a German army, might well be permanently severed from Great Britain, and with common assent erected into a neutralised, independent European state under international guarantees." All in effect that Casement gained from the German Government was one friendly and not very definite declaration, a certain amount of suspicion due to his British honours and affilia-tions, a small consignment of arms given only after great argument, and a collapsible boat to land him into the arms of the British hangman. And in spite of his sickness of mind and body, Case-ment went to this fate with his eyes open, bravely playing his rôle in the wake of Tone as Ireland's unofficial ambassador. He told Padraic Colum once that Ireland would be " saved by another Owen Roe O'Neill coming over the sea to her," and left no doubt in Colum's mind that Casement saw himself as that modern Owen Roe to the detriment of any living Irish rivals.[5]

Casement had thought out his new foreign policy for Ireland since 1910, and earlier. In that year, at the request of Bulmer Hobson, who was editor of the I.R.B. organ, *Irish Freedom*, and a

---

[5] "He is dead," wrote Maurice Joy, "this Knight of the Flaming Heart, hanged by the neck with a rope manipulated by a Rochdale barber, while the cheers of a Cockney crowd broke blasphemously through his last litany." *The Irish Rebellion of 1916*, ed. M. Joy, New York, 1916, p. 301. Colum in his *Dublin Review* article defends Casement's moral character by quoting Robert Ford, Editor of the *Irish World*, who had him shadowed in U.S.A. in 1914, believing Casement was a British agent:
There is nothing in these charges; we had him followed everywhere, and he behaved everywhere as an innocent and honourable man,"

close friend of his, he drew up a memorandum on the subject. Hobson, according to his own account, wanted this document forwarded to the German Government, but nothing very definite was done until March, 1914, when Hobson during a visit to New York submitted it to John Devoy who showed it to Count von Bernstorff.[6] Casement's *Irish Review* article was republished in the *Gaelic American* and *Irish Freedom* with other writings of his under pseudonyms in the same key. Of one of these, " The Elsewhere Empire ", Casement wrote to Wilfrid Blunt[7] wittily and candidly: " . . . .a most treasonable pamphlet. Read it if you are not shocked for it is not polite literature but a crude appeal to nationality versus imperialism." Apologising for another leaflet as " flamboyant ", Casement explained: " It was written for popular gatherings—in a style they like—and it is always something to get them, in Ireland, to read at all." Casement and Hobson were at one mind on an approach to the German Government before the war, and on a waiting policy, as opposed to an aggressive insurrectionist one, for the Irish Volunteers when the European war broke out. In this second object, they had the support of Eoin MacNeill. Hobson's statement of his views in *An t-Oglách*, June, 1931, may then be taken in general as expressing the outlook of this group, as opposed to that of Tom Clarke, Pearse, the I.R.B. and Connolly:

" Personally, I recognised that the Irish Republic was possible only in the event of the war being decisively won by the Central Powers. In preparation for such an outcome, which then seemed quite possible, Casement had gone to America, and then to Berlin, where he concluded a definite agreement whereby the German Government undertook to assist the establishment of an Independent Irish Government,[8] if the course of the war enabled them to do so.

---

[6] Devoy, writing in *Irish Freedom*, April, 1911: " The next great war will remake the map of Europe, and it is coming soon." Two articles in the same paper, October-November, 1911, " When Germany Fights England " by " Fergus Mac Leda " (Bulmer Hobson) anticipated Casement's *Irish Review* article; if indeed they were not inspired by Casement's conversations with Hobson. Hobson's account, above referred to, appeared in *An t-Oglách*, June, 1931.

[7] *My Diaries* (1888-1914) Wilfrid Scawen Blunt, pp. 969-71.

[8] A reference to the Treaty which Casement concluded with Germany. The text is given in Parmiter, Monteith, and in Devoy's *Recollections*: Devoy pointed out that this agreement was never ratified by any Irish body and that it contained a clause to which Clan na Gael and the I.R.B. leaders in Ireland were strongly opposed. The Treaty is based on " the

On the other hand, if the Allies won the war, or should it end indecisively, I considered that Dominion status, by whatever name it might be called, was the maximum which in the circumstances we could hope to achieve. To build up in Ireland a strong Volunteer force, which would be ready and able to take the initiative in either eventuality, was the central idea on which we worked at the time. As to the European war itself, our aim was to keep out of it, and to keep Ireland out, and to profit as far as we could from whatever turn it should take."

According to this statement of Hobson, his group recognised that in the case of war, the British Government would sooner or later make a move to suppress the Volunteer organisation: "To meet this eventuality a system of training for guerrilla war was worked out, principally by Colonel J. J. O'Connell, whom I had met in New York in the early part of 1914, and had asked to return to Ireland and help in the organisation of the Volunteers." Hobson gives "the three possible events" which the MacNeill group agreed would precipitate a struggle: A German landing in force (which Hobson did not regard as possible except in the case of a decisive German naval victory); an attempt to suppress the Volunteer organisation; conscription in Ireland. The plans in the case of suppression, secret organisation, small flying columns of "wanted" men, Hobson outlines, are those later mentioned in MacNeill's order issued on April 19, 1916, when rumours of suppression of the Volunteers were current.[9]

Casement's reliance on German aid was backed by an argument from history; he argued that no small nation could be freed except by the aid of a powerful foreign Power—in the case of Ireland, a strong naval Power. His policy was criticised from several

event of a German naval victory affording means of reaching the coast of Ireland," when "the Imperial German Government pledges itself to dispatch the Irish Brigade and a supporting body of German officers and men, in German transports, to attempt a landing on the Irish coast." Devoy dismisses the document as "a historical curiosity which had no influence on the course of events." *Recollections*, pp. 431-35. The objectionable clause referred to the employment of the Irish Brigade in certain circumstances in Egypt.

[9] MacNeill's order is quoted in full in *Life of P. H. Pearse*, Le Roux, pp. 349-50. It runs in part: "In general you will arrange that your men defend themselves and each other in small groups so placed that they may best be able to hold out. Each group must be provided with sufficient supplies of food, or be certain of access to such supplies." Hobson's 1909 pamphlet, *Defensive Warfare, A Handbook for Irish Nationalists* (Sinn Féin, West Belfast branch) advocated similar tactics.

quarters inside the Irish revolutionary movement. John Devoy, for instance, was very critical even of Casement's ability to state his case. An address to the Kaiser written by Casement on August 25, 1914, was accepted by the Clan na Gael, and the signatories included all members of its Executive, with Devoy's name first on the list. Devoy insisted afterwards that he and his colleagues would have worded it differently, and this may well be believed when its fawning and flamboyant rhetoric is read to-day: " Thousands of Irishmen are prepared to do their part to aid the German cause, for they recognise that it is their own," runs one sentence, at a time when Ireland was overwhelmingly pro-Ally, when Redmond had committed Ireland to the war, when thousands of Irishmen were flocking into the British Army. The main argument was Casement's familiar one finally pressed home in the last paragraph after repeated professions of Irish friendship for Germany, the unrelieved blackness of her enemies, and the righteousness of the German cause:

" We beg your Majesty to reflect that an Ireland freed by German victory over Britain becomes the sure gage of a free ocean for all who traverse the seas. On these grounds alone, did not natural sympathy and admiration for a people fighting against such odds lead us to address your Majesty, we should hope for a German triumph over an enemy who is also our enemy. We pray that triumph for Germany; and we pray with it your Majesty may have power, wisdom and strength of purpose to impose a lasting peace upon the seas by effecting the independence of Ireland and securing its recognition as a fixed condition of the final terms of settlement between the great maritime Powers."[10]

In September, Casement, to Devoy's annoyance and surprise, wrote another statement, and, without consulting Clan na Gael, had taken other Irish-Americans not in agreement with Clan policy such as Bourke Cockran and John Quinn into his confidence.

---

[10] The German Ambassador in Washington looked at matters much more coldly. A month later, September 27, 1914, von Bernstorff informed Berlin: " We are likely to find friends here if we give freedom to oppressed peoples such as the Poles, the Finns, and the Irish. . . . The decisive point seems to me to lie in the question whether any prospect of an understanding with England is now in view or must we prepare ourselves for a life and death struggle? If so, I recommend falling in with Irish wishes, provided that there are really Irishmen prepared to help us. The formation of an Irish Legion from Irish prisoners would be a grand idea if only it could be carried out." *Documents relative to the Sinn Féin Movement*, p. 3.

Devoy, as much as ever Lenin or Hitler, believed in an absolute party discipline, and his career was marked by many collisions with the individualistic temperament of Irish revolutionaries who preferred to act on their own. While he admired Casement as a man of intellect and an authority on foreign affairs, he distrusted his emotionalism and his almost unbelievable capacity for trusting the first comer. There is no justice in the charge that Devoy was jealous of Casement as it is all too clear that he had nothing to be jealous of, and that his criticisms of Casement's methods and temperament were in the main true, and provoked by an honest anger at Casement's mistakes. Devoy's long years of conspiracy and negotiations with every Power and force hostile to the British Empire over forty years, with the Russians, the French, the Spaniards and the Boers, with Zulu and with Afghan, with Communist and Royalist alike, made him an authoritative and formidable judge of the matter. He had run guns for the Fenians, he had changed the history of the 'eighties with his New Departure which united constitutionalist and physical forces, and he had interpreted for Clan deputations to diplomats. More than any man he had spread Fenianism among Irish soldiers in the British Army half a century earlier. On the eve of the war he had clashed with Casement and Hobson on their willingness to submit to Redmond's ultimatum for control of the Volunteer movement. Nor had he waited for Casement's arrival to begin negotiations with the German Ambassador; so far back as 1911 he had advocated an Irish-German understanding, and prophesied a European war. As has been noticed already, his main informant on Irish affairs, Tom Clarke, was thoroughly opposed to Casement as an intermediary with Germany.

The Clan na Gael approach to Germany was made directly and explicitly as soon as war broke out. In August, 1914, a special committee from the Clan interviewed Count von Bernstorff at a reception held in the German Club, New York. Captain von Papen, Military Attaché; Wolff von Igel, von Papen's assistant; Herr Dernburg; George von Skal, and others of the Embassy staff were present. Devoy and his colleagues attended openly without any pretence of secrecy. Their conversation with the Ambassador was screened by an apparently casual ring of members of the Embassy staff so that the other guests could not approach within hearing distance. The discussion was

short and to the point: Bernstorff was informed that the
I.R.B. in Ireland, with the sympathy and support of the Clan,
intended to use the war's opportunities to overthrow British
rule in Ireland and establish an independent Government by
armed insurrection; that the Irish at home lacked arms and
trained officers; that they wanted Germany to supply arms and
trained officers so that the work might begin; one thing, however,
was not wanted, and would be accepted under no circumstances,
money. These points were stated clearly, and repeated to Count
von Bernstorff so that he thoroughly understood the position. It
was urged that it was to Germany's advantage in a military sense
to aid the Irish revolutionary movement; that a rebellion in Ireland
must divert British forces in large numbers from the western front.
This was language more tuned to the German ear than Casement's
romantic and idealistic appeals, even when spiced with courteous
compliments and baited with the freedom of the seas. Bernstorff
was impressed, asked many questions, and agreed to send the Clan
na Gael's statements and application to Berlin.

The Irish-American proposals were wirelessed to Berlin immedi-
ately. Several written statements were sent to supplement these
messages through Holland and Switzerland from the German
Embassy and the Clan. John Kenny, for instance, according to
Devoy's account in his memoirs, left New York for Germany on
August 21. He handed in a copy of the statement at the German
Embassy in Rome, and, furnished with a special passport, went
to Berlin where he delivered the message personally to von Bülow.
Then, at a favourable opportunity, John Kenny travelled to Dublin,
and laid the details of the Clan negotiations and his Berlin visit
before Tom Clarke. Devoy never stated specifically whether the
Clan used Casement's earlier statement brought to America by
Hobson earlier in the year, although as Casement's relations with
the Clan were at first friendly, it is very probable that they used
it, especially as his expert knowledge of foreign affairs was highly
esteemed by the Clan leaders. (This statement in fact had been
conveyed to Bernstorff by Devoy himself who had refused to
allow Hobson to approach the Ambassador personally as Hobson
was returning to Ireland, and Devoy argued that no trails whatever must be left for the British Secret Service to pick up. Devoy
also forbade Hobson and Pearse in the early months of 1914 to
attend any Clan meetings in case secret agents were present.)

Later, as noted, Casement's address to the Kaiser was submitted to the Clan and forwarded to Germany.

Devoy admitted that Casement, while, in his opinion, ineffective in obtaining military aid from Germany, and failing badly to organise an Irish Brigade there through wrong methods of approach to the Irish prisoners of war, succeeded admirably in educating German public opinion, and far wider circles on the Irish situation: " Casement was the first to call the attention of the world to it when it was in a receptive mood."[11]

The second critic, and one as trenchant and as dangerously effective as Devoy himself, of the Casement-Hobson policy in Irish militant circles was James Connolly whose criticisms of Hobson and MacNeill in particular were, from the outbreak of war, marked by a personal rancour unusual in his propaganda. He knew that Hobson was the most dangerous opponent of insurrection in the Volunteer camp because Hobson in discussions with him never disguised this opposition, and stated it very openly to Connolly himself. Their relations at one time had been very friendly, so friendly that Connolly had urged Hobson to give up Sinn Féin propaganda and devote himself to a left-wing Labour movement. Hobson himself sincerely admired Connolly's force of character, and was puzzled by his fiery 1914-16 mood. Connolly once in exasperation snapped at Hobson that the situation in Ireland was a revolutionary one which a spark would explode. Hobson retorted to Connolly's annoyance that if he wanted images then Ireland was a damp bog which would extinguish many a torch, and many a gunpowder barrel. Probably, too, Connolly resented Hobson's friendly but neutral attitude in *Irish Freedom* towards the 1913 upheaval, even if Hobson was quite sympathetic to the Labour cause, and critical of Griffith's open hostility to the Irish Labour movement of the time. Connolly, apart from such personal animosities, was smarting under the double disillusion of the defeat of the Dublin workers, and the collapse of the Labour movement internationally in 1914 on the outbreak of war. Across the broad front of Liberty Hall defiantly streamed the slogan already noted as to serving neither King nor Kaiser. He would have preferred even an unsuccessful attempt at social revolution throughout Europe; when that hope failed him very promptly, he turned, and accepted the revolutionary choice to his hand: " In times of war, we must act as in war."

---

[11] *Recollections*, Devoy, p. 416.

The third quarter from which proposals of German intervention in Ireland came under sharp scrutiny was from idealist Volunteer leaders like Terence MacSwiney. "From the moment the European war was declared," wrote Mary MacSwiney in Erskine Childers' Republican organ, *Poblacht na h-Eireann*, April 20, 1922, " there was no doubt that the more thoughtful Volunteer officers were fully alive to its possibilities for Ireland, and planned accordingly. ' England's difficulty: Ireland's opportunity ' was their watchword then and now, as in the past. The history of the communications between Ireland, America, and Germany will show that Ireland's fighting men were quite ready to accept genuine help if they could get it from any enemy of England, as they were perfectly justified in doing, but they were not prepared to act as Germany's cat's-paw ' to create a diversion ' for Germany, irrespective of the advantages to Ireland.[12]

" In this connection it is interesting to note that the leaders in Cork were fully alive to the possibilities of such a desire on the part of Germany. About three weeks before Easter, Tomás MacCurtáin, Traolac [Terence MacSwiney], and Seán O'Sullivan [the leading Volunteer officers in charge of Cork area] had a discussion on that very point in the Volunteer headquarters in Cork, as a result of which Traolac went to Dublin to get fuller particulars of the expected help, and an assurance from the Dublin headquarters, that the chestnuts were for Ireland only. The result of his visit was satisfactory and the details he received of the material expected filled him and his colleagues with joy."

The Germans on their part were not impressed by a visionary like Casement or by Irish idealist nationalists with an inconvenient crotchet of insisting on regarding everything from the purely Irish point of view. They certainly found John Devoy the clearest-headed man they had to deal with, even if they foolishly ignored his warnings against their national mania for keeping files and disregarded his advice to keep dangerous secrets in their heads rather than in too obvious places for the British and American Secret

---

[12] Miss MacSwiney was obviously commenting on the publication of Casement's 1916 diary, and his accusations of German bad faith, which Devoy so strenuously denied in the de Lacy letter already quoted. The Casement diary was published in April, 1922, in the Irish press. The Casement and MacSwiney attitudes were not opposed, but it is evident that MacSwiney was more critical of German intentions than Casement originally was. Connolly's reservations were confined to the German Imperial Government; for the German people he had a deep affection.

Services to gather up at leisure. They made some effort to meet Casement in the organising of the Irish Brigade and agreed that it should never "be employed or directed to any German end." The real negotiations as to arms for Ireland, however, they finally conducted with Devoy and Dublin behind his back. The Foreign Minister, Zimmermann, through a friendly feeling for Casement, urged him as strongly as he could to remain in Germany and not accompany the *Aud*. In general, the Germans kept their word and ran the limited help they thought the Irish expedition merited with skill and courage through the formidable British blockade. To their own undoing, however, they disregarded the truth of the Irish situation set forth to them by Casement, by Plunkett, and Devoy.

The German view was given later in the official German naval history of the 1914-19 war, and a translation of this was published in *An t-Oglách*, the Irish Army journal, July 24, 1926. This account very candidly sets out that German interest in the 1916 insurrection was based solely on military, naval and strategic considerations: such an uprising would shake British morale and divert British forces from the west. It was taken for granted that any such Rising would be "squashed." In the main, this brief account is a repetition of Karl Spindler's own story of his brilliant guiding of the *Aud* through the British blockade. The amount of German aid is briefly listed as 20,000 rifles, 10 machine-guns and ammunition. A diversionary attack by German naval forces on Lowestoft is mentioned. The discovery of the code messages between the Irish-Americans and Berlin, their seizure and decoding, and the United States warning to the British on April 17, 1916, that a German arms landing in Ireland was intended, is noted without mention that German file-mania was in any way responsible.[13] Comment is laconic: " The failure of the rebellion

---

[13] Devoy and other Irish-American leaders had warned von Papen and von Igel that the New York office of the German Embassy would be raided, for more than a year before the raid of April 18 by American Secret Service men, and these warnings were supported without effect by members of the German Embassy staff with more experience of American conditions. *Recollections*, p. 463; 466-71. Devoy tells the story more tersely in his letter to de Lacy: " They got in the raid on von Igel's office a note of mine—the transcript of a message received in cipher from Dublin and wirelessed to Berlin the day before, April 17—a request not to land the arms ' before the night of Sunday 23rd.' That was its meaning, but it used the words ' Goods '. It was at once given to the English. . . ." Spindler, however, declares that information of the *Aud*'s

certainly rested on the shoulders of those who commenced too soon," and " It was no more than Germany's war rights to help the sorely-pressed Irish people, especially when the latter had asked her help." There was great sympathy, it is added, in Germany with the Irish victims of British callousness after the Rising. Casement is described as " the Irish leader in Germany " with whom towards the middle of March, 1916, the German General Staff held long discussions and " decided to support the rebellion."

Doubt, scepticism and a final decision to back an Irish venture as an outside chance mark this account as of most German references to the Irish. Much in the same spirit Herr Banse in his *Germany Prepares for War* scoffed at the Sinn Féin visionaries who failed to rise in real revolt when Germany and England were at war, but after Germany's defeat foolishly turned to fight the powerful British Empire on their own. Even in Zimmermann's generous tribute to Casement after his execution the same sceptical attitude towards the 1916 insurrection breaks out:

" It was never my lot to know a man of loftier mind, of higher honour, or of more burning love of home. It was a matter of personal grief to me when I had heard he had made up his mind to accompany the expedition, which I greatly feared was fantastic. So I urged him, so far as I could in propriety, to remain with us and to do work among the prisoners. I felt sure Casement could not escape capture, and I knew what that meant. But he only shook his head, saying: ' I must go—I must be with the boys.' "[14]

Monteith's narrative of his experiences fills in some of the gaps in the German official version of the negotiations with Casement, who, however, was in the end by no means the real negotiator, as the Devoy letter already quoted makes clear. The final negotiations in 1916, and indeed in 1915, were carried through by the Revolutionary Directory of the Clan na Gael on urgent instructions from Ireland.

---

departure and cargo was sent from Germany.   He also notes that German code messages by wireless between Washington and Berlin had been decoded by the British. (*Mystery of the Casement Ship*), pp. 168, 263.

[14] " Roger Casement and the German Plot ", Frau Dr. Agatha M. Bullitt-Grabisch, *Voice of Ireland* (1924), pp. 118-20. The same writer claims that Germany had no more than twenty submarines at the time of the Irish expedition, and few troops to spare—apart from all considerations of the British blockade—for the expeditionary force Casement urged, as the war fronts, especially in the East had been greatly extended. Spindler (p. 275): " In those days we were suffering from a shortage of submarines."

CHAPTER III

CASEMENT IN GERMANY

An American journalist, Gilbert Hirsch, who met Roger Casement in Germany, declared afterwards that no one he met there during the war, not even Karl Liebknecht himself, leader of the German Social-Democratic militant anti-war minority, seemed to be so deeply shocked by the horrors of the European war as the Irishman who was finally placed on trial and charged with trying to extend that war to his native land.

" It is horrible," Casement said to Hirsch the last time they met. " Ghastly. In the first few months the excitement and the novelty, and the sense of the ideals for which men were fighting were foremost. But the longer it goes on the more it becomes slaughter, murder. The whole world has become a terrible place."[1]

Hirsch was convinced that Casement meant what he said:

" Everything about him—his tall, thin figure; his incredibly long thin face with the deeply lined forehead and the sensitive lips and nostrils; something shy about his manner; something abstracted, half-apologetic about his way of speaking—all indicated a man extremely susceptible to suffering. But the perpetual sparkle of humour and intrepidity in the clear grey eyes made it clear that it was the suffering of others to which he was quivering rather than to his own."

The American insists that Casement's situation in Germany had been difficult indeed, attacked as Casement realised he was in England, America, and even in Ireland while the Germans found it almost a physical impossibility to understand this chivalrous and fantastic " Irish gentleman "—even apart from their respect for constituted authority. This respect, Hirsch noted, had made them instinctively sympathise with England against Ireland before the outbreak of war and regard the Irish much as they thought of their own irreconcilable Alsatian, Polish and Danish subjects, not to

---

[1] *Evening Post*, May 1, 1916, quoted *Gaelic American*, May 6, 1916.

forget the Czechs, who forbidden by the German censorship to conduct diatribes against Germany in Bohemia, had evaded the ban by using the word "Irish" when they meant Czech and "England" when they meant Germany.[2]

Casement, in spite of his final friction with the German authorities and his suspicions of their bad faith, admired the German character, in particular its kindliness which he advanced to Hirsch as a conclusive argument against the Bryce report on "German atrocities." Though he spoke with respect of Bryce personally, whom he knew well since his own agitation in the Congo, Casement denounced the Bryce report with fury, and then, "just as one expects him to begin to moralise, he always breaks off and smiles at his own intensity. Although he seemed sad while he was in Berlin, he was never solemn . . . there was nothing of the conspirator about him."

Two statements in Casement's diaries summarise his mood and the results of his German mission, over which shadows of doubt fell almost at once. On November 2, 1914, as he sat on a sofa in the German Foreign Office, waiting for his first interview with Zimmermann, Secretary of State for Foreign Affairs, these were his thoughts:

"I thought of Ireland, the land I should almost fatally never see again. Only a miracle of victory could ever bring me to her shores. That I did not expect—cannot in truth hope for. But, victory or defeat, it is all for Ireland. And she cannot suffer from what I do. I may, I must suffer—and even those near and dear to me—but my country can only gain from my treason. Whatever comes that must be so. If I win it is national resurrection, a free Ireland, a world nation after centuries of slavery. A people lost in the Middle Ages refound and returned to Europe. If I fail—if

---

[2] In September, 1915, officers of the Irish Brigade issued a manifesto, part of which read: "We are only doing what many other soldiers of the 'small nationalities' are doing or are being asked to do by the Allied Governments of England, Russia, France and Italy. . . . At the present moment there are some twelve regiments of Bohemians, with special uniforms given by the Czar, in the Russian Army, fighting against the Austrian Army to which they belonged. If these things be loyal and right . . . then how much more right is it for Irishmen to volunteer to fight for Ireland and for that cause alone." Many other examples are given of the enrolment of similar corps by Allied Governments in this manifesto. Quoted, Recollections, Devoy, pp. 440-41. Devoy notes that the American Press refused to publish this defence of the Casement Brigade, which appeared only in the Gaelic American.

Germany is defeated—still the blow struck to-day for Ireland must change the course of British policy towards that country. Things will never be again quite the same. The 'Irish Question' will have been lifted from the mire and mud and petty, false strife of British domestic politics into an international atmosphere. That, at least, I shall have achieved. England can never again play with the 'Irish Question.' She will have to face the issue once and for all. With the clear issue thus raised by me she will have to deal. She must either face a discontented conspiring Ireland—or bind it closer by a grant of fuller liberties."

On December 12, 1914, Casement wrote:

"In my heart I am *very* sorry I came. I do not think the German Government has any soul for great enterprises—it lacks the divine spark of imagination that has ennobled British piracy. The seas *may* be freed by these people—but I doubt it. They will do it in their sleep—and without intending anything so great."

He had already come to distrust German diplomacy, and on the first of the same month wrote in his diary:

"They wanted—and want!—'English friendship.' The military machine, however (and happily), is under no such illusions and desires mightily to get at England—and . . . the military mind in Germany dominates the civil power in every way and also has absorbed far the ablest minds in the land, so that German intelligence is much better represented in Army and Navy circles than in the Foreign Office and governing administration. This is evident! If the men who have controlled German 'diplomacy' and brought this country to its present state of colossal isolation had the war machine to run, I guess the French and Russian armies would now be near Potsdam."

Casement was to live to revise his views of German military and naval intelligence, in Irish affairs at least.[3]

Monteith gives a picture of Casement when he first met him in Munich in October, 1915, very şimilar to that given by Hirsch. Monteith, who had been practically deported to the United States for his activities as an Irish Volunteer organiser, was sent to Germany by Tom Clarke to take charge of the Irish Brigade.

---

[3] Casement warned his friend, Dr. C. E. Curry, who later edited his German diaries that: "I often say things in them I should not like to stand over. . . . My remarks are often unjust, hasty and ill-considered." *Sir Roger Casement's Diaries*, Curry, p. 197.

Casement, by then, regarded his mission to Germany as a failure. He was despondent at the course of the war, and convinced that America would eventually side openly with the Allies. His outspoken expression of this belief had added to his difficulties with the Germans. Moreover, he had already stopped any serious attempt to continue recruiting for his brigade, a work which Monteith persuaded him to resume, or rather to be allowed to undertake on his behalf.[4]

His depression was deepened by his troubles over the " Findlay affair," which had become an obsession with him. This was the alleged plot by the British Minister in Norway, M. de C. Findlay, to kidnap Casement in October, 1914. This official was stated by Christensen, Casement's Norwegian servant, to have offered him £5,000 to assist in kidnapping or " knocking Casement on the head." Devoy's opinion, already partly set forth in the de Lacy letter, was that Christensen himself first concocted the scheme and approached Findlay for his own gain, and in the sequel so upset Casement's balance that " he lost for a time his sense of proportion when the greatest war in history was going on," as Devoy acidly put it. Colum, who took the same view, commented:

" If the British Minister had really wanted—and why should he not?—to destroy Casement, he could not have taken a better way than by projecting an unaccomplishable plot, for the obsession that thwarted Casement externally and internally was more destroying than any kidnapping could have been." Among the most pathetic episodes in Casement's sojourn in Germany was this Findlay affair with Casement's own gins and traps for Findlay, his frenzied demands on the Germans to publish the documents against Devoy's and Cohalan's appeals to him to wait, his nagging at the Irish-Americans to secure publicity for the plot when, as a news item, it was dead, his scheme—which fell through to his relief—to trap British battleships, the comic trips of Christensen to Findlay, and the spate of wearisome words in his own diaries on the matter.[5]

The Irish-Americans understandably enough were cynical. Why

---

[4] *Casement's Last Adventure*, Robert Monteith, pp. 66; 74 *et seq.*; 97-9. The writer vigorously defends Casement against the criticisms of both friends and enemies already noted.

[5] Parmiter, pp. 154-165; Devoy, pp. 423-430; Colum, *Dublin Magazine*, October-December, 1931; *Sir Roger Casement's Diaries*, Curry (Munich, 1922). Pearse's opinion was given to the present writer.

C

shouldn't Mr. Findlay get Casement spirited away if he could, wasn't that his business if the chance offered?   The Germans, already irritated and disappointed, became suspicious. Christensen, then under police observation, was neither a credible nor a credit-able witness; his morals in Dr. Curry's careful expression were rumoured to be " rather loose." After fighting all Christensen's critics, and rejecting every German and Irish-American warning against his servant, Casement suddenly woke up to the facts of his personal character and his pronounced anti-German sympathies, even detecting in him a warm admiration for the reported ruthless disposition of Mr. Findlay. Casement certainly in this had " lost all his sense of proportion when the greatest war of history was going on."   Pearse shook his head dubiously over the famous " Findlay document," and Casement's version of the plot, as given in his letter to Sir Edward Grey, and commented: " A strange story, isn't it?   It's more like something you read in a sensational novel.   Mediæval, you might say."   His tone was sceptical and disturbed.

It is not surprising that the German Government, the Clan na Gael, and the I.R.B. leaders in Ireland—Tom Clarke, Seán MacDermott and Patrick Pearse—were, for different reasons, all sharply critical of Casement's management of his mission and the Irish Brigade.   Monteith, who was on the spot and, therefore, with some right to be considered as a first-hand witness, though his deep admiration for Casement may have prejudiced him to some degree, resented both German and Irish-American scepticism of Casement's independent methods and, so far as the second was concerned, what he regarded as an ignorance of German conditions and, in particular, the reluctance and delay in sending funds to the brigade.

Casement himself, however, stung by a taunt about " German gold," wrote in March, 1916, to Dr. Curry that he had declined offers, amounting to 50,000 marks, from German publishers for a sensational book on the Findlay case, and added that since he came to Germany he had spent over £2,000 : " Far from my getting ' German gold ' it is the Germans have had Irish gold." Case-ment's further remark that certain lion-hunting Germans who deserted him when he fell into disfavour with official circles had done well out of him is no doubt true, but it is as well to record that when Count von Wedel learned of his wants, he raised a fund by private subscriptions among German friends, and placed it to Casement's account in a bank. Casement thanked him courteously, and never used the money. Casement's figures of the amount he expended in " Irish gold " is confirmed by a most critical source.

John Devoy later, angered by allegations that Clan na Gael had been slow to back Casement and his men financially, published figures of the Clan funds supplied to Casement: $2,500 in gold on his departure for Germany; $1,000 more in December, 1914; $1,000 in April, 1915; and over the remaining months of 1915 five remittances of $1,000, somewhat over £2,000 in all. Casement admitted that the Findlay fight cost him £300, much of which Devoy suspected Christensen had appropriated in swollen expenses, though in fairness it may be added that that much-abused gentleman's conspiratorial journeys hardly could be conducted with strict economy. Devoy also claimed rather disingenuously that the Clan had expected the Irish Brigade not to be a charge on them but an integral part of any military force the Germans might use in an Irish expedition. The Clan had finally given way to Casement's desire to go to Germany in the hope that he would be able to persuade the German Government to give military and naval aid to such an expedition on a suitable opportunity. As neither Casement nor the Clan from a very early period in the war believed that Germany's naval position allowed her to risk an expeditionary force on a large scale in Ireland, and as both Casement and the Clan were adamant that no financial German aid should be accepted under any circumstances whatever, it is obvious that Casement, whatever his mistakes in expenditure, had an arguable case in this controversy.

The Clan view, according to Devoy's memoirs, was that if Casement succeeded in getting any Irish prisoners of war to join an Irish contingent to volunteer for a fight in Ireland, then the Germans, as part of their war effort, would feed, clothe and maintain such volunteers for the future Irish expedition. In Devoy's opinion—and as a former Fenian organiser in the British Army who had won over Irish soldiers in regiment after regiment, he was certainly a most competent critic—Casement hopelessly mishandled and bungled his Irish Brigade, which in the end numbered no more than fifty-two men. Some of Devoy's criticisms of Casement in this were based on incomplete and hostile information. The real clash between Devoy and Casement was that Devoy looked upon the arming of Ireland as a work far more important than Casement's mission to Germany, and upon Casement as a dreamer, an egoist, and not a revolutionary. Again Devoy's own record and experiences as the man who had helped to arm the Ireland of the eighties gave him some authority as a judge in this. A haze of sentiment and pity has inevitably blurred the faults of Roger Casement on his last adventure, and very understandably so, in the eyes of his own nation at least. Yet his own diaries and the facts of the case prove Devoy's criticism of him as a poor conspirator and a visionary who pursued his way regardless of protest to be only too well founded. He had not the relentless revolutionary will of Devoy, Clarke, or Connolly, nor the single-minded resolution of Pearse.

Connolly and Devoy both had a grasp as wide as Casement's of international issues and, with Pearse and Clarke, believed that the most important blow would and could be struck only in Ireland, and that if the chance of the European war passed without militant action then Irish nationalism would inevitably sink to the level and inefficacy of a Jacobite legend. Devoy was insistent that the Irish Volunteers and the I.R.B. should have first claim on the Clan's often strained resources for arming and equipping the men in Ireland.

It was all these currents and controversies which came to a head in the message that startled Monteith and Casement in March, 1916. When it arrived Casement was in a sanatorium near Munich, resting after a severe attack of malaria some months before, still weak in body and depressed in mind, resentful and shaken by obvious German evasiveness and some outspoken Irish-American criticisms which the Germans had communicated to him.

Monteith, or so his own account suggests, was informed verbally that a dispatch had been received from the Irish Revolutionary Directory, of which a true copy could not be shown him as some passages had to be verified. A Rising had been ordered for Easter Sunday, April 23, 1916. The German Government was asked to help by sending an arms ship with field guns, gun crews and officers, machine-guns and rifles. It was requested that the arms ship be accompanied by a submarine escort, and that she should reach Fenit, County Kerry, on Easter Sunday night. It was suggested that the German Fleet should make a demonstration in the North Sea and that a submarine should be dispatched to Dublin

Bay. Sir Roger Casement was requested to remain in Germany in his capacity as ambassador. After giving him these details, the officer—by name Von Frey, according to Casement's account—representing the General Staff asked Monteith to think things over and let him have any suggestions necessary. Monteith then went to the Admiralty and discussed plans for the landing and had a long and, finally, heated argument on the number of rifles that could be sent. Three naval officers and a staff officer were present at this discussion. Monteith's efforts to obtain more than 20,000 rifles were useless, and he left uneasy and deeply disappointed. He wrote that night to Casement, who, however, was too ill to travel to Berlin, and Monteith, at his request, went to Munich, and gave Casement full details of his interview.

Casement immediately jumped to the conclusion that Devoy had been deceived by the Germans through the instrumentality of " that ass von Papen," Military Attaché at Washington, and that Ireland was to be tricked into a Rising " foredoomed to failure " in the interests of a mere military diversion to suit German interests. He realised that he was being deliberately kept in the dark, although he did not guess the reason. The Military Council in Dublin was responsible for keeping Casement in ignorance, because even before he left Ireland the insurrectionist party knew that Casement was opposed to an insurrection unless backed by great German naval and military assistance. The Military Council, moreover, had received an emphatic message in the same sense from Joseph Plunkett when he returned from Berlin in the summer of 1915. They knew that Casement's anti-insurrectionist views were also those of MacNeill and Hobson, both of whom Casement had deeply influenced in policy.

When Joseph Plunkett informed Casement in April, 1915, that a Rising was being planned to take place in Ireland before the end of the war, Casement told him bluntly that no insurrection could possibly succeed without the naval and military support of a great continental power; that a Rising in 1915 would be criminal stupidity; and, finally, added: " If you do it, if you are bent upon this act of idiocy, I will come and join you (if the Germans will send me over) and stand and fall beside you. Only I deprecate it wholly and regard it as the wildest form of boyish folly. I am not responsible for it, and while I strongly disapprove it, if these boys break out I could not, in honour, refuse to stand beside them, since however vain and futile their fight might be, it would be a fight—an act, a deed, and not talk, talk, talk. I, who have always stood for action (but not this action, and certainly not in these circumstances), could not stay in safety in this land while those in Ireland who have cherished a manly soul were laying down their lives for an ideal."[6]

Casement sent back a message by Plunkett to the Dublin leaders that he " saw no way whereby Germany could help Ireland," that he regarded his mission to Germany as ended, and that " the course of the war would probably render all hope of German help a vain expectation."[7] In December, 1914, he had secured a definite Treaty with the German Government as to the Irish Brigade, writing in his diary that he could not accept the responsibility for " putting Irish soldiers in the treason pot unless I get very precise and sure promises both in their regard and for the political future of Ireland." In the first fortnight in January, 1915, Casement decided that there was little hope of a German naval victory, and the failure of the Germans to reach the Channel ports increased his doubts. He gave up all attempts to proceed with recruiting for the brigade and candidly informed the Germans about his doubts and reasons. Plunkett urged him to resume the work, and he succeeded in enlisting some fifty-three men at Limberg, after scenes in which Plunkett was mistaken for him, and roughly handled.[8] From then on Casement's mind was racked with anxiety for his men to an extent which affected his already failing health considerably.

The meeting with Plunkett was also mentioned in a letter from G. Gavan Duffy to Patrick Cahill, Vice-Commandant of the Tralee Volunteers,[9] when asked to comment on a statement of Austin Stack in his *Kerry Champion* narrative of the events in Kerry in 1916 that Monteith had given him a message from Case-

---

[6] Quoted from an unpublished diary of Casement's, Parmiter, p. 218.

[7] Quoted Maloney, p. 116. Both Maloney and Parmiter base their quotations on Casement's papers and diaries deposited in the National Library of Ireland. The diary of Casement's life in Germany was published in the United States in 1920 and 1923; by Dr. Charles Curry in Munich in 1922, already noted. The Casement diary relating to 1916 was published in the *Irish Independent*, April, 1922, and in the American Press.

[8] Monteith in his account denies vigorously that any demonstration was made in Limberg against Casement. Parmiter suggests Plunkett made a speech there, was hooted, and mistaken by some for Casement.

[9] *An Phoblacht*, September 13, 1930.

ment after their landing that a Rising at the moment would be
" pure madness," that Casement had come to put this view before
the Volunteer leaders, and that " if he failed to persuade them, he
would do his duty as an Irish Volunteer and go out and fight with
the others."

Gavan Duffy—who knew Casement's mind very well, as his
friend and legal defender at his trial—replied:

" Your quotation from Austin is an accurate statement of Roger's
mind. As to the leaders in Dublin—what they were concerned
about was the landing of the arms. Plunkett had seen Roger in
Germany some time before and I suppose that the leaders knew
that he might come, but did not know his object in coming. He
had tried to convey to them by messenger that the Germans had
' let them down ' and felt that he must come himself, because he
doubted if they had got his message or, having got it, if they really
appreciated it. He believed they relied on German help much
more than they really did."

Casement was ignorant of the negotiations which Devoy, at the
request of Dublin, had conducted on their behalf during 1915 for
German help for the Rising which the Supreme Council of the
I.R.B. had decided on in August, 1914, and confirmed in
December, 1915. The Germans had refused aid on the scale
requested on the understandable grounds that British control of
the sea forbade it; but, apart from that, they had refused appeals
to send arms in small quantities by submarine. Plunkett's visit to
Berlin was one attempt by the Military Council to come to a
definite agreement, and he was sent as an envoy from the revolutionary party. His journey to Berlin was taken via Spain, Italy,
Switzerland. He grew a moustache and beard, made tortuous
divagations to throw any spies off his trail, and changed his name
to " James Malcolm." The details of his negotiations in Berlin
are naturally somewhat obscure, and the accounts of his mission
are somewhat fanciful and contradictory.[10]

Plunkett found Casement somewhat overscrupulous during their
tour of the prison camps. Casement insisted that the patriotism
of the Irish soldiers should be the sole basis of appeals to join
the brigade. Plunkett, according to Casement's account, pressed

---

[10] See *An Cosantóir*, " Joseph Plunkett," Donagh MacDonagh, November, 1945. A general character sketch which also deals with his Berlin
visit.

him to get on with this recruiting work even on the most modest
lines, "the effect of its existence would be felt in Ireland and
would act as a great deterrent to recruiting." Casement agreed,
and again resumed the task he had, before Plunkett's arrival, felt
compelled to abandon. He was shocked by Plunkett's impetuous
and somewhat cynical remark: "We'll get them if we have to
kidnap them." Plunkett, who used himself up in the service of
Irish freedom, and whose playful Machiavellianism and notorious
reticence to his closest colleagues has left him with a mantle of
mystery around him, was probably speaking only as a practical
revolutionary with more zest than guile, bent on using all material
to his hand with the utmost speed.[11] Indeed, according to Donagh
MacDonagh's account, presumably based on family tradition and
records, Plunkett in reality had little enthusiasm for the brigade
experiment, and looked for little success from it.

Even in Irish-Ireland circles of the time there were many who
regarded the Casement Brigade with some misgiving, mainly on the
grounds that the Irish soldiers had in the majority of cases joined
the British Army in a spirit of national enthusiasm following the
Redmond appeal, and had taken an oath of allegiance voluntarily.
Casement himself admitted the moral issue implicit in the oath,
which he left to each man's conscience, merely stressing that two
parties to an oath have equal obligations. In his view faith had
not been kept by the British, quite apart from the orgy of oath-
smashing which the Allies were applauding among Czech, Pole
and Alsatian. To which the Irish critics had retorted that these
nationalities had all been recruited against their wills into conscript
armies. It was an old problem. The honeycombing of the
British Army in another generation by Fenian emissaries had
troubled the conscience in retrospect of even such a determined
agent in that work as John Boyle O'Reilly.[12] Patrick Pearse and
John Devoy had no such misgivings.

---

[11] Quoted Parmiter, p. 218.

[12] *Reminiscences,* Justin McCarthy, Vol. 1, pp. 241-44. Joseph Cowen,
Radical M.P. for Newcastle, speaking in the House of Commons, August
1, 1876, in favour of the release of the Fenian military prisoners, pointed
out that Great Britain had paid £300,000 in pensions to Polish refugees
of the 1831 insurrection, "and many of them—the leaders especially—
had taken the oath of allegiance to the Czar in the same way as the
Fenian soldiers had taken the oath of allegiance to Queen Victoria. They
broke their oath to the Emperor, and led a rebellion against his authority.
How can the Government, with any consistency, patronise and pension

While in Berlin Plunkett had interviewed von Bethmann Hollweg, and discussed the possibility of securing a cargo of arms and ammunition, with German instructors for the insurgent forces in Ireland. He encountered obviously enough some scepticism as to the power and the reality of the revolutionary movement, as the story of the awkward and very reasonable question hurled at him during discussions with officers of the German General Staff: if Ireland really wanted freedom why had she not at once risen in revolt in August, 1914? Plunkett countered with an equally awkward and reasonable question: what would have happened in Posen if the Poles had risen against Germany in the same month? The answer came promptly: such a Polish revolt would have been crushed in a day. But Plunkett had not to point out a second time that there was an obvious parallel between the Polish and Irish positions.[13]

Plunkett is said, by those close in touch with the Military Council, to have informed its members on his return that the Germans had only committed themselves to send captured arms to Ireland, and that no others were then available. Yet Plunkett and his colleagues appear to have entertained hopes until the end of securing substantial aid from Germany in spite of these declarations as their repeated demands for German officers and a submarine to Dublin Bay (later revealed in intercepted messages) go to show. Moreover, the Military Council appears to have been under the impression that if a blow was struck in Ireland during the war, then Ireland would be backed at the Peace Conference as a belligerent by Germany. Zimmermann, it may be noted, pointed out very clearly to Casement that any representations on an Irish

---

rebellious Russian soldiers, and at the same time punish with such severity a handful of Irish soldiers who have done identically the same thing as the Poles did? If the Home Secretary can explain the difference of treatment, it is more than I can do." *Life and Speeches of Joseph Cowen, M.P.*, Evan Rowland Jones (London, 1885), pp. 296-300. Pearse's attitude was that no oath could bind an Irishman to serve British interests against Ireland, especially in such a crisis as 1914-16.

[13] *Banba* (Dublin), May, 1922, p. 41. Gerrard, *My Four Years in Germany*, p. 63, states the Germans believed that a general rebellion would break out in Ireland the moment that war was declared. Le Roux, *Life of Patrick H. Pearse*, p. 318, declares Plunkett "returned to Dublin full of hope that the Germans would send a full Expeditionary Corps to Ireland." The same writer traces Plunkett's journey to Berlin in some detail.

settlement from Germany to Great Britain in peace deliberations would be difficult, especially in the case of a German defeat.[14]

The phrase in the Proclamation, " gallant Allies in Europe," and certain expressions of the 1916 leaders before their execution, point to a hope that the insurrection would win German benevolence and aid for the Irish claims after the war.   An intercepted letter from an unnamed correspondent, apparently of John Devoy's, in the south of Ireland, transmitted by Bernstorff in June, 1916, to Berlin, cites Tom Clarke as having mentioned " certain documents in our favour."[15]   Pearse, in his conversations at St. Enda's before the Rising, spoke in similar terms when defending his policy of militancy: he argued, when confronted by the objection that British armed force would make short work of any revolt by the Volunteers, that even if that were true (a) a blow struck during the war would burst up the belief that the British Empire was united in favour of the war; (b) that " Germany had pledged her word that if this blow were struck during the war, Ireland would come into the peace terms as a belligerent."   Pearse's final declaration to his courtmartial that " he had asked for and accepted a German expeditionary force," is also worth noting.   It is, of course, open to the explanation that he was exaggerating his responsibility to draw as much blame as possible on himself, and thus save other leaders and his followers.   In his statements at St. Enda's, to the writer and others, he never stated anything more than that he had asked for German assistance in arms and munition, and hoped for a few German officers.   His final courtmartial statement might be taken as meaning that he expected German assistance on a larger scale.   The documents published by the British and Germans later are most definite evidence that no man in his senses could expect any landing of German troops on a large scale, the sense in which Pearse alone understood " expeditionary force."

In his arguments and conversations at St. Enda's Pearse, as the crisis grew nearer, often discussed the clash of opinion in the Volunteer leadership with a few of his senior pupils and members of his teaching staff.   Then he always stressed that MacNeill, Casement and Hobson were agreed that no successful uprising could or should take place without the aid of a minimum German

---

[14] Quoted, Maloney, p. 116.
[15] *Documents relative to the Sinn Féin movement*, p. 18.

expeditionary force of 50,000 troops, or in " equal forces to the British." This Pearse considered to be the same thing as saying that no Rising whatever should be attempted, and sometimes, with a courteous impatience, he said that " MacNeill is Grattan come to life again." Pearse thus implied that he himself considered aid from Germany on such a scale as the wildest of dreams or the most subtle caveat of all against insurrection. His use of the term " expeditionary force " was always in the sense of the large force of 50,000 men, and he would certainly not, in the usual course, describe the *Aud* expedition—the full details of which were perfectly well known to him through messengers from America—in any such grandiose terms. There is not one atom of fact to indicate that he or any of the 1916 leaders were deceived into expecting any such " expeditionary force " when they actually rose in arms, all propaganda whitewash notwithstanding.

The Germans, whatever else they may have been, were certainly blunt and to the point. They listened with patience to Casement when he told them openly that he doubted their victory so much that he must decline to continue to recruit for his Brigade, and scarified their tactless handling of Irish prisoners of war, but to those who negotiated for arms behind his back they made no pretence of their ability to provide arms except on the smallest scale, and that grudgingly and dubiously. They professed no enthusiasm for Irish freedom nor ever made Irish independence a war aim. There is, however, every evidence that the Germans certainly wanted the 1916 Insurrection if the Irish were prepared to make such a desperate gamble with the most modest of resources.

Evidently the German official mind was divided on the question as to whether Ireland was worth using. Karl Spindler declared bluntly in *The Mystery of the Casement Ship* that the German Admiralty was interested in the Irish expedition and a successful Rising there as a means of obtaining submarine stations along the Irish coast while the German General Staff " did not take the initiative out of a pure friendship for Ireland but simply because it reckoned on the possibility of a timely end being put to the war as the outcome of a successful Rising." Devoy himself resented the muddling caused by the friction between the German Foreign Office, Admiralty and General Staff whereby their various agents interfered with the others' plans. In particular, Devoy denounced the foisting on Casement of untrustworthy meddlers by the German military authorities, without the authority of himself, Bernstorff or von Papen.[16]

" The Germans," cried Casement bitterly at the end, " want cheap Irish blood!" There was some excuse for his outburst. He did not know certainly that the instructions to the German submarine commander of U.19 which brought him out of Germany were that Casement was not to be allowed to land before the *Aud's* cargo was safely ashore. His anger and suspicion were aroused by the determined effort and the great pressure exercised to persuade first himself, and then Monteith over his head to embark the Irish Brigade on the arms ship, and by the impression of callousness and duplicity left upon both himself and Monteith during the discussions in March-April, 1916, with the General Staff. Captain Nadolny of the General Staff outlined the German proposals which, he tried to persuade Casement, would place the Irish in the position of dictating terms to the British Government and securing at least autonomy: " If sincere, and he believed what he said, he was a bigger fool than any I had yet met—and if not sincere he must have taken me for that man," wrote Casement later.

" We have no idealistic interest in Ireland," said Nadolny, " no revolution, no rifles. If it were not that we hope for a military diversion we should not send the rifles." There was a further clash when Nadolny threatened to inform Devoy that because of Casement's criticism of the inadequacy of the aid, the Germans were compelled to withdraw their offer, " and leave your countrymen in Ireland in the lurch." He also tried to insist that the Casement treaty with the German Government was null and void and that the Irish Brigade would be sent to Ireland in spite of Casement's objections: Casement retorted sharply and the Brigade remained in Germany. Unknown to Casement, the Germans were extremely embarrassed as to what they could or could not tell him. Devoy had asked them to keep Casement in Germany as he thought Casement's presence in Ireland would merely bring confusion.[17]

---

[16] *Recollections*, pp. 444-48. For Spindler, see his book, p. 265.

[17] *Recollections*, Devoy, p. 472. For Casement's discussions with the German General Staff, see Parmiter, p. 242; Maloney, Ch. 8; and *Irish Independent*, April 18, 1922. Spindler, p. 240, quotes a German Admiralty statement urging, on February 28, 1916, the use of Irish prisoners of war, *i.e.*, the Irish Brigade, on the gun-running trawlers, first proposed for the 1916 expedition.

To add to all this play of cross-purposes, Casement next dispatched a messenger to Ireland behind the backs of the Germans with a message giving details of the German help proposed and a warning that any Rising dependent on such help should be called off. When Nadolny discovered that the messenger, John McGooey, had gone, he denounced it as a " gross breach of faith." Other members of the German General Staff expressed the fear that Casement in fact had sent McGooey to stop the Rising. Casement replied that he was not the master of the Irish revolutionary body and, whatever he might say could be only advice or suggestion. Casement's messenger, a Glasgow Irishman who had come from the United States to help the Brigade, never reached Ireland.[18]

Apart from the German announcement that a Rising had been fixed for Easter Sunday, Casement received on April 6 the same information from Joseph Plunkett, who had asked his father, Count Plunkett, then on the Continent on his way to Rome, to transmit the following message:

" BERNE,

5th April, 1916.

' Ashling.'

DEAR ROGER CASEMENT,

I am sent here as a delegate by the president and supreme council of the Irish Volunteers, and through the courtesy of his Excellency the German Ambassador am enabled to give you this urgent message from Ireland:

(1) The Rising is fixed for the evening of next Easter Sunday.

(2) The large consignment of arms to be brought into Tralee Bay must arrive there not later than the dawn of Easter Monday.

(3) German officers will be necessary for the Volunteer forces. This is imperative.

(4) A German submarine will be required in Dublin harbour.

---

[18] According to Maloney, p. 253, he was captured by the British and " secretly executed at Kirkwall." Spindler, pp. 244-45, quotes Casement's previous demand through Monteith, March 7, 1916, that Casement, McGooey, and another member of the Brigade should go by submarine to Ireland to lay the German offer before the Dublin leaders. The demand was refused.

The time is very short, but is necessarily so, for we must act of our own choice, and delays are dangerous.

Yours very sincerely,

A FRIEND OF JAMES MALCOLM."[19]

The code word "Ashling" showed Casement that the letter came from Plunkett. He wired to Berne details of the arms cargo and stated that no German officers were going to Ireland. The message was never forwarded and was returned to him before he left Germany. Plunkett's message certainly gave Casement good grounds for believing that Dublin was in somewhat of a fog regarding the exact aid Germany was sending. Monteith recalled the incident very clearly as it was one of the few occasions on which he had ever known Casement to lose his temper, and he lost it very thoroughly upon this occasion.

A curious fog had certainly settled over the Dublin revolutionary councils. It was not the fog that Casement feared, but it was a fog in which he and Plunkett alike were to perish, the fog of ill chance and last minute bungling which through history so fatally pursued the romantic insurrectionists of Ireland. One bungled date, and Casement and his comrades were to go the road of Emmet and Tone.

---

[19] Another version of this document, slightly differently worded, is given in *The Irish Republic*, Dorothy Macardle, p. 155, wherein (2) Easter Saturday, and not Easter Monday, is given as latest date for arms landing. The above version is quoted from Casement's diary as given by Parmiter, pp. 244-45, quoted from *Irish Independent*, April 22, 1916. The Military Council, as will be seen, about the same time dispatched Miss Philomena Plunkett to Devoy with a warning that the arms must not be landed before the night of Sunday 23rd, and an inquiry as to whether a submarine would come to Dublin Bay. The Casement diary version would then seem to be a slip. Monteith, writing in *An Phoblacht*, November 15, 1930, accepts the "Easter Saturday" version as accurate, but describes the version of Casement's reply quoted by Spindler as not "quite accurate."

CHAPTER IV

THE KIDNAPPING OF JAMES CONNOLLY

ON January 19, 1916, James Connolly disappeared without a word to his family or closest intimates. No message reached his family in Belfast; no word was left with Michael Mallin or any other officer of the Citizen Army. From the afternoon of that day until late on the night of January 22, all trace of Connolly was lost.

The tone of his *Workers' Republic* for some weeks had been an open incitement to immediate insurrection, the leading article written before his disappearance, and published in the issue of January 22, unusually so: a campaign that stopped with his reappearance. In the first week in February, Connolly attended a meeting of the Military Council in Eamonn Ceannt's house, Herberton Road, Rialto. Pearse, Clarke, Plunkett, Ceannt, and MacDermott were present, MacDonagh was absent, and Connolly was in high spirits and on excellent terms with those present. He now knew the date of the Rising, and had reached a final agreement to act with the Military Council, to moderate the violent campaign in his paper, and abandon his openly declared intention to strike independently with the Citizen Army. From then onwards, Connolly regularly attended the meetings of the Military Council.

Behind all this lay a mysterious episode, which even to-day is none too clear, and of which the full details have remained a secret. From the outbreak of war, Connolly came more and more in touch with the leaders of the I.R.B. and Irish Volunteers who were working for insurrection, although he made no formal and binding alliance with them until the summer of 1915 at least, and more probably only within a few months of the Rising. The final agreement can be read between the lines of the brief " Notes " on the front page of the *Workers' Republic* of January 29:

" Our notes this week will be short. The issue is clear and we have done our part to clear it. Nothing we can say now can add point to the argument we have put before our readers in the past few months; nor shall we continue to labour the point.

" In solemn acceptance of our duty and the great responsibilities attached thereto we have planted the seed in the hope and belief that ere many of us are much older it will ripen and blossom into action.

" For the moment and the hour of that ripening, that fruitful blessed day of days we are ready. Will it find you ready?"

When Patrick Pearse read these words, he looked unusually thoughtful and commented: " Dangerous enough. Perhaps Connolly thought those were the last words he would ever write."

There are two explanations of Connolly's disappearance, and both are upheld by men of considerable knowledge and authority in the I.R.B. of that time, and by Connolly's own associates. The first explanation is that the Military Council kidnapped Connolly and held him prisoner until he agreed to co-operate with the I.R.B. plans for the insurrection and make no more calls in public for action. The second explanation is that Connolly disappeared of his own free will in order to round off his *Workers' Republic* campaign by forcing the Military Council to consent to immediate insurrection. The difficulty in deciding between these two explanations is that Connolly himself never confided even to his closest friends or the members of his family the reasons for his absence, while on the I.R.B. side there was almost as complete a reticence.

In January, 1916, Patrick Pearse in a conversation with the present writer at St. Enda's made the nearest reference he ever made to this incident in Connolly's life. He asked for a copy of the *Workers' Republic* of January 29, read it carefully and, as mentioned above, described the leading article as " dangerous enough," adding that Connolly possibly thought these were the last words he would ever write. Pearse then said that Connolly had planned to lead out the Citizen Army alone as a means of forcing the Volunteers into action; that Pearse had learned of this, taken every means to prevent it, and had not slept for a week. Pearse made no reference to kidnapping or hinted that any such action had been contemplated or had occurred. He said that, believing that Connolly was determined to take action at once on his own, both Seán MacDermott and himself had gone to Connolly, and urged him as strongly as they could to hold his hand, that he would ruin well-laid plans if he did not, and that he would have the Volunteers as allies if he waited. Finally, after what Pearse described as a terrible mental struggle, Connolly turned to Pearse with tears in his eyes, clasped his hand warmly, and said: " I agree, but God grant, Pearse, that you are right!" As he told this, in a lower room in St. Enda's, Pearse added emphatically: " God grant that I was . . perhaps after all, Connolly was right." And turning back to read the *Workers' Republic* again, Pearse said with deep feeling: " Connolly is a great man . . . what a great man."

Beyond recording what happened between himself, MacDermott, and Connolly at this meeting, Pearse's story throws no light on what preceded it. At Christmas 1915, he had in another conversation described the relations between Connolly and the militant Volunteer leaders as a state of " armed neutrality." About the same time, Pearse with unusual sharpness commented: " Connolly is most dishonest in his methods. In public he says that the war is a war forced on Germany by the Allies. In private he says that the Germans are just as bad as the British, and that we ought to do the job ourselves. As for his writings in his paper, if he wanted to wreck the whole business, he couldn't go a better way about it. He will never be satisfied until he goads us into action, and then he will think most of us are too moderate, and want to guillotine half of us." Pearse smiled, and went on: " I can see him setting up a guillotine, can't you? For Hobson and MacNeill in particular. They are poles apart. What can he do anyway just now? Riot for a few days." Later, Pearse summed up his position towards Connolly and the Citizen Army and certain Volunteers who sympathised with them as having had to " do his best to restrain people with whom he really agreed and thought in the right."

The rumour went round the Citizen Army that Connolly had been captured by the Volunteers and held prisoner. A Volunteer —unnamed—was quoted as boasting: " Our people have him safely where he'll do no harm." In an article in the *Free State*, 1922, George A. Lyons openly stated for the first time that Connolly had been kidnapped by order of the Supreme Council of the I.R.B. and held prisoner until he agreed to fall in with their views. The statement was repeated even more definitely by P. S. O'Hegarty in his book, *The Victory of Sinn Féin* (pp. 16-17), two years later. Seán MacDermott was quoted as saying in May,

D

1915, that the Military Council had had a lot of trouble with Connolly, expected more, and that unless he could " be brought to reason they were afraid that he would say or do something which would put the British on the alert." Mr. O'Hegarty declares that the trouble culminated in the kidnapping and detention of Connolly " for several days until he agreed to fall in with the I.R.B. plans and arrangements."

As Mr. O'Hegarty had been a member of the I.R.B. Supreme Council, and Mr. George A. Lyons was well known to be an authority on the I.R.B., such definite statements at first seemed to settle the question once and for all. One objection to this explanation was obvious : Connolly was the last man on earth to be easily intimidated, and, moreover, the agreement reached with the Military Council was just what he wanted, and what he had agitated for. It has even been suggested that if Clarke and MacDermott set a trap for him, he cheerfully walked into it with his eyes wide open. Yet the Citizen Army had the greatest difficulty at any time in persuading him to tolerate any personal bodyguard even when rumours of British intentions to seize or assassinate him were current. Connolly's quarrel in any case was not with the Military Council who, he knew very well, were wholeheartedly for insurrection, but with those of the Volunteer leaders, in turn described as would-be Wolfe Tones, " legally seditious and peacefully revolutionary."

Connolly was known to have been absent at other periods before and during his preparations for final revolt, and this had been urged to explain his absence in January, 1916, as a personal tour of inspection on his own of suitable positions for occupation and a survey of military barracks including the Curragh Camp. Connolly, however, had already made sure of obtaining a very accurate idea of the strength of military garrisons through several friendly sources, and his actual inspection of the Easter Week positions was certainly carried out in the company of various Volunteer commandants, including Thomas MacDonagh. Moreover, his last absence thoroughly alarmed the Citizen Army, which insisted, on his return, in overruling his objections to a bodyguard to the extent that he at last agreed to have some armed men within call to be summoned by a blast of a special whistle. After the shock and unrest in the Citizen Army caused by his unexplained absence, Connolly could no longer refuse although he only then agreed when his officers pleaded with him that otherwise the " men would go wild and do something desperate."[1]

Michael Mallin, Connolly's chief lieutenant, told Frank Robbins, also an officer of the Citizen Army, that he had a very uneasy time during Connolly's absence in January, and finally insisted on interviewing the Military Council and warning its members that if Connolly did not return within a specified period, the Citizen Army men would take up positions in Dublin, and begin action on their own, especially if they attempted to arrest Mallin himself.

Eamonn Ceannt, who was present, resented Mallin's ultimatum, and said sharply: " What could your few numbers do anyway?"

Nettled, Mallin retorted:

" We can die, and it will be to our eternal glory, and to your shame."[2]

Ceannt was merely expressing bluntly the simmering anger and alarm of the Military Council caused by Connolly's tactics, and using language used by Pearse and the other members some months before. Of all the members of the Council, Ceannt was the nearest to Connolly's social views, Pearse alone excepted. Ceannt had defended the workers in 1913 in the columns of *Sinn Féin* against Griffith's criticisms, and had studied social theories closely, yet, first and foremost, especially from the rise of the Volunteer movement, he was a soldier, and given to very downright and even contemptuous expressions when roused by what he considered slackness, evasion or indiscipline. Then indeed, Eamonn Ceannt no longer fitted the apt phrase of his friend, Stephen MacKenna, who compared him to a remote and tranquil harvest moon, and more wittily to a good-humoured uncle telling his Volunteer nephews to use their little fists for their rights like little men. He regarded Mallin and Connolly as endangering the hard work of months, he suspected their sincerity in this wild ultimatum, and he rapped out his full mind in the bluntest words that came to his tongue, with nothing of harvest moon or kind uncle in his manner.

Pearse was touched by Mallin's retort, and restored peace between Ceannt and Mallin by saying with the persuasive passion

---

[1] Nora Connolly O'Brien, *Portrait of a Rebel Father*, pp. 249-52. His daughter found that Connolly desired no discussion of his disappearance or even any reference to it.

[2] *Torch*, August 14, 1943.

that gave his words a peculiar power, usually on a platform, only in rare moments in private:

" Yes, by God, you are right, and here is one who is with you!"

In fact, the entire Military Council was with Mallin even if they had kidnapped his leader, and preferred their own plans and their own moment for insurrection.   Pearse, however, had eased the tension, MacDermott and Clarke discussed the matter with Mallin in a friendly spirit, and finally he agreed to wait until the next day when Connolly in fact reappeared without a word of comment or apology.

Mallin, moreover, by force of circumstances, was not a free agent. His abrupt approach to the Military Council was a desperate move to control the Citizen Army, or a large section of it and some of its officers, who had grown more and more restive the more Connolly's disappearance remained a mystery, and inquiries in Dublin and Belfast failed to bring any news of him. Mallin knew quite well that the British were unlikely to spirit Connolly away, and leave the other Citizen Army and Volunteer leaders in peace. He guessed and guessed rightly that the Military Council had more interest in the removal of Connolly at that particular time.   Madame Markievicz was urging action on the Citizen Army, and it needed great nerve and patience to avoid her precipitate counsels and incitements, which he was very well aware could not be carried out except at the risk of suicide, while the blunt warning he received in the course of his meeting with the Military Council showed him that the Volunteer organisation could not be dragged into action in these circumstances, as the leaders of the militant party which controlled them had warned him they would then be as hostile to action as the more moderate MacNeill group obviously would be. In his difficult game of calming the Citizen Army, controlling Madame Markievicz and her backers, and daring the Military Council, Mallin played a bad hand with skill.

These pre-Easter days were days of mystery and cross-currents. Even Denis McCullough, a member of the Supreme Council of the I.R.B. at the time, thirty years later strongly denied that Connolly was ever kidnapped, and contended that the three days' disappearance was all part of a subtle ruse to force an immediate insurrection.[3] He declares that while a meeting of the Supreme Council was in session in Clontarf Town Hall, where Michael McGinn, an old I.R.B. man, was curator, Seán MacDermott reported that Connolly was missing and that he understood that an agreement existed between Connolly, Mallin and Madame Markievicz that if any one of the three were arrested, the remaining two would call out the Citizen Army to take up positions for a Rising. This, of course, especially in January, 1916, would be a grave threat, if not fatal altogether, to the completion of the I.R.B. plans for an arms landing and insurrection at Easter.

After a long discussion, MacDermott, according to McCullough's account, was sent to inform Mallin and Madame Markievicz that, if they took the threatened action, no help would be forthcoming from the Irish Volunteers so far as the Supreme Council could prevent it, and, in addition, the Supreme Council would repudiate the Citizen Army action. MacDermott was also authorised to inform them that the Supreme Council had decided that a Rising would take place but the arrangements and date were matters for the Supreme Council and the Military Council which it had appointed, that Connolly's disappearance was regarded as an attempt to rush them, which they would not permit, and that Mallin and Madame Markievicz would be well advised to refrain from their threatened precipitate action which could only spoil the plans made and being made by the I.R.B. Two hours later, MacDermott returned to Clontarf Town Hall with a semi-assurance that no Citizen Army action would be taken for the present. Such is McCullough's recollection of what happened at the Clontarf S.C. meeting. The following week he returned to Belfast and soon heard that Connolly had not only turned up but was working in harmony with the Military Council.

Others present at this meeting disagree with McCullough's impression: the members of the Military Council were silent, and Clarke in particular, though well aware that Connolly was captive, " never batted an eyelid." He had in fact sent several friendly warning messages to Connolly from time to time, assuring him that

---

[3] *Torch*, September 4, 1943; March 4, 1944. Mr. McCullough's account followed one by Frank Robbins, already mentioned, and replies by George A. Lyons, November 27 and December 4, 1943, in support of the kidnapping theory. In the same paper, J. J. Burke, in the issue of November 13, 1943, described the interview between himself, Ceannt and Connolly mentioned later in the text.

everything possible had been done, and urging strongly that Connolly's impatience and general tactics were endangering the insurrection plans. (To reconcile Mallin's story to Robbins with McCullough's account, obviously Mallin's encounter with the Military Council must have taken place before the Supreme Council met.)

In his considered defence of the kidnapping theory, George A. Lyons insisted, in spite of the McCullough denial, that in January, 1916, the I.R.B. leaders in Dublin decided to have matters out with Connolly once and for all. His writings in the *Workers' Republic* week by week intensified the lack of understanding between the Volunteers and the Citizen Army. Pearse, Ceannt and MacDermott interviewed Connolly and returned disturbed and distressed afterwards. A secret convention of I.R.B. Centres considered the position and passed a resolution that "members of the organisation shall be warned against being led into any irregular or unauthorised conflict with the British forces, and in the case of any unexpected disturbance members shall report to their mobilisation quarters and await orders through the Executive of the Volunteers." This resolution was circulated to all I.R.B. circles, and a similar resolution was adopted by the Volunteer Executive and circulated to all companies.

In the I.R.B. of the time, Mr. Lyons states, there was not unanimity in the higher circles: " Seán MacDermott was very keen on fighting under any circumstances; others seemed to be building on a fifty-fifty chance of success. Young Colbert declared that if any shot was fired for Ireland by anyone he would second it unless he got very definite orders not to do so, whereupon he was told that he would get very definite orders."

Connolly, continues Mr. Lyons, openly defied this order in the *Workers' Republic,* and said that he would draw the Volunteers into a fight in spite of their leaders. Some time after, Connolly vanished for three days, and George A. Lyons was informed by a member of the Supreme Council of the I.R.B. that he had been arrested by " the Military Emergency Committee of the I.R.B.", and this story was generally accepted at the time. The Supreme Council and the Military Emergency Committee would naturally be inclined to deny it.

Denis MacCullough denied after the Lyons' statement was published that any All-Ireland Convention of the I.R.B. was held or contemplated during his membership of the Supreme Council, although there might have been a Convention of Dublin or Leinster Centres, and repeated that the Supreme Council " was as much surprised and concerned at James Connolly's disappearance as were his more intimate friends in the Citizen Army."

Within the Volunteers and the I.R.B. there were many officers as well as rank and filers who sympathised deeply with Connolly's propaganda for a revolt before the war ended, as indeed appears from the Lyons' statement quoted, which is moreover confirmed in one important detail by Connolly's defiant article in the *Workers' Republic*, January 22, 1916: "What is Our Programme?" This far more than his brief statement on his reappearance deserved Pearse's description—" the last words he thought he would ever write." This "What is Our Programme?" is the nearest approach to a personal testament that Connolly left behind him, not excluding his courtmartial statement: all his social ideals and his philosophy of revolt are here. One passage in particular is plainly the answer of a man who has been in heated and lengthy controversy with the Volunteer and I.R.B. leaders, and is replying to a definite warning: " . . . .insist that in the crisis of your country's fate, your first allegiance is to your country and not to any leader, executive or committee, and you are forthwith a disturber, a factionist, a wrecker. What is our programme? We, at least, in conformity with the spirit of our movement, will try and tell it.

" Our programme in time of peace was to gather into Irish hands in Irish trade unions the control of all the forces of production and distribution in Ireland. We never believed that freedom would be achieved without fighting for it. From our earliest declaration of policy in 1896 the editor of this paper has held to the dictum that our ends should be secured ' peacefully if possible, forcibly if necessary. . . . '

" What is our programme now? At the grave risk of displeasing alike the perfervid Irish patriot and the British ' competent military authority ', we shall tell it.

" We believe that in times of peace we should work along the lines of peace to strengthen the nation, and we believe that whatever strengthens and elevates the working class strengthens the nation. But we also believe that in times of war we should act as in war. We despise, entirely despise and loathe all the mouthings and mouthers about war who infest Ireland in times of peace, just as we despise and loathe all the cantings about caution and restraint to which the same people treat us in times of war.

"Mark well, then, our programme. While the war lasts and Ireland is still a subject nation we shall continue to urge her to fight for her freedom. We shall continue, in season and out of season, to teach that ' the far-flung battle line ' of England is weakest at the point nearest its heart; that Ireland is in that position of tactical advantage; that a defeat of England in India, Egypt, the Balkans or Flanders would not be so dangerous to the British Empire as any conflict of armed forces in Ireland; that the time for Ireland's battle is NOW, the place for Ireland's battle is HERE; that a strong man may deal lusty blows with his fists against a host of surrounding foes, and conquer, but will succumb if a child sticks a pin in his heart.

"But the moment peace is once admitted by the British Government as being a subject ripe for discussion, *that moment our policy will be for peace,* and in direct opposition to all talk or preparation for armed revolution. We will be no party to leading out Irish patriots to meet the might of an England at peace. . . . We are neither rash nor cowardly. We know our opportunity when we see it, and we know when it has gone."

This expresses Connolly's mood and conviction at the time—or most of it. He could hardly have believed, though he often hinted so in his propaganda, that peace was a probability in 1916. There is an anticipation in his words of Lenin's judgment on 1916: " A rebellion in Ireland has a hundred times more political significance than a blow of equal weight would have in Asia and Africa." He was to strike his blow, and hope a distant future would vindicate him, not foreseeing that in fact an insurgent Ireland would rise " against the might of an England at peace."

J. J. Burke, a Dublin Volunteer closely in touch with Connolly and the *Worker's Republic,* had some sharp words with him in Liberty Hall in January, 1916. Connolly told Burke abruptly and with intense feeling that the Citizen Army would move within a week on its own and under his leadership. Connolly declared that he did not believe that the Irish Volunteer leaders meant to move or would move only too late. " The ' bide your time doctrine '," Connolly went on, referring to the examples of the 1798, 1848, and 1865-67 insurrections, crippled or frustrated by British Govern-

ment swoops on the eve of action, " has ruined Ireland's chance of
success before, and the same doctrine will ruin it now." Burke
retorted that the Volunteers would move, and quoted Pearse,
MacDermott, Clarke, Ceannt and The O'Rahilly as men who were
not likely to let the war's opportunities pass. Connolly agreed,
but pointed out that other important leaders in the movement
were in favour of a waiting policy. After further argument,
Connolly consented to Burke telling his Commandant, Eamonn
Ceannt, what had been revealed about the Citizen Army plans,
with full permission to communicate them to Pearse and The
O'Rahilly.

Ceannt acted quickly after Burke delivered Connolly's message.
The following day a meeting took place between Ceannt, Pearse,
The O'Rahilly and Connolly in Liberty Hall. Later Connolly
informed Burke—just before the raid on the newspaper shop
attached to Liberty Hall on Eden Quay, March 24, 1916—that,
" we have arranged everything. The date is not as soon as I would
like, but it is definite. You were not long in getting in touch with
your leaders and I am glad." (In his article in *An t-Oglách*,
February 6, 1926, Burke placed the date of his talk with Connolly
in February-March.)

In truth the relations between Connolly and the insurrectionary
leaders are even yet obscure. He certainly made a similar statement as to the date being perilously late, in the autumn of 1915
after the Rossa funeral to Cathal O'Shannon. There are those
who maintain that Connolly began to work in co-operation with
the Military Council just before the O'Donovan Rossa funeral
in July, 1915. Seán McGarry, as the editor, approached Connolly
and asked him to write an article for the literary souvenir of the
Rossa funeral then in preparation. To McGarry's surprise, Connolly
curtly refused this request with an outburst of irony and scepticism,
bitterly phrased: " When are you fellows going to stop blethering
about *dead* Fenians? Why don't you get a few *live* ones for a
change?" McGarry somewhat nettled by this gruff reception said
he had not come to discuss such questions but merely to ask for an
article. He reported what had happened to Tom Clarke, who
smiled and said: " Send him to me. I'll fix that." Connolly and
Clarke had a heart-to-heart talk, and Clarke apparently fixed it
all because Connolly wrote an article in which he managed to turn
a dead Fenian into a live incitement to revolution, precisely as

Clarke, Pearse, and the other members of the Military Council had, according to Fenian precedent, decided to do before him:

" The burial of the remains of O'Donovan Rossa in Irish soil, and the functions attendant thereon must inevitably raise in the mind of every worker the question of his or her own mental attitude to the powers against which the departed hero was in revolt. That involves the question whether those, who accept that which Rossa rejected have any right to take part in honour paid to a man whose only title to honour lies in his continued rejection of that which they have accepted. It is a question each must answer for himself.

" But it can neither be answered carelessly nor evaded.

" The Irish Citizen Army in its constitution pledges its members to fight for a Republican freedom for Ireland. Its members are, therefore, of the number who believe that at the call of duty they may have to lay down their lives for Ireland, and have so trained themselves that at the worst the laying down of their lives shall constitute the starting point of another glorious tradition—a tradition that will keep alive the soul of the nation.

" We are, therefore, present to honour O'Donovan Rossa by right of our faith in the separate destiny of our country, and our faith in the ability of the Irish workers to achieve that destiny." (*Rossa Souvenir,* " Why the Citizen Army Honours Rossa," p. 19.)

From then onwards, according to this theory, Connolly worked in co-operation with the Military Council although it is not clear that he was then formally a member of it, and certainly with many displays of temperament, scepticism, and almost open opposition. Connolly appeared to several I.R.B. leaders to be a very hard man to work with, and his tactics, as before noted, even made them suspect his good faith in part, and his intelligence altogether. He seemed to them unduly suspicious, quarrelsome, and obsessed by the idea that an independent blow by twenty Citizen Army men would lead to an all-Ireland insurrection, while his views on military tactics appeared hopelessly amateur, short-sighted and reckless. Above all, he refused to admit that the British would ever shell Dublin, " because a capitalist army will never destroy capitalist property." Connolly not only antagonised the I.R.B. leaders and the more level-headed of the Volunteer military leaders—in spite of the respect for Connolly which persisted in spite of his escapades in word and act—but incurred the criticism of such Labour men as Seán O'Casey who said Labour had lost a leader, and such sympathisers as Francis Sheehy-Skeffiington who once publicly expressed the hope that " Connolly would return to the ways of peace."

Connolly's relation with the insurrectionary leaders, and his attitude to the war in general display the agony of a strong mind, bitterly disillusioned and wrestling with contradictions in his beliefs, and struggling with an iron despair against the force of the world hurricane.

He was in a mood of bitter disillusion because the Socialist and Labour movement to which he had given so many years of work and propaganda had collapsed in face of the war, because his union, the Irish Transport and General Workers' Union, was almost bankrupt in members and funds after the Dublin struggle of 1913, because the attitude of British Labour and Irish national-ism alike had angered him during that very bitter and stubborn lock-out. Friction, co-operation, alliance one day, grim neutrality and recrimination the next, incitements to open revolt and per-sonal attacks on those whom he considered moderate and vacillat-ing, were the steps on the road to complete agreement and an offensive alliance with the I.R.B. Military Council.

Connolly met Pearse in the autumn of 1914 both at a meeting in September at the Gaelic League Dublin headquarters at Parnell Square and on other occasions. At the Parnell Square meeting Tom Clarke, Seán T. O'Kelly, Eamonn Ceannt, James Tobin, Pearse, Seán McGarry, Arthur Griffith, Connolly, William O'Brien of Dublin, and others representing various national and Irish-Ireland organisations discussed the war situation as it affected Ireland and to what degree co-operation could be carried on between them. This conference discussed the situation in general terms. At a later conference after Redmond's Woodenbridge speech in favour of recruiting the Volunteers for the war abroad, and the split which at once took place in the Volunteer organis-ation, a desperate plan was put forward to seize and hold the Dublin Mansion House where a joint recruiting appeal by Red-mond and Asquith was announced for September 25. Connolly was strongly in favour of the proposal, which was only abandoned when it was learned that the confusion and defects in the plans arranged to seize the building and occupy it by armed force against all comers had given the British military authorities ample time and opportunity to be in position first with a strong detachment of soldiers and machine-guns. Connolly was then fully prepared to participate in this desperate venture, and shrugged his shoulders with a wry and disappointed expression when it had to be called off. In a letter to his friend William O'Brien, later published in the Glasgow *Forward*, December 28, 1935, Connolly said it " was a desperate situation," that he was " afraid our friends of the conference have not got sufficient dash and desperation," that everything planned for the Asquith demonstration would be backed by British military force: " In a sense all our future is on the cast of that die. I am ready for any call."

Piaras Beaslai, who was present at the final conference in Parnell Square (then Rutland, to be precise) on September 25, where eighty armed Volunteers and Citizen Army men with Connolly, MacDermott, Pearse, Clarke and others were present, describes Connolly as the leading spirit in this undertaking, and speaks of his " relentless determination ".

On November 23, 1915, Connolly writing to decline an invitation from his Scottish Socialist friend, Arthur McManus, to address an anti-conscription meeting in Glasgow, showed an equally relentless determination in the terms of his refusal: " I would gladly accept . . . but every moment in Dublin just now is full of tragic possibilities . . . and my presence is required here in constant watchfulness. . . . We in Ireland will not have conscription, let the law say what it likes. We know our rulers; we know their power, and their ruthlessness we experience every day. We know they can force us to fight whether we wish to or not, but we also know that no force in their possession can decide for us *where* we will fight. That remains for us to decide; and we have no intention of shedding our blood abroad for our masters; rather we will elect to shed it if need be in the battle for the conquest of our freedom at home." (*Socialist*, Edinburgh, April 17, 1919.)

It was against such a background that the final tussle between Connolly and the Military Council took place in January, 1916. Details of his detention—if detention it was—are few and vague. A house in the Lucan district has been mentioned as the spot, but those rumoured to have been concerned have guarded an impenetrable silence on the subject. Those who deny the kidnapping ever occurred believe that Connolly never left Dublin but remained in hiding studying the plans for the Rising. Where Connolly went to, who held him captive if captive he was, all this still belongs to rumour and conjecture.

James Connolly returned to Madame Markievicz's house in Leinster Road on the night of Saturday, January 22, unobtrusively. William O'Brien, who called to see Madame Markievicz, was surprised when he was told that Madame Markievicz was out and asked " if he would like to see Mr. Connolly, who is upstairs." Connolly was silent about his absence, so significantly and grimly silent that William O'Brien saw at once that it would be useless to question him.   Miss Helena Molony next arrived and asked Connolly point-blank where he had been, and received the smiling and evasive reply: " That would be telling you." Nor was Madame Markievicz on her return more successful in her cross-examination beyond one remark extracted from Connolly that he had been " through hell!" There was very little information for anyone in his final word to Miss Molony that he had walked forty miles that day.

Although the constitution of the I.R.B. had always provided for a Military Council, attached to and subject to the Supreme Council, in February, 1916, objection was raised to the constitutional status of the existing Military Council which was then reorganised. It was to this reorganised body that Connolly was formally admitted a member after the events of January, 1916, and his final agreement to follow the plans and direction of the I.R.B. There is no clear evidence as to whether Connolly himself was ever formally sworn into the I.R.B. although his name was believed to have been circulated to the Dublin Circles of that organisation some time before Easter. Connolly was fully aware of the activity of the organisation after his return to Ireland in 1910. His opposition to and open contempt for secret societies was often very vigorously expressed in his earlier propaganda. Yet on the outbreak of the war, he expressed his desire to his friend, Cathal O'Shannon, who, he knew, was friendly with several prominent Belfast and Dublin leaders of the I.R.B., that he wished to get in touch with that organisation and was willing if necessary to swear a hundred oaths if that would help to establish friendly relations between militant Nationalist and Labour elements. Connolly's pact with the Military Council was not made known to the Dublin officers and rank and file of the I.R.B.—a mistake in the opinion of George A. Lyons.

From February, 1916, the " war party " in the Citizen Army, the I.R.B., and the Volunteers was a united bloc. The meeting of the Supreme Council at Clontarf had, with apparently some reservations on the part of some of its members, reaffirmed the resolution on an insurrection before the close of the war decided on in 1914, and reaffirmed it with one dissentient. According to Seán T. O'Kelly, *An Phoblacht*, April 30, 1926: " If it were not for Connolly the Rising might not have taken place just exactly at that time." The decision took the Clan na Gael leaders in America by surprise as they had not expected action so soon and regarded the war situation as unfavourable to the effort at the time. As Devoy states in his memoirs, however, they conceded the right of those in Ireland to decide the question, and at once threw all their support and efforts behind the insurrection.

Eoin MacNeill, Connolly and Pearse also had an interview early in February at MacNeill's own request. He was disturbed and alarmed by Connolly's evident intention to force a clash between the national armed forces and the British at the earliest possible moment. MacNeill's main argument to Connolly was an insistence that Connolly's revolutionary insurrectionist policy, his " start first, and get the rifles afterwards " propaganda, his contemptuous " between the Molly Maguires and the Molly Coddles we'll be landed in the soup ", were all very fine to start with but very bad and uncertain guides to carry through a prolonged and successful fight against British power. MacNeill even urged that rather than cede a Republic under stress of war, Britain would withdraw every available soldier from the West. MacNeill further stated, that though a separatist by conviction and sentiment, he was convinced that Irish independence would come by stages, and that—short of an overwhelming British naval and military defeat —a Republic was not an immediate possibility. He made a strong appeal to Connolly to change his tactics and to talk less about aggressive action during the war. Connolly refused to be swayed by MacNeill's long and courteous argument, and said sharply: " I am glad to know where we all stand." In the end, Connolly went away and left MacNeill and Pearse together. Pearse, according to MacNeill's own account, agreed that Connolly was a little unreasonable, but that perhaps Pearse himself might persuade Connolly.

This is the story Le Roux gives in his *Life of Pearse*, based " on

an unpublished memorandum of MacNeill" which on the publication of Le Roux's biography MacNeill agreed was an authentic
document. William Pearse gave the writer substantially the same
story of the Connolly-MacNeill interview, adding that MacNeill
did not understand how far he had really committed himself.
Pearse, according to his brother, welcomed MacNeill's declaration,
at this or at an earlier interview that he was a separatist and their
ultimate national ideal was the same. Cathal O'Shannon's own
account of the same interview to the writer added the detail of
Connolly's sharp retort.

Pearse did not inform MacNeill that he and the Military Council
had made peace with Connolly only by revealing to him that they
were resolved upon insurrection on a specific date; nor that
MacNeill himself was being consistently kept in the dark, and used
as the best possible screen for preparations for a revolt to which,
in the circumstances, he was outspokenly and consistently opposed.
That MacNeill was as much in the dark, however, as some of his
defenders and admirers have contended, is very difficult to credit.
He should have suspected the real purpose of Pearse, MacDermott,
Clarke and Connolly from their characters, their own very explicit
declarations and actions. He probably underestimated their intelligence although in the war of wits between him and his conspiring colleagues, it was he who won in the end by one single
stroke which did more to localise and curb the insurrection of 1916
than all the power of Britain.   Yet the testimony of his closest
friends of the time—confirmed by his actions in Holy Week, by his
very vacillations and changes of mind as the crisis broke upon him
—is unanimous: almost to the end he suspected nothing. He lived
the life of a secluded scholar, disliked meetings, which he rarely
attended, and never answered letters. Fortunately for his
immediate peace of mind, the circumstances of James Connolly's
disappearance and its sequel in the conferences with the Military
Council were then unknown to him.[a]

---

[a] See Appendix VII.

CHAPTER V

As the plans of the Military Council for insurrection matured, on the Monday before Easter, most opportunely a document was made public which alarmed the general public and hardened the militant temper of the Irish Volunteers to such a degree that even in the ranks of Sinn Féin and the Volunteers there were those who asked with delighted scepticism: " Whoever forged this?"

It was a very natural question. This document purported to outline very drastic measures decided upon by the British military authorities against not only the Irish Volunteers but against Sinn Féin, the Gaelic League, and the Redmondite National Volunteers with just the methods best calculated to put the British in the wrong before the average citizen in Ireland, and to send up the temperature to a height very favourable to those who had already fixed the date of the armed uprising, and were then busy putting the finishing touches to the good work. This document was indeed not the least skilful of the touches, with its provocative suggestions of occupation of Irish-Ireland centres, isolation of premises, deportations, arrests, and even action against the Archbishop of Dublin.

After a brief attempt to prevent publication in the daily and weekly Press, the British military authorities lifted the ban on publication, and declared indignantly that the document was " an absolute fabrication from beginning to end and did not contain a word of truth," adding that the " object of this fabrication " was obvious.

Eoin MacNeill for the moment disagreed and declared to his colleagues of the Volunteer Executive at a meeting in his house: " The Lord has delivered them into our hands!" Patrick Pearse also scouted the military denial, and showed Liam Mellows— then hiding in St. Enda's—with some show of pleased excitement this list of proposed arrests, the formal list of premises to be raided, the details of the proposed military round-up, above all the references to a swoop on The O'Rahilly's house, on St. Enda's College,

Joseph Plunkett's armed camp and bomb factory at Kimmage, Madame Markievicz's home, James MacNeill's rustic retreat near Rathfarnham, Liberty Hall, on Irish Volunteer and National Volunteer premises alike, and, above all, that most helpful suggestion of British provocation and stupidity, the isolation of the Archbishop's House at Drumcondra. And Pearse went ahead with his preparations, into that adventure which he now often described as " a race between us and the Government." Whether Pearse himself really believed in this document is not certain. He certainly was very reticent in discussing it, although he is said to have told some enquirers that it had been obtained from a friendly source in Dublin Castle. MacNeill's enthusiasm did not last. Scepticism soon gripped him after Bulmer Hobson and Captain J. J. O'Connell examined the document more carefully and discovered certain points in it which made them doubt its authenticity.

This document read:

" The following precautionary measures have been sanctioned by the Irish Office on the recommendation of the General Officer Commanding the Forces in Ireland. All preparations will be made to put these measures in force immediately on receipt of an Order issued from the Chief Secretary's Office, Dublin Castle, and signed by the Under-Secretary and the General Officer Commanding the Forces in Ireland. First, the following persons are to be placed under arrest: All members of the Sinn Féin, the Central Executive Irish Sinn Féin Volunteers, General Council Irish Sinn Féin Volunteers, County Board Sinn Féin Volunteers, Executive Committee National Volunteers, Coisde Gnotha Gaelic League. See list A 3 and 4 and supplementary list A 2. . . . Metropolitan Police and Royal Irish Constabulary forces in Dublin City will be confined to barracks under the direction of the Competent Military Authority. An order will be issued to inhabitants of city to remain in their homes until such time as the Competent Military Authority may otherwise direct or permit. Pickets chosen from units of Territorial Forces will be placed at all points marked on Maps 3 and 4. Accompanying mounted patrols will continuously visit all points and report every hour. The following premises will be occupied by adequate forces, and all necessary measures used without need of reference to Headquarters. First, premises known as Liberty Hall, Beresford Place; No. 6 Harcourt Street, Sinn Féin

E

Building; No. 2 Dawson Street, Headquarters Volunteers; No. 12 D'Olier Street, *Nationality* Office; No. 25 Rutland Square, Gaelic League Office; No. 41 Rutland Square, Foresters' Hall; Sinn Féin Volunteer premises in city; all National Volunteer premises in the city; Trades Council premises, Capel Street; Surrey House, Leinster Road, Rathmines. The following premises will be isolated, and all communication to or from prevented: premises known as Archbishop's House, Drumcondra; Mansion House, Dawson Street; No. 40 Herbert Park; Larkfield, Kimmage Road; Woodtown Park, Ballyboden; St. Enda's College, Hermitage, Rathfarnham; and in addition premises in list 5 D, see Maps 3 and 4."

The *Aud* and Casement were already near the end of their voyage to the Irish coast. The warning from the British Admiralty that a gun-running ship had left for Ireland had already reached Dublin Castle where the reservation made as to the authenticity of the report lulled Viceroy, Chief Secretary and General Officer Commanding the Forces alike, and the last two left for London in the pleasant hopes of a quiet Easter. It was then this most opportune document emerged from whispers in Dublin drawing-rooms to an open debate at Dublin Corporation and, after a brief interval, was published in the Press. Neither the British military authorities, nor the military leaders of the Irish Volunteers, outside the Military Council, expected full-scale insurrection.

So the general public and even large sections of the Irish Volunteers received the news of a pending British military swoop with indignation and alarm, for this action inevitably meant an armed conflict. Public pledge after public pledge had been made, and warning after warning given by Volunteer leaders from Eoin MacNeill downwards that the Volunteers would surrender their arms only with their lives. Already a police raid on a Volunteer Hall at Tullamore in March had led to an exchange of shots and casualties while sections of the British and Irish Press, controlled by the Unionists, were calling for suppression of all anti-British activities, aided by solemn and pointed diatribes by Mr. Justice This and Mr. Justice That, and the sinister pressure from within Dublin Castle of certain military and police officials.

It was obvious enough even to the most indignant readers of the document that the British military and civil powers would have been greater fools than their most savage critics imagined if there had in fact been no record of the more dangerous Sinn Féin, Volunteer, and Labour leaders and rank and file, and their centres no precautionary measures in outline to deal with such obvious contingencies of wartime as an insurrection long-threatened on many platforms and in many seditious and subversive papers, a German landing or attempted gun-running. General Friend by implication admitted that such measures in outline were most certainly ready when he informed the Royal Commission in 1916 that this document, although " a pure invention," was indeed " very cleverly got up, except that some places were named that we should never have thought of seizing . . . the Archbishop's house was named . . . it was one." (Comm. Report. Evid. P. 67.)

General Friend in these words put his finger on the very point which had already perplexed his enemies in their inner and heated circles. The document had been first brought to the attention of the Military Council and the Executive of the Irish Volunteers by Joseph Plunkett, who had perfected and fabricated it into its final form of a threat of imminent British aggression on the basis of what he knew or could surmise of the genuine precautionary measures drawn up by the British military authorities. Whether Plunkett really knew of these measures in whole or in part, whether he obtained certain hints of what these measures actually were from a friendly official in Dublin Castle, or whether he boldly forged the entire document with the help of his combined poetic and military imagination is not of great importance. Romantic as is the haze which screens his memory, and courageous as was his bearing when, a half-dying man, he went into insurrection, his contemporaries very often regarded him as an adult Tom Sawyer trimming a revolution with conceits borrowed from romances. He revelled in passwords, ciphers, and the mummeries of dusty conspiracies. His involved and ceaseless arguments irritated them as much as his Machiavellian shifts and elaborations for the simplest mission. In Berlin his assurance infuriated some German observers who told an Irish sympathiser in good American: " That blowhard Plunkett thinks he can teach our General Staff how to run the war!" The Irish Volunteer officers he sent on missions took his instructions more charitably as the ways of a poet, laughed at his passwords, promptly disregarded them and went the straightest way to work. ("You will meet a man in X outside the Railway Hotel, he will polish the radiator of a car with grass as you approach, you will ask: ' Are you Thomas?' He will answer: ' Do you come from William?' You reply: 'I am William!' He will salute, and say: 'I will now lead you to Thomas in his house behind the Market Square.' This order was much simplified by the formula: 'I'm So-and-So. Take me to Tommy Mac.'")

In the form Plunkett presented the document to the Volunteer Executive and through them to the general public at that time of all times, it was in effect a ruse of war to create an atmosphere for the Rising, or more bluntly, if the reader prefers, a clever forgery to deceive Eoin MacNeill, Chief of Staff of the Volunteers, the rank and file of that organisation, and the Irish people in general, a calculated deception, obscured with a characteristic mystification of codes, maps 3 and 4, list this and that, all for the benefit of not enemies but of friends and colleagues. And this is made clear from the very circumstances of the document's publication, and confirmed even more by the attempts made very much later to vindicate its authenticity.

Forgery is a strong word, but that in its final form the document was a forgery no doubt can exist whatever, and General Friend himself shrewdly indicated this in his reference to the improbability of any British action against Archbishop Walsh—who ironically enough regarded the Rising as madness, and deplored that a Government with ample force at its command had not prevented it, or in a word, had neglected to adopt those very precautions supposed to have been planned against himself. The introduction of his name was merely a nimble exploitation of popular respect for the Archbishop, whose reputation as a patriot stood higher than that of any other member of the Catholic Hierarchy from the Land League until his death.

The Archbishop's message to the people of Dublin immediately after the Rising ran: " In this time of unprecedented excitement and danger through which our city is at present passing, I deem it a duty to exhort, with all earnestness, our Catholic people to take to heart the warning that has been issued by his Excellency, the Lord Lieutenant, of the danger of frequenting places, of assembling in crowds." (Quoted *Banba*, May, 1922.) The Archbishop, though his sympathies were always strongly Nationalist, had not clashed with the British authorities as Bishop O'Dwyer of Limerick had already done, and like Bishop O'Dwyer he evidently regarded an armed uprising in the circumstances as theologically unjustifiable. He was certainly the last man in Ireland the British had any reason to antagonise or to regard as a public danger to them in a time of crisis, nor was it until much later that he pronounced definitely for Sinn Féin. The British had already repressed the itch of the military authorities to arrest the already openly defiant Dr. O'Dwyer; it was most unlikely they should attack Dr. Walsh for no reason whatever.

The Archbishop, however, strongly resented an attempt made by Sir James O'Connor, later an Irish historian of sorts but then an unknighted law officer of the Crown, on Easter Monday, 1916, to persuade him to call upon the insurgents to lay down their arms unconditionally and denounce the Rising publicly as a mad enterprise. Dr. Walsh agreed that in his own view the Rising was a folly which must end in defeat, but told the excited and panicky messenger from the Castle that his suggestion was preposterous, and that both he and his Government ought to resign as incompetents who, with ample force at their disposal, had failed to avert the bloodshed. He spoke to his own secretary of his resentment that such an incompetent administration should have the effrontery to attempt to make a cat's-paw of him, and try to suppress the Rising by spiritual weapons. (*William J. Walsh, Archbishop of Dublin*, Walsh, p. 592. Dublin, 1928.)

Nothing has ever been proved by the defenders of the authenticity of the " Bogus " or " Castle " document except, of course, that some precautionary measures existed, while all the evidence points either to an incredible carelessness on the part of the British military and civil authorities, or a sinister complacency, on the part of some at least in allowing the insurrection to mature and break out in the hope that both Sinn Féin and any prospect of Irish autonomy alike could be both defeated. The *Aud* commander asked himself again and again during his voyage whether the British naval patrols which hovered round his ship and then let her pass unchallenged were silly or subtle; the definite Admiralty warning to Dublin Castle of the departure of the German arms ship was very casually received; Eoin MacNeill after his arrest was invited by the same Major Price, who thought the murder of Skeffington was a public service, to implicate Dillon and Devlin in the preparations for the Rising. Seen in retrospect, one of the mysteries of that time is the casual conduct of both Dublin Castle and the insurgents in most vital matters. In this

crazy pattern of chance and error, a chapter of accidents defeats
an All-Ireland Rising, the *Aud* evades the blockade, and insurrection breaks out.

Early in March, 1916, Rory O'Connor informed Mr. Patrick J.
Little—editor of *New Ireland*, and later de Valera's Minister for
Posts and Telegraphs—that a certain official in Dublin Castle
occasionally had an opportunity to consult certain files, and had
discovered in them a document in code which set out plans for
the military occupation of Dublin. This most sympathetic
official had decoded the plans at odd moments as he had the chance.
Mr. Little agreed to publish this information in *New Ireland*, and
thus defeat the militarist plans, for Mr. Little no more than most
people had any inkling that the Military Council had determined
on insurrection. A committee was formed to give the alleged
British plans so wide a publicity that they could be defeated. The
members were: F. Sheehy-Skeffington, L. P. Byrne (Andrew E.
Malone), Dr. Séamus O'Kelly, and Mr. Little. They all acted to
prevent bloodshed and they were all in fact opposed to any attempt
at insurrection. They acted in good faith and were all convinced
at the time that the document was genuine. Not one of them
really knew or suspected that, British plan or no British plan, bogus
document or genuine document, the date for insurrection had been
fixed by the Military Council of the I.R.B. two months before.

According to Mr. Little's account,[1] Rory O'Connor produced
the document in two parts during meetings at Dr. O'Kelly's house
in Rathgar Road, and other witnesses of these meetings are agreed
that the code messages were produced at the meetings piece by piece
while the friendly official in Dublin Castle snatched his rare and
precious glances at the originals. James Connolly, who apparently
had enough sensations on his hands, generously informed Mr.
Little that he would not publish anything on the matter in the
Workers' Republic, and left a clear scoop to *New Ireland*.
Connolly was convinced, document or no document, from his
reading of the history of Irish insurrections that the British Government would inevitably swoop on the militant forces and their
leaders in its own chosen time. He knew, doubtless, that any
charge made by *New Ireland*, then the organ of the left wing of
Redmondite constitutionalism, would be more effective than any-

---

[1] *Capuchin Annual*, 1942. " A 1916 Document," P. J. Little, pp. 454-62.

thing published in the *Workers' Republic,* which had predicted action against the Volunteers in nearly every issue for weeks on end.

The real tension and temper of the times are best recalled in a remarkable letter written by Sheehy-Skeffington on April 7, which was addressed to the London *New Statesman,* and published after Skeffington's murder in its issue of May 6, 1916. Skeffington was convinced that a grave danger of disaster existed because of the temper of the military party in Dublin Castle, and believed that the document showed its mind and immediate plans, and this inspired his outspoken warning of the explosive situation in Ireland. Prophetically and vividly he summarises the situation on the eve of the outbreak, and the summary reveals his own attitude against insurrection as a pacifist, and his sense of impending tragedy. This summary makes clear why he very naturally accepted the document as genuine:

" There are two distinct danger-points in the position. In the first place, the Irish Volunteers are prepared, if any attempt is made forcibly to disarm them, to resist, and to defend their rifles with their lives. In the second place, the Irish Citizen Army (the Labour Volunteers) are prepared to offer similar resistance, not only to disarmament, but to any attack upon the press which turns out the *Workers' Republic*—successor to the suppressed *Irish Worker*—which is printed in Liberty Hall.

" There is no bluff in either case. That was shown in Tullamore on March 20th, when an attempt at disarming the small local corps of Irish Volunteers was met with revolver shots and a policeman was wounded—fortunately not seriously; in Dublin on March 25th and following days, when, at the rumour of an intended raid on the *Workers' Republic,* the Irish Citizen Army stood guard night and day in Liberty Hall—many of them having thrown up their jobs to answer promptly the mobilisation order—armed and prepared to sell their lives dearly. The British military authorities in Ireland know perfectly well that the members of both these organisations are earnest, determined men. If knowing this, General Friend and his subordinate militarists proceed either to disarm the Volunteers or to raid the Labour Press, it can only be because they *want* bloodshed—because they want to provoke another '98, and to get an excuse for a machine-gun massacre. . . . Twice already General Friend has been on the point of setting Ireland in a blaze

—once last November, when he had a warrant made out for the arrest of Bishop O'Dwyer of Limerick; once on March 25th, when he had a detachment of soldiers with machine-guns in readiness to raid Liberty Hall. In both cases Mr. Birrell intervened in the nick of time, and decisively vetoed the militarist plans. But some day Mr. Birrell may be overborne or may intervene too late. Then, once bloodshed is started in Ireland, who can say where or how it will end?

" In the midst of world-wide carnage, bloodshed in our small island may seem a trivial thing. The wiping out of all the Irish Nationalist and Labour Volunteers would hardly involve as much slaughter as the single battle of Loos. Doubtless that is the military calculation—that their crime may be overlooked in a world of criminals. Accordingly, the nearer peace comes, the more eager will they be to force a conflict before their chance vanishes. Is there in Great Britain enough real sympathy with small nationalities, enough real hatred of militarism, to frustrate this Pogrom Plot of British Militarist Junkerdom?"

Again General Friend admitted later during his evidence before the 1916 Royal Commission that he had prepared to raid Liberty Hall on several occasions but had been overborne, adding: " I was of the opinion that if we undertook anything of that sort we should make one big blow with an ample and sufficient force and arrest the leaders at the same time." He first suggested such action in October, 1915. (Evid. p. 7.)

Bishop O'Dwyer wrote to the *Munster News*, November 10, 1915, strongly defending the Irish emigrants who had been mobbed at Liverpool, and prevented from sailing on the *Saxonia* by its crew. This letter was described by Mr. Birrell before the same Commission " as one of the most formidable anti-recruiting pamphlets ever written. . . . It did not lend itself to proceedings." (Evid. p. 67.)

Skeffington was given no opportunity of appealing to the sympathy in Great Britain for small nationalities and against militarism until he had been murdered in Portobello Barracks by a crazy neurotic in charge of a panic-stricken garrison on the 26th of the same month, and Major Price, Director of Military Intelligence, Dublin Castle, had infuriated Sir Francis Vane with the epitaph: " Men like Skeffington are well out of the way."

It was into such an explosive situation that the squib of the

" Castle Document " was thrown. George Plunkett and Colm
Ó Lochlainn were given the task of setting up the document on
a small handpress in Kimmage, and printing it. Joseph Plunkett
at the time was in Miss Quinn's private nursing home in Mountjoy
Square. This was on April 13, 1916. An additional flourish was
introduced by Joseph Plunkett in his instructions to the compositors which Rory O'Connor delivered: punctuation and capitals
to be omitted as the original had no such marks. There was a
very serious error in this famous original which Colm Ó Lochlainn
detected and insisted should be referred back to Joseph Plunkett.
It was the mistake in the name of the Archbishop's House, Drumcondra, which was given as *Ara Coeli*—the name of Cardinal
Logue's house in Armagh. Jack Plunkett was at once dispatched
on his motor bike to the nursing home, and returned in less than
an hour with the laconic message from his brother: " Make it
' Archbishop's House '." The work of setting up was completed
with the exception of a line or two when Ó Lochlainn left.
Unfortunately, as Rory O'Connor was examining the forme later,
it was upset, the type scattered, and the whole task had to be
begun again.

Thirty years after, the slip about the " Archbishop's house "
was explained by Mr. Little as a natural " error of a stranger in
the British service." It is more probable that a stranger's
ignorance might also extend to the very name of Cardinal Logue's
house, and in fact neither the Plunkett brothers nor Rory O'Connor
detected the error until Ó Lochlainn pointed it out and insisted
on Joseph Plunkett being consulted.

The most serious point in the case of those who, like Mr. Little
and Donagh MacDonagh, contend that the document was genuine[2]
is a statement made to Mr. Little by an anonymous informant who

---

[2] The reference to Mr. Little's article has already been given. Donagh
MacDonagh, *An Cosantóir*, " Joseph Plunkett," November, 1945, relies
upon the same evidence as Mr. Little. He also claims that " Grace
Gifford, who married Joseph Plunkett, was present while he decoded
parts of the document." Le Roux, *Life of P. H. Pearse*, pp. 345-7, who
says the document " was either an extremist ruse of war or a genuine
summary of information in Joseph Plunkett's possession," mentions that
he had seen a copy of the code in Plunkett's own handwriting. Eimar
O'Duffy's satirical novel, *The Wasted Island*, upholds the forgery theory.
Miss Dorothy Macardle, *The Irish Republic*, p. 948, notes the *Ara Coeli*
slip in the original, and states, p. 164, that Rory O'Connor, Joseph and
George Plunkett " fabricated the document, embodying plans which they
knew to have been prepared in the Castle."

actually saw certain "precautionary measure" proposals on the files of Dublin Castle. The statement asserts that the document sent by Mr. Little, after he had received it from Rory O'Connor, to Alderman Tom Kelly, who read it at a meeting of Dublin Corporation on April 19, was certainly authentic. His admissions, however, weaken this confident claim:

"The document was an outline of the method (suggested by the G.O.C. in Ireland to the British Government) for grappling with the 'dangerous state of affairs' in Ireland. I was in a position to know, at first-hand, the entire contents of the suggested plan of operations and I can definitely confirm the truth of the contents of the document. *Only the reference to the maps and lists are unfamiliar to me and I assume these were inserted, presumably in London, but certainly after the matter had passed out of my sphere of duties. I cannot confirm that the plan of operations as suggested by the G.O.C. was ordered to be put into execution.*"

If anything this confirms General Friend's own admissions at the 1916 Royal Commission, but where are the codes and the evidence that action on the part of the British was imminent? The document was certainly a most opportune one. Further evidence at the Royal Commission shows that Plunkett had a shrewd idea of the measures the British military and civil authorities had in mind in the future, while the statement above quoted shows that precautionary measures proposed were in fact on the Castle files.

It was only on the very eve of the insurrection that the British finally decided to move. Lieutenant-Colonel W. Edgeworth Johnson told the Royal Commission that at a conference at the Viceregal Lodge on April 23, while discussing a proposed raid on Liberty Hall to recover explosives seized by the Citizen Army at a Dublin quarry, that he had urged stronger action than a single operation against Liberty Hall, as that was only nibbling at the fringe of the question:

"His Excellency asked me what I proposed. I urged the arrest of the leaders, military occupation of their strongholds, and disarmament. The Under-Secretary agreed to this finally. It was the unanimous opinion of the conference that this plan should be put into operation as soon as possible. . . . My view was that the police, assisted by the military, if necessary, should simultaneously arrest all the leaders, twenty to thirty of them, in Dublin, about 2 o'clock in the morning in their private homes, and send them across Channel either by special boat or by the mail boat, and intern them on the other side. Meanwhile their strongholds in Dublin to be occupied by strong pickets so that when the rank and file heard of the arrest of the leaders, and when they commenced to mobilise in these halls they would be met and disarmed by military pickets. Then I considered that immediately afterwards a house to house search should be carried out of the houses of all known Sinn Féiners who had arms, these to be taken from them, and anything in the shape of arming or drilling to be prohibited in the future." (Evid. pp. 53-4.)

On the eve of his execution, Seán MacDermott was asked what was the truth about the " Castle Document." He smiled and said: " That is a secret that is buried in Joseph Plunkett's grave— a secret that I and Plunkett will keep."

CHAPTER VI

EASTER EVE

On Palm Sunday, April 16, 1916, James Connolly with much military ceremony had the Green Flag flown over Liberty Hall. " On that day," runs his own description in the *Workers' Republic,* " the Irish Citizen Army, the armed forces of Labour, on the top of the Headquarters of the Irish Transport and General Workers' Union, hoisted and unfurled the Green Flag of Ireland, emblazoned with the Harp without the Crown, and as the sacred emblem of Ireland's unconquered soul fluttered to the breeze, the bugles pealed their defiant salute, and the battalion presented arms, strong men wept for joy, and women fainted with emotion."

In spite of all the cares of Holy Week, Pearse laughed long and gaily as he read this outburst, so unusually flowery even from Connolly on the eve of battle; reports of a second Palm Sunday gathering pleased Pearse less.

On Palm Sunday evening, at a Cumann na mBan concert in a Parnell Square hall, Mr. Bulmer Hobson was asked at short notice to take the place of a speaker who could not be present. As he then strongly suspected that the Military Council were moving towards insurrection, and as strongly held the belief that the majority of the Volunteers were opposed to that, he took the opportunity to issue a guarded warning. He said that it was first necessary for the Volunteers to perfect their organisation and pre- serve it so that it could influence the eventual Peace Conference in Ireland's favour when the war ended. It was not enough to rely on fighting forlorn hopes or leaving a glorious tradition behind yet one more failure. No man had the right to sacrifice others merely that he might make for himself a bloody niche in history. This speech startled the audience and was the first public hint of division in the leadership. There was to be a sequel to Hobson's speech on the very day that his friend Roger Casement landed in Ireland. Casement had left Germany four days before.

It was not until the middle of Holy Week that the real crisis

of Easter Eve began. Until then the Military Council pressed
ahead with its preparations. On Spy Wednesday evening, while
the Citizen Army drilled in a room in Liberty Hall, Connolly
sent an urgent message to the Citizen Army officers, R.
McCormack, Joseph Doyle and Frank Robbins, to meet him at
once in his office. He informed them that the insurrection had
been fixed for Easter Sunday evening. It would begin in Dublin
at 6.30 p.m. and at 7 p.m. in the provinces. He then assigned
them parts and positions in the Rising. The utmost secrecy was
to be preserved. A shipload of arms, including some artillery with
officers and men to operate it, was expected from Germany.[1]

Connolly outlined to one of the officers the methods to be used
to check the advance of British troops from Portobello so that the
Citizen Army detachment allotted to Stephen's Green could take
up posts and strengthen defences uninterrupted. This place had
been selected because it commanded so many points for rifle fire:
Grafton Street, Harcourt Street, Leeson Street, Kildare Street, and
it was intended to seize the Shelbourne Hotel and other buildings
in the Green. Connolly had already informed the Citizen Army,
and won their consent to his proposal that the force should co-
operate with the Volunteers in various positions although the
Citizen Army men would have preferred to fight as one unit. The
Stephen's Green position in fact was held by the largest single unit
of the Citizen Army in the Rising but the plans there were based
on a full mobilisation of Volunteers and Citizen Army there. The
Green was to be surrounded by barricades across the main
approaches. Later developments were in fact to turn the position
into a death-trap and a shambles although the original scheme was
sound.

To allow uninterrupted occupation of the Green and the neighbouring posts Connolly assigned sixteen men under Joseph Doyle
for an occupation of Davy's public-house at Portobello Bridge.
They were to allow the British forces to advance within a reasonable distance, surprise them with heavy volleys of rifle fire, and
continue firing until the troops retreated. James Joyce, grocer's
assistant working at Davy's, was to assist them to seize the house
from within. Another section of sixteen men under Michael Kelly,
on the railway bridge crossing the Grand Canal were to support

---

[1] Frank Robbins, *Irishman*, "Citizen Army and Easter Week," May
19, 1920.

the Davy's men and cover their retreat. Captain John O'Neill in turn was assigned to support the Kelly contingent by posting men on the railway bridge overlooking Harcourt Road so as to check military reinforcements sent along the South Circular Road. Captain McCormack was to be installed in Harcourt Street Station with a section while Frank Robbins with twenty men would operate in Hatch Street. His work was the building of barricades at each end of the street to provide a safe retreat for the whole company through a gateway leading to the Green; to defend the Hatch Street area and prevent men on all these dangerous tasks from being surrounded and cut off. The Harcourt Street Station garrison was to assist the barricade building by dumping all material available into Hatch Street while Robbins's men were at work. These plans were based on a full mobilisation of the Volunteers and Citizen Army.

Connolly's preparations were not restricted to Dublin. He sent William Partridge, one of his best known organisers, to Tralee to arrange for the handling of the *Aud* cargo and its discharge on arrival at Fenit by members of his union. Drivers and firemen were detailed to meet Austin Stack on Sunday morning to receive instructions about the train arrangements at Tralee for the distribution of the arms to Cork and Limerick.[2] Connolly and MacDonagh made a thorough tour of the Camden Street area and surveyed Jacobs' factory.

In Dublin the Volunteers thronged Lawlor's shop in Fownes Street buying bandoleers, and belts and haversacks, water bottles, swords and bayonets to complete their equipment, hunted through chemists' shops for first-aid outfits and emergency rations, shifted arms from dumps, worked late into the nights filling their canister bombs with scrap, explosives and fuses, or empty shot-gun cartridges with lead pellets, discussing rumours. From the publication of the " Castle Order " in the Press, numerous armed vigils were added to their activities.

Throughout the country feverish activity also prevailed among the Volunteers, and there, too, rumour winged its way. Quaint cipher messages reached Volunteer officers from messengers Pearse sent southwards. There were constant comings and goings of messengers to the country and Volunteer officers arriving in Dublin

---

[2] P. Cahill. "Who Blundered in Ireland?" *An Phoblacht*, September 13, 1930.

for instructions and for information. Mysterious packages were unloaded from side cars at Dublin hotels and were borne away with a quick eye for the watching " G " men at railway stations.

Down on the Kerry coast Austin Stack, William Partridge, Patrick Cahill and their helpers were thinking hard. Pearse had visited Tralee in the last week in February; Stack, Dublin early in April. MacDermott and Michael Collins held conversations in Kimmage and soon from there Keating and Daly were to leave with the cryptic words: " Much will have happened before we see you all again." But it was not in February or March or April that the Military Council and the Kerry leaders had begun their work to give the *Aud* a welcome.

Cotton and Stack were summoned to Dublin in the autumn of 1915, and had a long interview with Pearse at St. Enda's, Rathfarnham. According to Cotton's account, they were informed by Pearse, under a pledge of the strictest secrecy, that an insurrection had been arranged for Easter, 1916, that arrangements had been made with Germany to land rifles, machine guns and explosives in Tralee Bay, that they would have to make the local arrangements for the landing and distribution of the arms. Only a general plan of the Rising was given without details.

There was to be a general mobilisation of the Volunteers throughout the whole of Ireland, and more detailed instructions as to positions and objectives in each area were promised for a later date. Pearse stated that in broad outline it was proposed that the Cork Volunteers would move towards Macroom and link up with the Kerry Brigade, which, in turn, would be in communication with the Volunteers in Clare, Limerick and Galway. Ultimately a line would be held from the Shannon through Limerick and East Kerry to Macroom. Volunteers from Ulster would occupy positions from the Shannon to South of Ulster. The Rising would begin with the declaration of the Republic and seizure of Dublin with action against the British troops in adjoining counties while moves would be made by country Volunteer forces towards the capital to relieve the pressure on the Volunteers who had seized the ring of positions inside. The arms and ammunition landed at Fenit were to be distributed to the Kerry, Cork, Limerick and Galway Volunteers. Stack and Cotton were to have a goods train ready to leave Fenit with the arms. Part of the armament was to be left at Tralee for distribution to the Cork and Kerry Brigades, and the remainder sent on by goods train to Limerick where arrangements would be ready to distribute them to the Galway area. At Fenit a pilot must be on the alert for signals agreed upon with the arms ship, meet it, and guide it into the pier. A cable in code was to be sent to the U.S.A. announcing the proclamation of the Republic.

Pearse ordered Stack and Cotton to preserve secrecy to the very last minute, and to give the barest minimum of information to the men selected for the various preparations. Nevertheless, Stack and Cotton then insisted on a very thorough discussion of the plan and the general situation. They raised the questions of the difficulties of running the British blockade, the risks of delay by storm or fog, and the uncertainty of the ship arriving at Tralee to a strict time-table. Cotton, who had great experience as a Volunteer organiser and was then acting Vice-Commandant of the Tralee Battalion, suggested that it would be wiser to arrange for the landing of arms round the coast in small quantities of 500 and 1,000. In that case there would be no danger of any serious clash with the British, and the gradual arming of the Volunteers would hearten them and bring more recruits to their ranks, and the force would be so strong that the British would hesitate to attack in the war situation, as a fight with a really well-armed and determined Volunteer force would only endanger British chances of victory in the war. Pearse said shortly that Germany would not agree to any such gradual landing of arms. The plans made were final, and preparations must be made in the hope that these plans would work out successfully. Pearse did not tell Stack and Cotton in detail what they were to do in their area. He only indicated in very broad outline what the plan was, leaving them to fill in and work out the necessarily complicated local details. Tralee post office was to be seized to control telephone and telegraphic communications; the railway station was to be occupied and the goods train made ready for the conveyance of arms at Fenit; R.I.C. barracks were to be either rushed or isolated by snipers covering their exits, and similar measures taken with barracks occupied by small forces of British troops; any British troops hurrying to Tralee as soon as the arms were landed and the Rising in progress were to be ambushed *en route*.

These and many other details were later considered by Stack

and Cotton and not discussed closely during the first interview with Pearse. Stack had two other interviews at least with Pearse in 1916. Cotton was served with a notice by the British authorities forbidding him to return to Cork or Kerry when he visited Belfast in March, 1916.[3] Ironically enough, Cotton had previously established Volunteer camps where a few Volunteers spent week-ends near Banna Strand and close to Fenit. His intention as the crisis drew nearer was that small armed parties should be encamped there during the critical days of the proposed arms landing. Seán MacDermott, however, ordered him to obey the British order and not to return to Kerry, although Cotton was anxious to return there in disguise. MacDermott pointed out that above all no attention must be drawn to the Kerry coast. Cotton reflected later that so close was the watch kept on him from the moment the order was served that there was much wisdom in MacDermott's precautions. No effort was made to continue these camps, in Cotton's absence.

From the O'Donovan Rossa funeral there was great activity on the part of the Military Council, and a minor crisis with Connolly who pressed publicly for insurrection. There is some evidence that the Military Council considered an earlier date than Easter for the insurrection, and rejected it. Seán MacDermott held consultations with a South of Ireland Volunteer commandant on plans for a landing of arms in the West of Ireland during the late autumn of 1915. Pearse warned some Volunteers who had to leave Dublin at that time that if they received code messages in letters from himself or Ceannt asking them to return a certain book by a particular date that they would understand that on that date there would be fighting in Dublin. The plans for the western landing were abruptly dropped; no messages in code reached those warned to be on the alert.

A month before the insurrection Stack was summoned again to Dublin for further discussions. He met Terence MacSwiney in Dublin, and travelled back with him as far as Mallow. They " discussed the situation at length, the hope of getting material aid from Germany being a matter which loomed largely before us,

---

[3] These details in the text are based on a very full account given by Cotton himself in an article, " Kerry's Place in the General Plan, 1916," in *Kerry's Fighting Story* (*Kerryman*, Tralee, 1947), and accounts by other Volunteer officers concerned in the Kerry landing.

F

as this was bound to have a very great effect on the prospects of the insurrection." [4]

Stack records nothing further of his conversation with MacSwiney who, in fact, during this same visit to Headquarters had expressed great uneasiness about the danger that Germany might use Ireland in her own interests, and was presumably reassured.[5] Certainly a very easy task as German scepticism as to the possibilities of exploiting the Irish situation was then profound, German aid strictly limited to a minimum of captured weapons, and communication with Germany sporadic and roundabout. The two men parted, each in turn to grapple with a tragic choice that haunted both until their deaths.

Under cover of preparation for the Easter manœuvres there was great activity in Volunteer circles in the country areas. Three weeks before the Rising Commandant Michael P. Colivet of the Limerick Brigade received orders to speed up battalion and brigade organisation. He had eight battalions in his command, one in Limerick City, three in County Limerick, including one in Tipperary, and four in County Clare. With the exception of the city battalion, most of these were not very well armed, and his battalions were at less than full strength, numbering some 200 men per unit, at best not exceeding more than 1,600 men in all. The plan of operations on which the Limerick Brigade worked had been based on holding the line of the Shannon from the Clare side. Colivet had already had one surprise about plans for holding the line of the Shannon. On a visit to Limerick, Pearse had asked Colivet about holding that line " in the event of hostilities," and indicated that that would be one of the Volunteers' tasks. Colivet was somewhat amused at Pearse's faith that the Limerick Brigade was yet numerically strong enough to do this, and replied that it would be a problem rather than a task as the Limerick Brigade would have to be spaced out, one man for every three hundred yards. Some time later, Eoin MacNeill was reviewing a local contingent of Volunteers at Lough Gur. Colivet, who was present, mentioned these instructions of Pearse. MacNeill looked blank, answered vaguely, and finally said he would look into the

---

[4] *Kerry Champion*, August 31-September 21, 1929, with notes by the editor, Patrick Cahill; also in abridged version, Silver Jubilee 1916 Souvenir (Tralee, 1941).

[5] Mary MacSwiney, Easter Number, *Poblacht na h-Eireann*, April 20, 1922.

affair after his return to Dublin. A sharp reproach next reached Colivet from Pearse as Director of Organisation which stated that his instructions had been confidential and should not have been repeated. Colivet was in touch with I.R.B. and Volunteer circles but suspected nothing of any possible cleavage in the leadership. He had merely assumed that Eoin MacNeill as Chief-of-Staff was entitled to know all Volunteer plans and Headquarter Staff instructions. The incident went out of his mind. On the Tuesday of Holy Week, Seán Fitzgibbon, then a captain on the Volunteer Headquarters Staff, arrived with a message very much concerned with operations along the Shannon.

Fitzgibbon had been sent down by Pearse with orders to get in touch with Colivet in Limerick and Stack in Tralee, and had been informed by Pearse that the orders he was to carry out were approved by Eoin MacNeill.[6] He was to superintend the landing of arms from a German ship in Kerry within a week or less. Fitzgibbon was an obvious man for Pearse to choose for one reason, and a dangerous man for a second. Fitzgibbon was a member of the Volunteer Executive, close friend of Arthur Griffith and MacNeill, and had superintended the Kilcoole gun-running a week after the first arms for the Volunteers had been landed at Howth. He was not a member of the I.R.B., and he was a supporter of the policy of the Hobson and MacNeill group. The choice of Fitzgibbon for such a task proves that the Military Council had determined to sweep everyone possible into the insurrection from MacNeill down. That Pearse was deliberately deceiving Fitzgibbon, however, does not follow.

It illustrates Pearse's extraordinary one-ideaed outlook on insurrection in which he believed so strongly that he persuaded himself that everyone must at heart agree with him. He sounded some members of the Hobson-MacNeill group, dropped vague hints of coming events, and was certain until events undeceived him that they would turn up with their guns when he wanted them. Pearse's safeguard in this was that he talked so much of insurrection that his listeners grew to expect it from him and to disregard it. He dropped " as broad a hint as I dared " to an ex-pupil of his who had in fact very decided Redmondite views, and always assumed his ex-pupil would " come over and join us "

---

6 So Fitzgibbon informed the writer shortly before his death in April, 1948.

until his ex-pupil, in fact, astonished him by fighting as a British officer in France. "He went to MacNeill," said Pearse sadly, "and no doubt heard from him that I was talking nonsense and that nothing would happen." Quite oblivious of their hurt looks, Pearse would peremptorily inform very moderate Volunteer officers about what practice might be useful for "the day we rise in arms." Plunkett, who preferred to keep his own counsel, was rather startled at Pearse's outspokenness, and remonstrated with him. Pearse made his stock defence that there had been so much talk of insurrection for years that neither Dublin Castle nor MacNeill would suspect anything amiss. Undoubtedly, Pearse lent himself on the eve of Easter Week to adroit moves to capture, control and compromise as many men as needed to ensure that the Rising would take place and that it should be general. He was convinced he was acting rightly in this. For one thing, he believed his speeches and propaganda had committed him to the use of armed force in the circumstances of 1914, and that to postpone action "until the next war," as Casement and Hobson urged, would lead to a wave of national cynicism. Like Connolly he was a prisoner of the formula that the lesson of the Irish insurrections of the past was that "the only failure is the failure to strike." Moreover, as Chairman of the Military Council of the I.R.B., he felt himself bound to carry out the militant policy which had been agreed upon soon after the outbreak of war. As a last resort, Pearse would have relied upon the hard core of the I.R.B. in alliance with the Citizen Army.

This deception of MacNeill and Fitzgibbon, apart from any moral issue involved, was to prove fatal to the plans for the general rising. John Devoy, when he learned the full story, refused to defend the deception of MacNeill. It cannot be denied that the Military Council were fanatically bent on having their way, and this blinded them to the slickness of the methods employed to involve their colleagues, and to any moral issue at stake in their resort to what can most mildly be described as equivocation. "The war party," said Pearse himself very sadly when Italy entered the war against Austria, "always wins because the war party is always restless, ruthless, and aggressive." Pearse, however, as will appear, had a case against the conduct of his moderate critics, and in particular against MacNeill. It must not be forgotten that the Military Council believed that they would eventually gain MacNeill's consent to their policy.

Fitzgibbon carried out his mission in Limerick and Tralee. He discovered when he discussed the H.Q. orders with Colivet that they clashed with the plan of operations on which the Limerick Brigade had hitherto worked. According to these new instructions of Pearse, Colivet was to receive the arms landed at Fenit at Abbeyfeale, take what he wanted for his area, and send the rest by train to Galway. Colivet realised that insurrection was intended because Pearse's instructions also included attacks on police and military positions in Limerick City to cover the transfer of the arms train in safety across the Clare line. Later the outlying battalions were to march on Limerick City and, as soon, if ever, as the position was stabilised, to move eastwards to relieve the fighters in Dublin. Colivet was as much in the dark as Fitzgibbon and assumed that these orders came from MacNeill and Pearse united on one plan and one policy. This was so great a change from the H.Q. orders which he understood he was expected to follow that, after discussion with Fitzgibbon and on Fitzgibbon's advice, he determined to go to Dublin and get clear and definite instructions once and for all from Pearse himself. It was only long afterwards that he recalled the hint he had already had of a difference between MacNeill and Pearse. Strangely enough, MacNeill was very soon to remember Colivet's obscure question about operations on the Shannon in the event of hostilities, and fit it into a pattern that appalled the until then unsuspecting Chief-of-Staff of an army well on the way to battle without his knowledge.

Pearse arranged a meeting with Colivet when he arrived in Dublin on Wednesday at the North Star Hotel near Amiens Street Station. Pearse confirmed the instructions sent by Fitzgibbon immediately, and ordered Colivet to cancel all previous arrangements, and to concentrate on the arms landing. The discussion between the two men was disguised by Colivet pretending to be a tight-fisted farmer and Pearse a haggling buyer. This was a precaution against being overheard by an embarrassingly over-attentive waiter. Whenever the waiter approached he heard Colivet insisting: " I can't really let you have more than thirty bushels," and Pearse, who thoroughly enjoyed the game, replying impatiently: " But I must have more, and you must find them somewhere," and so on with many refusals and appeals on both sides.

With the waiter well out of sight, Colivet asked Pearse point-blank:

" Of course this means insurrection as soon as the arms are landed and we get them?"

" Yes," said Pearse, " you are to start at 7 p.m. on Sunday. You are to proclaim the Republic and, as soon as things are secure in your own district, move eastwards."

Again Colivet asked another direct question:

" Are the Germans coming in force?"

Pearse hesitated, and would give no definite reply until Colivet asked whether he was to understand that the Germans were not coming, and Pearse said briefly: " No!" The impression left by Pearse's attitude and words, however, was that the Germans were coming although Pearse seemed prevented by some promise or agreement from saying so.

Finally, Pearse informed Colivet that he must work out the local plans for the revolt without any more definite line from H.Q. than Pearse's conversation with him and the orders already conveyed by Fitzgibbon. Colivet left Pearse and walked out into the sunny street towards Nelson Pillar, watching the peaceful crowds, mothers with their children, loitering citizens, joking passersby, and thinking on the changed scene the streets would present the following Sunday when insurrection startled those same happy-go-lucky and careless crowds. He also thought of the big task before him of planning in detail a Rising at less than a week's notice.

As soon as he reached Limerick he summoned his Brigade Staff to a meeting that night at George Clancy's house. Clancy was the Vice-Commandant of the Limerick Brigade. A plan was agreed on without delay. Briefly, it was arranged that the Limerick City battalion should march out of the city at 10 a.m. on Sunday morning to Killonan, as if for the announced three-day manœuvres. The return to the city was timed for 7 o'clock in the evening when all police and military barracks in the city were to be attacked after first cutting telegraphic and telephone wires as well as railway communications with Limerick Junction and Dublin. The police and military garrisons were to be confined to their barracks by the attack, which was not to be pressed home but kept up as a diversion until the Kerry arms train had passed safely into Clare over Longpavement railway bridge. When the arms reached

Limerick the barrack attacks were to be followed up with the utmost energy.

As the train had to cross the Limerick lines to the south unnoticed and uninterrupted, this diversion of police and military attention was essential. At Newcastle-West on the following day Volunteer units were to be posted, poorly armed as those in West Limerick were, to take over the train at Abbeyfeale, to attack the police barracks at Newcastle-West and see the train through in safety, and to attack and disarm all police likely to interfere with the plans. The Volunteer unit at Newcastle-West was to watch the station very closely as it was a terminus where all trains and engines had to be reversed, and delay there offered dangerous opportunities for police and military interference. There was an insistent order from Dublin that any armed clash with police and military must at all costs be avoided until 7 p.m. on Sunday. (This particular order had been impressed very strongly by the Dublin H.Q. in all Easter Eve messages to the Volunteer commandants in the provinces. It was to weigh much with Stack when he was faced with urgent demands from some of his officers to attempt the rescue of Casement, it had as we have seen ended Cotton's scheme to keep a constant Volunteer camp near Banna Strand to cover the landing, it prevented sporadic outbreaks as soon as conflict of orders rained down on the country commands.)

The Limerick plan provided that all available Volunteers were armed and taken aboard the train as it proceeded towards Limerick. All possible reinforcements were to be gathered at the various stations. The Galtee Battalion was to attack Charleville Junction and put it out of action, attack all police units in their district, and advance on Limerick to take part in the fighting there. At Limerick Junction the Tipperary Volunteers were to take similar action, and after settling with the local police units, also to march to join the Limerick Volunteers. Doon and Castleconnell units were to deal with railway lines from Castleconnell to Killaloe, destroy Birdhill Junction, and make their way to the Limerick and Clare units operating in Limerick City. In County Clare Captain Michael Brennan and the Mid-Clare and East Clare Volunteers were to seize Ennis and all stations to Crusheen, and finally, after disarming the R.I.C. in various localities, take up positions on the north side of the Shannon at Limerick, complete its encirclement, and force a surrender of the hostile forces within.

In West Clare Captain P. Brennan was to take command of all available Volunteers at Kilrush, commandeer boats, cross the Shannon at Ballylongford or Tarbert, join the Kerry Volunteers at Listowel, and proceed to Limerick on the arms train. He was urged to come with as strong a party as possible so as to make sure that there would be no hitch or interference at the danger-point at Newcastle-West. The stationmaster at Castleconnell, Lieutenant McGee, was an active, although secret, supporter of the Volunteers. He was given charge of the work of making contacts and arrangements for the safe passage of the arms-train.

When all these plans were successfully carried through there was to be a general march on Dublin.[7]

In a word, the Cork, Clare, Tipperary and West-Limerick Volunteers were to seize railways and barracks in their immediate areas, disarm the police, surround Limerick and march into the relief of the city battalions. The plan assumed that the barracks would be taken without a hitch, the police overcome, the Limerick attack maintained, that the arms-train would pass without interference by police and military, and, most important of all, that the arms would be landed safely from the *Aud*.

On the Thursday of Holy Week, Commandant Liam Manahan, Galtee Battalion, Limerick Brigade, visited the Dawson Street Headquarters of the Irish Volunteers, as innocent of any suspicion of divided counsels among the leaders as Monteith, when he landed the next day on Banna Strand. He met Bulmer Hobson, J. J. O'Connell, and other Volunteer officers. In reply to his questions as to whether a crisis was near, they told him that they expected no exceptional developments. The publication of the "Castle Document" and the debate at Dublin Corporation as well as the rumours of impending military action had made Manahan, like many other Volunteer commandants in the various areas, uneasy, and he had, in fact, visited the Headquarters as the fit and obvious place to find out the truth. If he had asked Hobson and O'Connell the same question some hours later, they would probably have given him a very different answer, although they had already informed MacNeill that, in their opinion, the famous "Castle

---

[7] The statements in the text on Commandant Colivet's interview with Pearse, and the outline of the Limerick plans for the Rising were given to the writer by Commandant Colivet himself. The plans are described in detail in *Limerick's Fighting Story* (*Kerryman*, Tralee, 1948).

Document" was a forgery, and that a British military swoop was
not an immediate danger.

On his way out Manahan met Thomas MacDonagh, who became
excited and angry at the very sight of Manahan. MacDonagh was
greatly disturbed, he said, to find Manahan in Dublin at all and
not on the alert in Ballylanders. "There is danger of immediate
raids and arrests," said MacDonagh sharply, "yourself among
them. Are you armed and prepared to resist? You had better
rush for the one o'clock train home, and await orders there." This
was one of MacDonagh's favourite flourishes even in normal times.
He was always informing Volunteer officers and men that they
should be prepared to start into action at a moment's notice. On
this Thursday morning he was unusually peppery but a straight
question from Manahan calmed him.   "Why have Hobson,
O'Connell and the other members of the Volunteer Executive I
have just been speaking to, not been aware of these dangers and
warned me of them?" MacDonagh said vaguely that "they were
not in it," that he would like to give further information but was
not free to do so, Manahan had better, after all, wait for the evening train at 7.30, and see Pearse. Manahan returned to Ballylanders that night without seeing Pearse. On Friday night the
order came to him from the Limerick Brigade H.Q.:

"Mobilisation Sunday. All arms. March west and hold railway line between Adare and Newcastle-West. Seize any arms
possible, and do everything possible to avoid shooting the members
of the R.I.C."

In the meantime in Dublin the split in the leadership had at
last become an open one. Following a meeting of the Volunteer
Executive on Wednesday, MacNeill had, with the approval of
Pearse and the others present, issued an order warning the
Volunteers to be on their guard, that a plan for their suppression
by the British Government had been discovered, that the date of
putting it into operation depended only on a mere Government
order: . . . "in the event of definite information not reaching you
from Headquarters you will be on the look-out for the signs of any
attempt to put this plan into operation. Should you be satisfied
that such action is imminent you will be prepared with defensive
measures. Your object will be to preserve the arms and organisation of the Irish Volunteers, and the measures taken by you will be
directed to that end. In general you will arrange that your men

defend themselves and each other in small groups so placed that they may best be able to hold out. Each group must be provided with sufficient supplies of food, or be certain of access to such supplies." MacNeill, in his statement later, with good reason insisted that a policy of insurrection was not adopted or proposed at the two meetings at which this order was drafted and sanctioned.

On Thursday evening Hobson and O'Connell discovered definitely that the insurrection had been fixed for Sunday—through a conversation overheard either at the Volunteer Headquarters, or at an important meeting of the Volunteer Executive. They immediately went out to Dundrum and informed MacNeill. He broke out into a furious denunciation of the fraud practised upon him, and made the most emphatic declarations that his authority should not be flouted, acted in short with all the fury of a sedate professor transformed for a short space into a tough and walking terror. Hobson, who had been his unofficial backbone for years, was somewhat surprised as well as O'Connell, by MacNeill's demand that they should all three go at once to St. Enda's, a few miles away, rouse Pearse and tell him what they thought of him and the war party. It was after midnight but MacNeill, in a towering rage, insisted. Pearse was duly knocked up. The overheard conversation had dealt with certain of the orders which had been issued by Pearse for the Sunday, orders which could have no other interpretation than that insurrection was intended: demolitions, barracks attacks, seizure of railways. They informed Pearse that they had learned that these orders had been issued, and that they could be only intelligible as part of a general scheme of insurrection.

Pearse listened courteously to his visitors, and said quietly: "Yes, you are right. A Rising is intended."

MacNeill burst out into an indignant denunciation of the deception used by his colleagues against him, and Pearse said again, for he was determined to tell MacNeill all the truth he cared to hear that night:

"Yes, you were deceived, but it was necessary."

For the three men before him in his study that night Pearse had mixed feelings. He respected MacNeill in everything except his incapacity as a revolutionary leader. He knew though he was courteous enough to say it only in the brief words: "it was necessary" that MacNeill had run away from the truth that had stared him in the face if he had only the courage to face it: that Pearse, Clarke and Connolly had been bent on insurrection from the outbreak of the war. It was MacNeill's own evasiveness and refusal to come to grips with the real problem, his temperamental caution, his proneness to play for safety and non-action beyond the last possible minute that had moved Connolly to suspicion and active hostility, the astuteness with even a touch of cunning that led him to hide in bland isolation in his study behind barricades of platitudes and syllogisms, all these and more that were summed up in Pearse's sentence: "it was necessary". As he looked at MacNeill, majestic in wrathful innocence, outraged behind a flowing beard and waving mane, Pearse might well have thought that he and his scheming colleagues of the Military Council deserved some sympathy for their vain hope of trying to nail such a man to a set policy. It had been Pearse's policy to stand between Connolly and MacNeill and hold a balance. O'Connell he probably underestimated and, in any case, thought not too wisely that MacDonagh had learned as much military science in text-books as O'Connell in travels and an army. For Hobson he had a sincere respect though gradually the clash on policies had driven them apart.

The crisis of Easter Eve had come at last that midnight in Pearse's study. Nothing could then reconcile these four men, wide apart as they were in temperament, in character, in views of policy and tactics. Pearse had said as he left the Rotunda Rink the night two years before when the Irish Volunteers had been founded: "We have started an insurrection!" Hobson, MacNeill, and O'Connell had elaborated from a hint in Fintan Lalor a guerrilla and waiting policy. They believed that the reports they received in the Volunteer Headquarters showed that the organisation was hopelessly equipped for a general insurrection, and they were inclined to scoff at Connolly, Pearse and Seán MacDermott's interminable parallels from past insurrections as a guide to action. The course of the war, the state of Irish public opinion, then mostly pro-British and pro-Ally and Redmondite, the coldness of Germany to Casement's mission had deepened their belief in their own policy.

MacNeill, Hobson and Pearse had argued round all this before. Once Pearse staggered Hobson by answering very disingenuously: "I agree that your arguments against an insurrection now are unanswerable in reason and logic, yet I feel that I am right." Pearse was only saying very politely that his mind was made up, and that he intended to go his own way. His political writings are the continual argument he carried on within himself as to the pros and cons and the inevitability of an armed revolt of which he saw himself the predestined leader. If Pearse had remembered he might have quoted his aphorism to MacNeill: " The instinct of the Fenian artisan was a finer thing than the soundest theory of the Gaelic League professor." Or the apt historic parallel from the same essay in his " From a Hermitage ":

" The leaders in Ireland have nearly always left the people at the critical moment; have sometimes sold them. The former Volunteer movement was abandoned by its leaders; hence its ultimate failure. Grattan ' led the van ' of the Volunteers, but he also led the retreat of the leaders; O'Connell recoiled before the cannon at Clontarf; twice the hour of the Irish revolution struck during Young Ireland days, and twice it struck in vain, for Meagher hesitated in Waterford, Duffy and McGee hesitated in Dublin. Stephens refused to ' give the word ' in '65; he never came in '66 or '67. I do not blame these men; you or I might have done the same. It is a terrible responsibility to be cast on a man, that of bidding the cannon speak and the grapeshot pour."

Pearse was in the mood to " give the word," but he gave few words to his very critical visitors that April night. Hobson said little, O'Connell less, MacNeill in his anger talked on and on, reiterating his protest and his determination. Finally he informed Pearse for the last time that there would be no insurrection, no waste of the lives of the men for whom MacNeill was responsible as Chief-of-Staff, no calling out of a half-armed force. " I will do everything I can to stop this," said MacNeill, as he left, " *everything* except to ring up Dublin Castle!"

After his visitors had gone, Pearse sat alone in his study, silent and disturbed, and said briefly in answer to a question from his mother: " Oh, it was nothing. Some trouble with MacNeill, but it will come right."

Early next morning Pearse gave the news of MacNeill's midnight ultimatum to MacDonagh and MacDermott who went out to Dundrum, and after much debate succeeded in talking him into agreeing to do nothing for the present. He told them when they arrived that he had cancelled all Pearse's orders, and given Hobson and

O'Connell full authority over the Volunteers in Dublin and in the
country. MacDonagh and MacDermott then told MacNeill that
a Rising was indeed planned for Sunday, that it was too late to stop
it without disaster, and that an arms ship was on the way to Ireland
from Germany. It was this last news that seemed to have convinced MacNeill that nothing could be done, that a fight was
inevitable, and that they were all involved. Whether MacNeill
then formally surrendered his position as Chief-of-Staff or not is
uncertain, as his own memoranda have never been made public,
and this side of the history of the Rising is still obscure.[8]

What is certain is that this change of mind was not a lasting
one. MacNeill's reading of the possibilities of the situation was
in fact true. The arrival of the arms ship and its discovery by
the British authorities would lead to action against the Volunteer
organisation. Within a few hours Dublin Castle was debating its
course of action. MacNeill was later the same day in touch with
The O'Rahilly, Seán Fitzgibbon, and other members of his own
group whose arguments unsettled him again. That very morning
Casement had landed at Banna Strand from the German submarine, and a few hours later was a prisoner.

A frail boat had hurled three men, Casement, Bailey and Monteith on the lone Kerry coast with not a friend in sight among the
sandhills and the dark mountains that Good Friday, just after 3
a.m. The *Aud* was still in Tralee Bay. She had waited from
Thursday afternoon. Towards noon she left. By dawn next
morning she lay beneath the waters of Cobh Harbour with her
cargo, and Spindler and his crew were prisoners.

On Good Friday afternoon, Bulmer Hobson was summoned to a
meeting on the north side of Dublin. When he arrived, an armed
party arrested him by orders of the Military Council.

The O'Rahilly was still opposed to a Rising. When he heard of
Hobson's arrest and that an insurrection had been prepared without the knowledge of MacNeill and the non-I.R.B. members of
the Volunteer Executive he called out to St. Enda's on Good
Friday evening. As he entered Pearse's study he whipped out a
revolver and said : " Whoever kidnaps me will have to be a quicker

---

[8] The most detailed account so far published is to be found in Le Roux's
Life of Pearse, and *Tom Clarke and the Irish Freedom Movement.* The
account given above is partly based on Le Roux, a statement to the writer
by Mr. Bulmer Hobson, and the writer's own memory of the time at
St. Enda's.

shot!" Pearse said indignantly. "No one wants to kidnap you. Put away that gun." After The O'Rahilly had calmed down, the two men had a long and not too stormy interview, and The O'Rahilly, having made his protest, left.

A car arrived at St. Enda's very late on Good Friday night with a summons for Pearse to attend an urgent conference at Liberty Hall where he learned from Connolly the news of Casement's arrest, and that the arms ship had gone. He heard, too, of the arrest of Con Collins and Austin Stack and of Monteith's message and warning. Pearse and MacDermott again saw MacNeill early on Saturday and informed him. He still reproached them for leaving him in the dark but they believed that they had persuaded him that there was no alternative, that the British would swoop on the Volunteers, and there must be unity to meet the coming storm.

MacNeill had not yet made up his mind. He appears to have decided that the British might not move against the Volunteer organisation, and that it could be saved without a clash. That afternoon, after a talk with Seán Fitzgibbon and The O'Rahilly, he drafted an order: " Volunteers completely deceived. All orders for Sunday cancelled," and prepared to send it out with his signature as Chief-of-Staff to all areas by special messengers. He summoned a meeting at the house of his friend, Dr. Seamus O'Kelly in Rathgar Road. This was an informal discussion at which Arthur Griffith, Seán Fitzgibbon, some members of the Volunteer Executive and a number of others attended. Joseph Plunkett and Thomas MacDonagh came, too, but their stay was short. When MacNeill announced that he had issued orders to stop the Sunday mobilisation, both MacDonagh and Plunkett warned him that the Rising could not be stopped then without disaster to the whole movement, and that in any case, whatever he might do, they would go ahead. MacDonagh indicated his view of the informal meeting by saying: " These gentlemen are not my colleagues." He, however, promised MacNeill that he would return or send a message. He and Plunkett then got in touch with MacDermott and Pearse, told them of MacNeill's change of mind, and arranged a full meeting of the Military Council for Sunday morning.

Professor Liam Ó Briain who was present at the meeting[9] describes it as a very informal gathering to which MacNeill with an unusual show of agitation explained that he had already made

---

[9] *Comhar*, April, May, December, 1945.

up his mind to stop the projected Rising, and proposed to send messengers throughout the country to the Volunteer commandants in each area calling off all manœuvres on Easter Sunday. He emphasised that he had learned of the insurrection plans, but had been left in ignorance of them until three days before; that owing to what he knew of the unarmed state of the country Volunteer forces combined with the disaster which sent the German arms ship to the bottom of Cobh harbour, he regarded it as an imperative call of conscience to do his utmost to save the Volunteers from hopeless and useless slaughter. Before midnight, MacNeill had dispatched messengers to the country with his countermanding orders. Indeed by ten o'clock messengers had already left for Cork and Belfast and The O'Rahilly had hurried to Limerick. He also sent notices to the Press calling off the mobilisation. To MacNeill in his anguish the idea of insurrection seemed like a fantastic nightmare that he was determined to shake off. Until the shots were ringing in his ears, he steadily believed that it could not happen. In this strange mood, Seán Fitzgibbon and another member of the Volunteer Executive urged him to take every precaution that it should not happen, and insisted that he should send a written confirmation of his order to the *Sunday Independent*.

MacNeill then wrote a personal note confirming his countermanding order, and cycled to the newspaper office to make sure that it should be published. He also dispatched an order to de Valera—as Adjutant of the Dublin Brigade—to be conveyed to all commands of the Dublin Brigade that no movements of Volunteers should take place on Easter Sunday.

His fateful countermanding order read:

" Owing to the very critical position, all orders given to Irish Volunteers for to-morrow, Easter Sunday, are hereby rescinded, and no parades, marches, or other movements of Irish Volunteers will take place. Each individual Volunteer will obey this order strictly in every particular."

The confirming letter, authenticating the order ended:

" . . . Every influence should be used immediately and throughout the day to secure faithful execution of this order, as any failure to obey it may result in a very grave catastrophe."

That same Saturday evening at six o'clock, Eamonn Ceannt had told his wife that there would be an insurrection on Sunday, and that he would occupy the South Dublin Union. There was to be a secret session of the British Parliament which meant either peace or conscription. " We Volunteers," he went on, " an armed body, could not let this opportunity pass without striking a blow while England is at war. We would be a disgrace to our generation. So we strike to-morrow."

At three o'clock on Sunday morning he returned, saying: " MacNeill has ruined us, he has stopped the Rising. The countermanding order is in the hands of the papers." In his absence Cathal Brugha had left a message for him informing him of the MacNeill meeting. Ceannt then visited Liberty Hall to contact Connolly but the Citizen Army guard refused to waken Connolly. At the Metropole Hotel he called for Joseph Plunkett but Plunkett had given orders that he must not be wakened until nine. Ceannt went home, and fell asleep, saying: " If I sleep now I would sleep on dynamite."[10] Within a few hours he was at a conference of the Military Council at Liberty Hall where it was decided to confirm MacNeill's order to avoid isolated and premature acts from Volunteers—and to strike on Monday at noon. Ceannt returned home and told his wife the news, adding that the cancelling of the manœuvres would lead the British to believe that everything was all right.

Patrick Pearse and his brother returned to Rathfarnham. Pearse was silent and dejected, and hardly spoke. He wrote to MacNeill that Thomas MacDonagh would call on him that afternoon and that the Dublin parades for that day had been countermanded by MacDonagh on Pearse's orders. Pearse also notified MacNeill that he had confirmed MacNeill's countermand " as the leading men would not have obeyed it without my confirmation."

On Sunday two other very interesting letters were written. When Thomas MacDonagh came back to his home in Ranelagh after his talk with MacNeill and Fitzgibbon at Dundrum he wrote a statement, noting that it was just 8 p.m. He had had a long conversation with them " upon many aspects of the present situation," and hoped he had made clear to them his loyalty to Ireland, his honour as an Irish Volunteer, and " what for obvious reasons " he had not said plainly in so many words, his intention to act with the Military Council: " My future conduct may be different from

---

[10] *The Leader*, Dublin, " Looking Back to 1916," Mrs. Aine Ceannt. April 20, 1946.

anything now anticipated by MacNeill and Fitzgibbon, two honest and sincere patriots, though I think wrong in their handling of the present situation and in their attitude to military action. They and my countrymen must judge me on my conduct. . . ."[11]

In a word, Thomas MacDonagh knew that " freedom's war was knit at length." The Liberty Hall conference, that morning, had been brief and to the point. Tom Clarke had argued that the original plans should be followed, that if Dublin rose on Sunday the country Volunteers would conclude that MacNeill's countermand was a hoax, and support the insurrection, that if they were dispersed it would be difficult to mobilise them again. Clarke, though disappointed that even Seán MacDermott and Pearse rejected his arguments and voted against him, wasted little time on argument and agreed. Connolly and the majority insisted that MacNeill had thrown everything into chaos, and that it would be impossible to get the men out that night. This was an accurate reading of the situation in the country on Sunday. The criss-crossing of conflicting orders, and rival messengers, MacNeill's countermand, the news of Casement's arrest and the sinking of the *Aud* had shaken the Volunteer organisation outside Dublin where alone they were comparatively well-armed, and their communications good, although even there the MacNeill stroke was felt. It was clear that MacNeill's word would carry the greater weight with the majority of the Volunteers who knew nothing of the disagreement among the leaders. It was clear enough twenty-four hours later that the Volunteers in the provinces were weak in transport, in control of communications, in numbers, in resolution, above all in arms. In the light of events there is no doubt that the *Aud* cargo of rifles and machine-guns would not have greatly altered the situation, assuming that they had been distributed and the British had not intercepted them. Men who went through the Easter Rising said bitterly later as the collapse weighed on them: " In April, 1916, the best place for the *Aud* and its Russian rifles and its ten machine-guns was at the bottom of the sea. God Almighty sent it there!" They meant that leaders and men and the majority of the Irish people were unready in hand and mind for the national revolution that came two years afterwards.

Pearse would not have agreed. He thought that the people once

[11] This statement is given in full in a facsimile of MacDonagh's own handwriting, *Capuchin Annual*, 1942, p. 368.

G

in insurrection would fight as well as in '98. Ceannt told his wife:
" If we last a month, the British will come to terms." Connolly said
that the failure to take the offensive was the death of all revolutions,
that in every revolt the advantage was all on the side of the established order, that if they won they would be all great fellows, and
if they lost they would be the greatest scoundrels in all history.
It was in fact to be the other way round, but the muse of history
for once could not enlighten Connolly.

There was no scruple any longer about consulting MacNeill.
The decision to strike was unanimous. It was clear to the conference that a British swoop on the leadership and organisation
would be even more dangerous than all the risks of a hurried
Rising. The movement would collapse amid general ridicule.
Grim was the choice and searching the test of will and mettle that
confronted the leaders. Thomas MacDonagh was ordered to
mobilise the Dublin Brigade, and the mood in which he did so,
after a last courteous word with MacNeill and Fitzgibbon is
written in his Sunday statement after the interview. His mobilisation order was received with relief by many Volunteers, with
scepticism by others who departed for the races. All had been
shaken by Sunday's surprises. Sunshine soldiers and fair-weather
patriots there were, to be sure, who faded away. Some disillusioned
Volunteers had already burned their uniforms and smashed their
rifles, vowing that never again would the will o' the wisp of an
Irish movement waste their time, that never again would they
commit themselves to a wordy fiasco. Rumour and disaster had
already done their work. For the most part, however, the Dublin
Volunteers knit by the discipline of their organisation and their
ideal waited to see whether the Flag would go up or not.

A second letter written that day by Lord Wimborne to
Mr. Augustine Birrell, Chief Secretary, then on a few days holiday
in London, would have shortened the Military Council session and,
in particular, would have edified Joseph Plunkett. The British
had decided to move at last against the Volunteer organisation
and arrest the leaders. It was all set out by Lord Wimborne with
a candour that would have set Ireland ablaze if its contents were
known:

" Nathan will not have time to write by this post, so I send this
in haste to let you know that this morning two men held up the
caretaker of the magazine of the quarry works at Tallaght, ten

miles south-west of Dublin, and abstracted 200 lbs. of gelignite which they conveyed to Liberty Hall. . . . Nathan proposes, and I agree, that Liberty Hall, together with two other minor Sinn Féin arsenals—Larkfield, Kimmage, and the one in Father Mathew's Park—should be raided to-night. I have strongly urged him at the same time to put his hand on the ringleaders, who having countermanded their Easter Day parade, are probably sitting in conclave plotting against us. Our friend (Casement) landing from a German ship full, probably, of gold and rifles is met by Collins (he of the G.P.O.) with thirty-five sovereigns and a revolver in his pocket—now in custody with a Tralee man named Stack on charge of conspiracy to land arms, etc., who is in the thick of the suspect gang. The whole of them could be arraigned for supporting the King's enemies and there is our internment policy safely in port. I am afraid if you stir up the hornets' nest and leave the hornets that we may have serious trouble. This haul, if successful, even will not deprive them of all their ammunition. As for our ' friend ' (Casement), what a stroke of luck, and what credit to the police and Executive. I hope there will be no nonsense about clemency. He must be made an example of. He expects nothing else, I understand. These fellows have enjoyed too much immunity already. After all, it is nothing else than to create a diversion in favour of the enemy and detain three or four divisions here to deal with it—at a critical moment, too. I want to implicate as many of the Sinn Féin as I can with the landing—invasion, in fact. It has changed everything, and justifies us altering our attitude. A public trial, if there are not bad difficulties in the way, would bring it home best. I fear that they will deny here in Berlin the identity of our prisoner. I will write you more coherently to-morrow. This is in great haste for the post. I hear there is still a possibility of conscription. All the more reason for getting our suspects packed away. We shall never get a better opportunity or justification. If you agree, do write and ginger Nathan. I have never made much of their movements, or have been or am now an alarmist, but if you don't take your chances they do not recur."[12]

At a conference at the Viceregal Lodge at 10 p.m. that night it was decided to arrest from sixty to a hundred leaders, and raid and

---

[12] 1916 Commission, Minutes of Evidence, pp. 36-7, 53, 59.

disarm six or seven hundred of the " prominent rank and file of the Irish Volunteers in Dublin ", and occupy their strongholds within a few days as soon as the Chief Secretary's consent had been obtained and preparations completed. It was decided not to call reinforcements from the Curragh and Athlone from the fear that any undue military activity would alarm the Volunteer leaders. MacNeill's order had disarmed not the Volunteers but the Castle.

CHAPTER VII

WHY THE ARMS LANDING FAILED

AT dawn on Good Friday morning, Roger Casement, Monteith and Bailey were thrown half-exhausted among the sandhills of Banna Strand, at the foot of the Kerry mountains, after a desperate struggle of some hours with the stormy waters of Tralee Bay in a collapsible boat into which they had been hustled from U.19. That evening Casement was a prisoner in Tralee R.I.C. Barracks under the same roof as Austin Stack, Commandant of the Tralee Volunteers, Bailey had informed the police of what he knew as to plans for an arms landing and insurrection, Monteith was a fugitive grappling with the tasks of an approaching Rising, the plans of which were unknown to him, and Karl Spindler, captain of the German arms ship, the *Aud* which had lain in Tralee Bay for twenty-four hours, unchallenged, unsuspected, and unwelcomed by pilot or Volunteer, was sailing slowly towards destruction at the mouth of Cobh Harbour, guarded and escorted at a respectful distance by British warships and patrol boats. The arms landing had failed, and the fatal hitch in the insurrectionist plans was already spreading doubt and disaster through the provinces, and was soon to cause havoc in the Dublin councils. Already romantic insurrection was proceeding according to history's somewhat fatalistic plan, and 1916 was well on the way to an inglorious fiasco. Only a last-minute and determined act of will in Dublin was to shatter that depressing and too-familiar pattern of history, and change the path of Irish history for ever, although at a cost of blood, tragedy and tears. Or in a word, seven men in Dublin, who by one slight slip, had ruined months of work and planning, saved their cause at the cost of their lives. Fate, which had served them badly, relented then, and gave them victory in their graves.

Yet the failure of the arms landing, which was within a hair's-breadth of success, was not due to Casement, to the Germans, to the Kerry Volunteers or their leaders, but to an almost inexplicable oversight, and a lack of very obvious precautions. So late as April

9th, that is up to the day that the *Aud* sailed from Lübeck, no message reached Devoy or the Germans that Dublin wished to alter the landing dates already agreed upon, that is between Thursday, April 20 to April 23. A last-minute change of mind occurred in Dublin, and a message was rushed to Devoy that the landing must not take place until the night of April 23. The reasons for this change are not known although the desirability of timing the landing as near as possible to the outbreak of insurrection, and the difficulties of conducting a large-scale arms landing unobserved by police and coastguards have been suggested as plausible explanations. What is surprising is that Dublin took no precautions against the arrival of the *Aud*—as in fact happened—on the first date named by the Germans. Yet the *Aud* sailed into Tralee Bay, and remained there for nearly twenty-four hours, with the cargo on which the insurrection depended on board, without a single scout detailed for a lookout or a camp in waiting to cover a most obvious contingency. On the eve of arrival, Dublin discouraged any move whatever that might arouse the suspicion of the British coast watchers, and any suggestions made from Kerry for unofficial rivals in this business were severely frowned on. Some Volunteer officers from Dublin, who had organised Volunteer summer camps in the vicinity of Banna, so late as March, were ordered not to return to Kerry by the British authorities. Although they offered to go on the run or disguise themselves as fishermen, Dublin ordered them not to return to Kerry as nothing must be done to alarm the enemy or increase the tension in the country until Easter Sunday.

It is even more instructive to follow the tangle in which Casement, Stack, MacNeill, the Military Council leaders, and the forces of insurrection throughout the provinces were in turn involved step by step.

On February 5, 1916, Tommy O'Connor, steward on an Atlantic liner and regular messenger for the I.R.B., brought the I.R.B. Military Council's first intimation to Devoy that an insurrection had been fixed for Easter, and aid from Germany was necessary. It was definitely stated that arms must be landed " between April 20 and 23." A week later the message was confirmed by a second message, also in the difficult I.R.B. cipher reserved for such occasions, which was handed to Devoy by Miss Philomena Plunkett, Count Plunkett's daughter; the message had some supplementary information concerning preparations for an arms landing. Nine days after the first message, the German reply was handed to Devoy by von Papen:

" It is possible to send two or three small fishing steamers, with about ten machine-guns, 20,000 rifles, ammunition and explosives, to Fenit Pier in Tralee Bay.   Irish pilots should wait north of Inishtooskert Island from before dawn of April 20, displaying at intervals three green lights.   Disembarkation must be effected immediately.   Let us know if this can be done."[1]

This message was taken back to Ireland immediately by Miss Plunkett. It was modified a week later in detail by the substitution of " one mercantile steamer of 1,400 tons," and due warning of this was conveyed to Ireland by O'Connor on his next voyage a few days later. The arrangement with Miss Plunkett was that no reply would be needed if the German offer were accepted while rejection or changes were to be notified by cable.

Berlin learned on March 12 through Bernstorff's wireless that " the Irish agreed. Will follow instructions. Details sent to Ireland by courier."[2]

The conspirators were somewhat hampered by the roundabout communications by wireless through the Germany Embassy in Washington in code, and later these coded cables had to be sent through South America and Madrid with inevitable delays and mutilation of messages. However, the plans for the arms landing went ahead smoothly enough (apart from Casement and Monteith's efforts to increase the scope of the armament, an effort which independently, and in a more subtle manner Devoy and the Clan were also making). Finally the *Aud* sailed for Ireland from Lübeck on April 9, 1916, and, three days later, Casement overcame German objections to his joining the expedition and departed with Monteith and Bailey by submarine from Wilhelmshaven.

The negotiations were also protracted by the slow passage of documents from the Foreign Office to the General Staff and thence to the Admiralty. Spindler comments on this slowness, and gives as typical of the progress under this system that the message of March 12 above quoted reached the German General Staff from

---

[1] Devoy, *Recollections*, p. 461. A similar message is given, *Documents Relative to the Sinn Féin Movement*, p. 10; and Spindler, p. 241.

[2] *Documents Relative to Sinn Féin Movement*, p. 11; Spindler, p. 255. The first authority also gives a similar message, same date, p. 10.

the Foreign Office on March 17, and finally the Admiralty only on March 21.

Spindler in fact agreed with Casement that the armament carried by the *Aud* was not the last word in modernity, and is quite candid in his expression of the inadequacy of " our old Russian rifles " to assist in repelling any attack on his ship. His realisation of the inadequacy of the same armament for a serious insurrection is very thinly veiled in his contemptuous summary of the help the German Army Supreme Command fixed as the maximum for " assisting a revolution, which apart from other things, was to serve to thin out the Western Front by the withdrawal of considerable masses of English troops, making it possible for the German Army to break through the Allied front and thereby end the war. And the Navy, which, in this case, had virtually only to see to the equipping of the ship, could not refrain from giving vent to misgivings," i.e., that as the quantity of arms to be transported was so small whether the undertaking was worth while.   The Navy, however, proceeded because, even if the Rising failed, the sending of arms to Ireland, by a German ship would be a " great moral victory " and " the mere fact that such a big-scale insurrection and German gun-running expedition were possible in face of the grip of the English blockade would in any case have a demoralising effect upon England and her allies."[3]

Yet for some days after the sailing of the *Aud* and the departure of Casement, plans for the landing ran duly to schedule—so far as Devoy and the Germans were concerned. Both of them understood the other's viewpoint. Spindler expresses his admiration for the Irish-American grasp of the situation, clearly outlined in a long memorandum of Devoy's on February 16, and comments that, even if their demands seemed stiff to the Germans, they evidently knew that revolution cannot be made " with a handful of blunderbusses and cartridges and without above all things a sufficient supply of artillery and machine-guns."   Their further demand after the German refusal to dispatch troops that " at least a few German officers

---

[3] Spindler, p. 242. In *Danger Zone* (London, 1934) Edward Keble Chatterton summarising the British Admiralty's report on the armaments found by divers sent down to examine the *Aud* wreck tartly comments that " the rifles which had been deemed good enough for the Sinn Féiners were by no means modern. The butts bore the stamp and date of Orleans small arms factory, 1902. The barrels were marked with the Russian War Office arms and near the same was the name ' Deutschland '."

of superior rank be sent across to Ireland, shows that the Irish in America realised how matters stood and knew how to tackle the business."[4]

It was when the negotiations were over, and the *Aud* and Casement alike were racing to Ireland, the first with arms, the second with a warning, that the Dublin leaders made their most fatal blunder. On April 14, Devoy was greatly surprised when Miss Plunkett again arrived in the *Gaelic American* office with an urgent message from Ireland in code. It was indeed to be a fatal Friday afternoon for the insurrection. Devoy realised that the code message she handed to him must be discussed in full privacy and brought her to James Reidy's office some distance away. The code took some time to decipher, and by the time Devoy had read the message it was five o'clock, and the Germany Embassy was closed. The message ran: "Arms must not be landed before night of Sunday, 23rd. This is vital. Smuggling impossible. Let us know if submarine will come to Dublin Bay." Next morning, von Papen was handed a copy of the message in typescript, and that evening it was wirelessed to Berlin.[5]

On Tuesday, April 18, United States secret service agents raided the New York office of the Germany Embassy, and seized, among other documents, three type-written sheets pinned together. The

---

[4] Spindler, p. 248. For full text of this memorandum of February 16, 1916, see his Appendix. The estimate of the Revolutionary Directory of the British forces in Ireland was 40,000: 30,000 troops " poorly trained, few competent officers, no trained non-commissioned officers, little artillery, and a few machine-guns. . . In Dublin 3,000, in Limerick 1,000 soldiers, all recruits. . ." Police, 10,000—" efficient, all armed with rifles, distributed in quite small detachments throughout the country." The Irish Volunteers were estimated at 40,000, " as efficient as American National Guard." It was also believed that 50,000 Redmond Volunteers, badly trained, would join the insurrection and " even for 100,000 rifles the necessary number of men would be obtainable." Support in arms and men was impossible from America. Devoy's memorandum was based on the Dublin message of February 5 which announced that aid was expected immediately after the Rising began. (*Recollections*, p. 458.) The R.D. memo which pointed out the weakness of the British in Ireland in artillery was lost on the Germans who refused to send any. The British, v. 1916 Commission, realised more clearly than the Germans what incalculable consequences a German landing of arms, even a small body of troops, backed by an all-Ireland Rising might have had. The Spindler documents show that the German military and naval authorities were very sceptical about the Irish revolutionary movement. So late as November, 1915, they refused a request to smuggle a small amount of arms into Ireland by submarine, even when backed by von Skal in U.S.A.

[5] Devoy, *Recollections*, p. 463; *Documents Relative to the Sinn Féin Movement*, p. 12. Spindler, p. 263.

first sheet was marked: " This was handed in by Mr. John Devoy."
The second was a copy of the new Dublin message, reading " goods
must not be delivered " for " arms must not be landed." The third
sheet contained a copy of the message with the German code for
each word written over it.   According to some, the German code
was not changed in spite of its disclosure in this raid.[6] The information was conveyed to the British Government, and in spite of a
lack of details was a plain warning that an arms landing in Ireland
was planned with German help.   On April 18 a warning reached
Dublin Castle " that a ship had left Germany for Ireland, accompanied by two submarines, but the news was accompanied by a
warning as to its accuracy."[7]   The first of these warnings was evidently unconnected with the von Igel raid in New York, and may
have been information from British agents in Germany who had
closely watched the movements of both Casement and the *Aud*.
The second, which followed the New York raid, according to
Devoy through the American Department of Justice communicating the news to a pro-British American journalist who " indis-
creetly " informed the British.   Dublin Castle, however, was only
very casually informed of the first warning—the only one it
received.   Events in Ireland conspired to throw the British authorities off their guard while the *Aud*—whether the British patrols had
it under observation or whether Spindler succeeded in persuading
them that his vessel was really a neutral or not—successfully ran
the British blockade and eventually reached Tralee Bay in
safety.

The *Aud,* however, had not been equipped with wireless, and

---

[6] Captain von Rintelen, *Dark Invader*.

[7] Report of Commission, 1916, p. 11.   Lord Wimborne in his evidence
stated that he was informed by the Under-Secretary, Nathan, that General
Stafford, the officer in command in the South, had written to General
Friend on the 16th conveying a warning from the Admiralty that the
German ship and escort had left on the 12th, due to arrive on the 21st,
that a Rising was planned for Easter Eve, " but the Admiralty was sceptical as to the reality of such an intention." (*Minutes of Evidence*, p. 36.)
The dates given, prior to the New York raid, rather support Spindler's
suspicion that the *Aud* was betrayed in Germany.   The American press
did not publish the von Igel seizures until September, 1917. Wimborne
added that this was the only warning that reached Dublin Castle, and
that he himself was under the impression that the boat was supposed
to be on its way from America, not from Germany.   *See* Nathan, ibid.
p. 10.   General Friend, ibid. p. 36, gave the rumoured date of the ship's
arrival, as " not later than the 22nd." That is the original landing date
fixed as the limit before Dublin sent the second message.   The *Aud* sailed
on April 9—Casement on April 12.

the Germans were unable to communicate with her or with U.19. Devoy contended that the change of date, with the circumstances that gave the British such a broad hint that an arms landing was imminent, was responsible for " turning what would have been the most formidable insurrection in Irish history, with a reasonable hope of success, into one which was confined almost solely to Dublin over the period of one week, and foredoomed to military defeat." In other words, if the *Aud* had been allowed to act on the original plan, the arms would have been safely landed or had the Dublin leaders in their first message really made up their minds that Sunday night, April 23, was the more suitable date, there would have been no neatly typed memoranda in von Igel's office to give the plot away. This assumes, of course, that the British had no other source of information, that the *Aud* was unsuspected by the British patrols, and that there was no other hitch in the plans or collision with Dublin Castle and the forces of insurrection in the interval.

Dublin Castle certainly was wrapped in an innocent slumber to all appearances. The one thing the British feared, and against which they took precautions was a German landing in force which they were well aware might have incalculable consequences. The Dublin leaders, who had to conduct a conspiracy through a fog of codes, cables and couriers, cannot seriously be blamed for not foreseeing what a wreckage the simple change of date would involve. It is clear, however, that they neglected some very obvious precautions. Devoy informed Monteith later that when he learned that the *Aud* had sailed and could not be contacted by wireless he at once sent a courier to Ireland to warn the Military Council " but for some reason the messenger did not arrive in time." (Monteith in *An Phoblacht*, November 15, 1930.) Joseph McGarrity later informed Patrick Cahill that a messenger was sent to Clarke and the others to warn them that the second message could not reach the *Aud* in time.[8]

The real riddle of the landing episode is the neglect of Dublin to guard against a premature arrival of the *Aud*. The defence made

---

[8] Cahill in his account of this to the writer added that McGarrity was convinced that the message was received by Dublin. Assuming that Devoy had a prompt answer to his cable of April 15 to Berlin, there was barely time for a courier to reach Dublin with the information. One explanation for the change in landing dates is that Good Friday was originally suggested for the Rising. The first Dublin message to Devoy, however, gives Easter Sunday. See footnote, p. 114, *infra*.

for the change of date is that a three-day mobilisation of the Volunteers was too dangerous as it might give the British a chance of taking the initiative. The weakness of this argument is that the Volunteers in fact were ordered publicly to prepare for three-day manœuvres, that the Military Council perceived this danger so late that it did not inform Germany of the change in date until mid-April, and that the Germans had specifically warned Dublin that the landing could not be predicted for any one particular day, —a warning hardly necessary when the fact of the British blockade was notorious. Again, all the pre-Easter arrangements for receiving the arms ship point to the expectation of Dublin that the *Aud* could not arrive before Easter Saturday at the earliest. The Volunteers dispatched by car from Dublin to erect a wireless station in Tralee left Dublin only on Good Friday morning. And the Kerry accounts, as given by Austin Stack, Patrick Cahill and others only deepen the puzzle.

Pearse, according to these, informed Stack in the presence of Father Joe Breen, Chaplain to the Tralee Volunteers, a month or five weeks before the Rising, that the arms landing was to be very early on Easter Monday morning when the arms ship was expected at Fenit. Pearse's last visit to Tralee was, in fact, on February 26. He reviewed the Volunteers the next day—several hundred from local areas—in a sports' field, and lectured the same night in the Rink on " The Nature of Irish Freedom." Father Breen stated emphatically that Pearse gave the early hours of Easter Monday as the landing date : " I am absolutely convinced of that because I discussed all the arrangements for the actual landing and distribution of the guns in my own room. . . . The boat, therefore, could not be and was not expected before Sunday."[9] This story is undoubtedly true, yet difficult to understand when contrasted with Devoy's account of the changed date and second message to the Germans. If Pearse could tell Stack on February 26-27 that the arms landing was to take place on Easter Sunday night, why were the Germans informed of the change only so late as April? The published documents prove Devoy's account correct in every particular : no intimation reached Germany until April 15 that their own dates, Holy Thursday to Easter Saturday must be changed to Easter Sunday night.

---

[9] " Who Blundered in Ireland?" P. Cahill, *An Phoblacht*, September 13, 1930.

Cahill himself was told by Austin Stack about a month before the Rising what Pearse had previously told him, Father Breen, and the Volunteer organiser, Alfred Cotton, which he finally agreed, at Stack's request should be told to Cahill. Two weeks before Easter Sunday, Cahill was sent to Dublin by Stack.[10] Seán MacDermott gave Cahill two signalling lamps for use by the pilot boat that was to meet the *Aud;* the lamps had green glass on the outside, and were to be shown close together from the pilot boat—the lamps were to be kept in the Volunteer Hall, Tralee, and to be taken on Saturday evening to the Maharees, Castlegregory where the pilot lived.[11]

Cahill also quotes a statement made by Mr. P. O'Shea, N.T., Castlegregory, who arranged to get in touch with the pilot. Mr. O'Shea states that Stack, three weeks before the Rising, " told me of the Rising that had been planned, and that one small vessel would leave a German port shortly, laden with arms and ammunition for the use of the Irish Volunteers. Austin asked me to make the necessary arrangements for procuring a pilot. *He stated quite definitely that the gun-runner would be off Inistooskert on the night of Easter Sunday or the morning of Easter Monday,—not before.* As the ship was to arrive at night or at dawn, we were to look out for a green light on her bridge. The answering signal was to be two green lights on the pilot boat. It was our intention to board the vessel accompanied by Mr. Mort. O'Leary and Mr. Maurice Flynn, both of Maherees. On Easter Saturday I went to Tralee to make final arrangements with Austin and to bring out the lamps which were to be used for signalling. I learned of the arrest of Austin and all those other events which are now a matter of history."

In the same narrative, Mr. Mort. O'Leary, the pilot, who was to

---

[10] Pearse informed Stack and Cotton at an interview in Dublin in Autumn, 1915, of the coming insurrection in general terms.

[11] Apparently MacDermott sent other signalling lamps to Tralee. A fortnight before Easter, D. S. Madden, now of Waterford, was asked by Stack, Father Breen, and Cahill to arrange for an important message from Dublin. At Stack's suggestion, Mrs. Madden who was visiting Dublin with her sister, Miss Kathleen O'Brien of Clonmel, agreed to bring back the message. On the Monday of Holy Week, Seán Heuston handed them a parcel at Geraghty's Hotel, Parnell Square. It consisted of two lamps, two feet high with square glass sides; one lamp had a red slide, the second a green slide. Stack took charge of these lamps and sent them away by two Volunteers on the Tuesday or Wednesday of Holy Week. (Statement in a letter to the writer.)

meet the *Aud* at Fenit, where the pier and railway were to be seized and the arms distributed, according to Stack's orders to Cahill, O'Shea, and others, gives his story of events. The only information he received was from a captain of the Castlegregory Volunteers who told him on Holy Thursday that a small arms steamer was due on Sunday night, and that he would give O'Leary full particulars if he called up to see him on Holy Saturday night: " When I went home that evening (Holy Thursday) I saw a small two-masted boat about a mile N.E. of Inistooskert, but having no information, and not expecting any boat until Sunday night, I took no notice of her. I found out afterwards it was the *Aud*. Really I did not expect such a big one from what Tadhg Brosnan told me. I was up early on Friday morning, at dawn, she was then steaming slowly west from Kerry Head. I took her to be a British decoy boat, as such were around at the time."

This statement of the pilot understandably aroused the ire of Karl Spindler when he read it. There was a truly casual method in the handling of the pilots, a what's everybody's business is nobody's business. Dublin, which had been informed by Germany that a 1,400 ton small steamer would come, as far back as mid-March, must have given Stack some idea, at least, that the expected arms would not arrive in a cockle shell. What is clear, beyond all doubt, is that Stack and the Kerry Volunteers were convinced from the Dublin instructions that the landing could not be expected before Sunday night, that the pilots cannot be blamed as they received orders only very late, and those vague and general ones, that the split in the Dublin leadership and the rush of tragic events which crowded upon the Kerry Volunteers created a confusion that nothing could have transformed into clear and definite action. Things all at once reached such a pass that even if the pilot had hailed the *Aud,* and discovered her true character, that even if Stack had realised the truth he could not have mobilised his men in time, that the Rising was already doomed by that fatal last-minute change of date.

The events that paralysed Kerry were: a tragedy at Ballykissane Pier, the sudden arrival of Casement, the arrest of Austin Stack. Nothing that Stack could have done could have saved the arms landing, and with the *Aud's* cargo gone the plans of Military Council fell to pieces. Sir John Maxwell's judgment that the Irish effort so far as the pre-landing arrangements went was all too casual unfortunately for the immediate prospects of the insurrection was true.

It was the first time for fifty years that insurrection had been attempted in Ireland, and there was to be, in Connolly's final words, too many of " the almost unavoidable incidents of a hurried uprising against long established authority." Pearse's *Singer* recaptures the clash of thought and policy in the divided leadership of the time. He, like Plunkett and Clarke and MacDermot, believed that a bold lead in 1916 would rouse the people, and inspire as fervent and militant an outburst as '98. The prestige of Eoin MacNeill, who had no such expectation, was strong among the rank and file of the Volunteers, and already there was a feeling among the Volunteers in the country that Dublin was better armed and prepared for action, and that difficulties and conditions outside the capital were not understood by the Dublin leaders.[12] The three conditions laid down by MacNeill for an insurrection, attack by the British, an attempt to enforce conscription, or a German invasion in force, would have been accepted, and in that order of importance by the majority of the Volunteers. There was, moreover, a growing body of opinion amongst them which realised that any struggle against British power would have to be fought out on guerrilla lines. The confidence of the 1916 leaders in a militant tradition among the people was only justified, and then slowly, when they had transformed the situation by their deaths—but the attempt at large-scale insurrection was never renewed.

There was some justification for German scepticism as to the vitality of the revolutionary movement. In the actual situation in the country—which remained for the most part pro-Redmonite and pro-Ally, with the Press, Church, the wealthy, the farmers almost solidly behind it, and with Sinn Féin and the Irish Volunteers in a most unpopular minority—there was certainly a mixture of faith and bluff in the messages from Ireland, and Irish-America to Germany. This was checked by reports from whatever German intelligence service operated in Ireland. German experience of the Casement Brigade experiment, and of Irish soldiers in general, for

---

[12] An unnamed correspondent of presumably John Devoy's is quoted, June 30, 1916, *Documents relative to Sinn Féin Movement*, p. 17: " We still think that Inner Council were not justified in keeping MacNeill in dark so long. . . . Provinces wished not to be left out of affair but there certainly was regrettable disregard of provincial conditions on the part of Dublin. . . . Dublin had been told that without arms, etc., we could do nothing." See also p. 232 *infra*.

instance, must have led to a cynical reception for such claims as the Irish message per Devoy-von Skal, February 10, 1916: "The Irish regiments which are in sympathy with us are being gradually replaced by English regiments." There was, in fact, a grain of truth in this statement, a tiny grain indeed, but the German anticipation that it was unreliable was, in practice, to be justified by bitter experience. Nor again was the claim of the Revolutionary Directory in February, 1916, that it was "anticipated that practically all" the "50,000 Redmond Volunteers" would "join the revolution," justified by the fact that this force so far as it really existed at all, and acted at all, took sides openly and at once against the insurrection.

The Revolutionary Directory estimate, so far as figures went, was plausible. Their reading of the weakness of the British forces in men and artillery was accurate. Their plan of insurrection was bold and possible. Their faith in the ultimate Irish revolution in the end moved the mountain. Yet the facts of the pre-Easter situation proved that the mass of the people and the Volunteers were not mentally ready for insurrection. The 1916 plan of insurrection was a gamble on one thin chance, a bold seizure of Dublin, an uprising in the country fed by German armament. As the hour of action came nearer, and as the *Aud* reached the Irish coast after its adventurous dash from Lübeck to the Arctic circle, with a sharp swoop past the Färöee Islands, to Tralee Bay, and Casement landed, the tangle of mischance in Kerry thickened.

First, the Ballykissane tragedy destroyed the insurgent plans to establish wireless communication with the arms ship and submarine and Germany. It was proposed to dismantle the wireless station at Cahirciveen, Waterville, and set up a transmitter in Tralee. Seán MacDermott, in company with Michael Collins, had discussed the scheme in two interviews with Dennis Daly and Con Keating. On Good Friday morning, Daly left Dublin in charge of the party which was to carry out the work: Con Keating, the one man of them all who was an expert on wireless installation; Dan Sheehan, of West Limerick; Charles Monaghan and Colm Ó Lochlainn, of Dublin. They separated at Kingsbridge and travelled to Killarney in different compartments. The five met there at a house in the town, and were met half a mile outside by two cars from Limerick which were an hour late. Ó Lochlainn set off in one car with Daly. The second car, driven by Thomas MacInerney, followed behind.

Keating sat beside him as he was the only man in the second car who knew the road to Cahirciveen. It had been arranged that Keating should keep the rear light of the first car in view. Half a mile between Killorglin and Milltown the rear car broke down, and was later held up a few miles outside Killorglin by a policeman who became so inquisitive and difficult that Keating finally drew a revolver and ordered him off. MacInerney drove through Killorglin, turned at the entrance to the town, and, mistaking the route, drove straight towards Ballykissane. The road ended, in fact, on Ballykissane Pier. The lights of the first car were no longer visible. MacInerney hesitated, and asked Keating if he was sure of the road. Keating replied very emphatically that he was certain and to proceed. MacInerney at once put on speed, and a few seconds afterwards the car shot over the pier-head, overturned, and, as the hood was up, trapped and drowned Monaghan, Keating and Sheehan. MacInerney managed to break free and swam towards lights he saw at some distance. They were lights shining across Castlemaine Bay. He heard a whistle and turned. A friendly resident, fortunately for him, had arrived on the scene with a light and directed him back to the shore. He entered a friendly house, where he managed to hide his revolver and some papers before he was arrested. Daly and Ó Lochlainn missed the headlights of their companion car, which they first believed to have taken a different and less fatal route over Beaufort Bridge, to proceed to Killorglin by the Beaufort road. They drove on and waited three miles west of the town. In the end, thinking the other car had gone on in front, they went towards Cahirciveen where they were held up by a police patrol. Their driver explained he was bringing two medical students to Waterville on a pleasure trip. After a casual search, they were allowed to proceed. They reached the meeting-place arranged with the other party an hour and a half after the time fixed, and waited for two hours. As Keating was the only one who understood wireless installation, they had to abandon their plans, return to Dublin and report, and they reached it by train on Saturday morning.[13]

Spindler comments that the Ballykissane drownings did not change the situation materially as, even if the party had arrived and

---

[13] Colm O Lochlainn later in the day had an interview with Joseph Plunkett, and, in company with Eoin MacNeill, another with Pearse at the Hermitage.

H

completed their work, the orders issued already to the Tralee Volunteers concerned a landing on Sunday night only, and it would have been impossible at such short notice to concentrate forces rapidly enough to cope with the landing. Casement and Stack were already prisoners. The German wireless had already flashed out warnings to all U-boats in Irish waters: *" Everything betrayed. Return immediately with the Aud."* The *Aud*, after a twenty-two hour wait, had sailed out of Tralee Bay.[14]

---

[14] Both William O'Brien and Miss Madge Daly have informed the writer since the first edition of this book appeared that Good Friday was seriously considered as the original date for the Rising. Tom Clarke so told Miss Daly early in 1916. James Connolly told William O'Brien that the date was later changed to Easter Sunday because Volunteer officers objected that a mobilisation on Good Friday was a departure from the usual rule that mobilisations were ordered only for Sundays and Holidays when the majority of men were not at work, and any change would cause comment and might also be a dangerous hint to the British. (See *Irish Press*, January 25, 1936. " Was the Date Changed?" William O'Brien.) Geraldine Plunkett (Mrs. Gertrude Dillon), *Irish Press*, January 3, 14, 1936, in two articles, " Casement and Easter Week," and " How Much Did the Castle Know?" argues that her brother, Joseph Plunkett, had definitely arranged for an arms landing on Easter Sunday, that this was later confirmed, and that Casement himself in his anxiety for the safe arrival and distribution of the arms took it upon himself to alter the date. This argument is at variance with Devoy's account of the messages from Ireland on February 5 and April 14, 1916, already quoted, although the Germans certainly acted to a certain extent on Casement's and Monteith's suggestions in loading the cargo. The Germans, however, were fully aware of the Dublin message handed to Casement from Plunkett as to the final date before the *Aud* sailed.

CHAPTER VIII

FROM 10 o'clock onwards on Easter Monday the Volunteers mobilised and by noon were marching off to take up their posts. It was a fine and sunny day, and the streets were filled with holiday makers. In Dublin Castle no one expected insurrection. Not even Eoin MacNeill as he cycled into the city past the mobilised Rathfarnham Volunteers could believe in it. He stopped and had a word with the officers, issued a paternal word of warning, and rode on to Dr. O'Kelly's house in Rathgar. Major Ivor H. Price, County Inspector, Royal Irish Constabulary, Inspector of Military Intelligence, Headquarters, Irish Command, had not even a suspicion of such a thing as he went down in very good humour to the Castle at a quarter to twelve in the ordinary course of duty. He entered the Upper Castle Yard by the picturesque gateway over which a figure of Justice holds the scales with her back to the hostile city, and entered the office of Sir Matthew Nathan, some twenty-five yards from the gate, and began a discussion of the measures that would soon put the Sinn Féiners and Volunteers in their proper places behind prison bars. It was not only the figure of Justice that had her back to Castle visitors that morning. Even the few soldiers on guard at Ship Street Barracks nearby were in a holiday mood.

Eoin MacNeill met Seán Fitzgibbon, another member of the Volunteer Executive, and Liam Ó Briain in Rathgar Road. Liam Ó Briain had carried the countermand through Leinster, to Edenderry, to Tyrellspass, and to Tullamore, feeling as if he was in a dream, and wishing he were back to take part in whatever the Volunteers would or would not do in Dublin, wondering at the queer world where people were giving a threatening turn to that worn old word, rebellion. He had turned Dublin upside down for a bayonet in vain on Saturday, but bought a Spanish blade in Lawlor's shop, and placed it beside his rifle and knapsack just before he was summoned to MacNeill's meeting by Arthur

Griffith, and found himself a courier. He had spent Sunday night with Seán T. O'Kelly, who advised him to report to MacNeill what he had learned in the country, but dropped no hint as to what might happen on Monday.[1] Seán Fitzgibbon cycled off to find out what the Volunteers were doing. MacNeill and Ó Briain entered Dr. O'Kelly's house, and MacNeill opened his mind. He still said he would move heaven and earth to stop the Rising. From the day the Volunteers were founded he had feared that some rashness might lose the Irish people what the Volunteer movement had given them, the right to carry arms in their own country. He wanted to keep the organisation intact until the war was ended, and the disillusioned remnant of the 100,000 Irishmen who had fought abroad returned and asked where was the Home Rule they had been promised. He had known vaguely that some members of the Volunteer Executive belonged to the I.R.B., but he had thought they were all working together with him. He knew nothing about the negotiations with Germany for arms, he knew nothing about the special orders for insurrection until a university student told him about an order to demolish an important bridge. He spoke of Hobson and O'Connell's information which confirmed this, of his visit to Pearse, of Pearse's retort that deception had been necessary, of the later messages given by MacDonagh and MacDermott, of the loss of the German ship, of MacNeill's own admission that, as the Government would then attack the Volunteers, and that, as MacNeill had often before said publicly, all must stand together in any such crisis. As Saturday passed, MacNeill continued, and the British made no move, and as he studied the reports of the wretched equipment and armament of the Volunteers outside Dublin, he thought an effort could still be made to save the Volunteers, and as his I.R.B. colleagues had not consulted him, he had as much right not to consult them, and advise the Volunteers to follow his path as Pearse and the other I.R.B. leaders had advised the Volunteers to follow theirs. Liam Ó Briain laughed and said that the Military Council should have kidnapped MacNeill as they had kidnapped Hobson, and MacNeill agreed that he wouldn't have been at all offended if that had happened. But he thought all danger of a Rising was now over. As for the Volunteers marching and parading through the city that

---

[1] *Comhar*, Nollaig, 1945, " An Méid aDúirt Eoin MacNéill," Liam O Briain.

morning, MacNeill thought it a very wise precaution, as the Castle might get suspicious if the Volunteers failed to take advantage of such wonderful weather. Lack of arms, at all events, would stop an insurrection as all the delegates at a G.A.A. Convention over the Easter had said, except one very wild fellow.

Seán Fitzgibbon burst in at that minute and told the two men that the fight was on. Even then MacNeill refused to believe it. Ó Briain promised MacNeill that he would go out and bring him back definite news. And very definite news indeed Liam Ó Briain brought back. Even while they were talking away, Major Price, too, saw something he could not have believed could happen without at least a hint beforehand from his Intelligence services. Men in green uniforms were dashing about the Upper Castle Yard, and the policeman on duty lay dead in a pool of blood inside the gate. A sentry who had fired one warning shot was racing for safety. The Major fired a few shots from his revolver, and the attackers began to break into one of the buildings opposite. The Major expected to see 200 soldiers marching up to his relief but no soldiers came. He realised that there was only a small guard on duty, ten in all, and that the Castle was at the mercy of the attackers if they pressed on, the Castle, Under-Secretary, himself and all. Twenty-five determined men, he said afterwards, could have taken the Castle. Fortunately for him, the attackers did not realise it. Nor had the Military Council realised that Dublin Castle was ever left with so weak a guard. Connolly had rejected the project of capturing the Castle as not feasible, and not desirable, even if feasible: the place was well guarded, it was a long and straggling collection of buildings difficult to defend and, moreover, there was a Red Cross hospital inside. The plan was to seal up the Castle by seizing the City Hall, the guard room in the Upper Castle Yard, the *Evening Mail* office, and other buildings facing the gates. Nor were there even twenty-five men, there were sixteen, and six took the guard room even while Major Price fired his gun, about turned, and looked in vain for an army.

Seán Connolly had headed the march to the Castle, demanded admittance, and when the policeman on duty slammed the gate to shot him dead. As the sentry fired and fled, six Citizen Army men led by Tom Kain opened the gate, rushed in, bombed and seized the guard room. They overpowered several soldiers, and tied them up with their own puttees, The six men settled down, determined to hold out against whatever forces came. If they had realised the weakness of the Castle guard, there is little doubt that Major Price would have had no complaint to make about lack of determination or that Connolly's cooler considerations would have weighed much with them. The instinct of any Citizen Army man or Volunteer of the time, offered the Castle as a gift would have been to take it, if only to burn it. Yet even the original plan of holding the Castle approaches had been gravely hampered by the weak mobilisation of the insurgent forces that morning, and a slight hitch in the plans had led indirectly to Seán Connolly's impetuous shooting of the policeman. James Connolly had secured a duplicate from an impression of the key of the City Hall main door, and the original plan had been to make the attack on the Upper Castle Yard and seizure of the guard room from the City Hall. There was some delay in securing this key and Seán Connolly decided to rush the Upper Castle gate and secure the guard room before the City Hall was occupied. James Connolly's orders had been to open fire on the first stroke of the Angelus bell. Noon struck as the first shots were fired.

Almost immediately afterwards Seán Connolly quitted the guard room garrison and returned to the City Hall. The frontal iron gates were climbed by his small band of ten men and nine women. Small parties of Citizen Army men and Volunteers at the same time took over the *Evening Mail* office on the corner of Parliament Street and Cork Hill, and Henry and James shop nearby. From the roofs and windows of these buildings snipers opened fire on the Castle. Six posts in all were taken. There were ten Citizen Army men in the City Hall, some forty others spread over the other posts in the area. Nine women also accompanied Seán Connolly on his march to the Castle. They took their place in the various dangerous posts. Seán Connolly's sister, Mrs. Barrett, was in the City Hall. Miss Helena Molony was with the party at the Castle gate. As Tom Kain and his party dashed through towards the guard room, a second policeman came round a corner. Miss Molony drew a revolver and fired in the air. That satisfied his curiosity, and he went away. Seán Connolly sent her to the headquarters for reinforcements, and at six that evening a small force of Volunteers and Citizen Army men arrived. Dr. Kathleen Lynn and Miss Molony saw the City Hall windows darkened by a hail of bullets from British rifles and machine-guns long before that.   Sniping began from the Castle almost at once, and as Seán Connolly on the roof of the City Hall hoisted the Tricolour he was shot dead.

Liam Ó Briain had continued his quest for news in the meantime.   He cycled towards Portobello Bridge.   There he saw the flashes and heard reports of rifles from the windows of Davy's public-house.   Ten Citizen Army men under Joseph Doyle were firing across the canal at a party of British soldiers crouched on the banks who, in turn, were peppering the Citizen Army post very vigorously.   From Portobello Barracks other parties of soldiers were dashing along the canal, rifles ready.   A machine-gun detachment appeared.   All the soldiers were shouting and cheering wildly.   Liam Ó Briain remembered his promise to Eoin MacNeill and returned to him.   MacNeill hesitated to believe the news even then.   He sat down, and remained silent for five minutes and more.   He was thinking deeply, tears in his eyes, then he spoke:

" I will go home for my Volunteer uniform, and go out and fight!   My friends and comrades are fighting and dying, and I must join them."

Liam Ó Briain was moved by the sincerity and mental anguish which lay behind MacNeill's words.   MacNeill, to be sure, changed his mind again.   Others who met him in the same mood were less sympathetic than Liam Ó Briain.   They said sharply that MacNeill could not make up his mind whether to go into the Rising in uniform or in plain clothes, and racked himself so much with metaphysical speculations on these points that the Rising was over before he had decided them.   MacNeill, however, had not spoken his last word that week nor made his last effort to save the Volunteers.   Three days later he and Arthur Griffith discussed an appeal over their joint names to the country to rise and support the Volunteers, but it was then too late, and there were no means of distributing the appeal.   In the end MacNeill was to beard Sir John Maxwell himself as Ireland lay under martial law, and the Army of the Republic lay broken.

Liam Ó Briain himself went out with the one care on his mind as to where and how he should meet his Volunteer company.   He went back to Portobello.   The soldiers were still firing at Davy's public-house.   No reply came from the fortress.   The garrison had withdrawn.   The soldiers eventually charged it in force, bayonets fixed, and ransacked it from basement to attic.   Panic tales of a coming attack on Portobello Barracks itself were rife among the garrison.   Liam Ó Briain had no time to watch the battle, one-sided as it was, unknown to the vigorous volleyers and shouting officers and cheering men.   A British officer pointed his revolver at Liam Ó Briain and told him to be off.   The officer was angry.   Round the corner at Earlsfort Terrace Liam Ó Briain found another very angry officer, a Volunteer officer—Harry Nicholls—an Ulsterman and a Protestant, beside himself with rage that he, a Volunteer Captain of Engineers, had received no summons to the fight.   Round the corner in Stephen's Green they both found all the battle any man of war could ask.   The Citizen Army had taken possession.   The gates were barricaded.   Picks and shovels were being flourished inside.   They approached the barricade and looked inside.   There was a typical crowd of Dubliners looking idly on.   Inside the gate there was a Citizen Army man—gun in hand—Bob de Coeur.   He was making a speech to the crowd.   Short and to the point: " If you are any bloody good, come in and fight for Ireland."   They spoke to him and told him they were Volunteers astray and looking for their company.   He told them that if they wanted fight, Stephen's Green was as good a place as any, that is, if they were serious Volunteers.   There was a burst of gunfire near at hand.   They decided that Stephen's Green was indeed a battlefield, and cleared the railings and said they would stay.   Bob de Coeur told them that his father was a Frenchman and that he, therefore, was a good man to guide them through a revolution.   He guided them to Madame de Markievicz who told them that they would only get a rope or bullet for their services, unless they managed to beat the British.   They said they didn't give a damn, and stayed.

That morning as the Stephen's Green Citizen Army contingent marched up Grafton Street in sections to take over the various posts Connolly had assigned them at his Wednesday conference, Frank Robbins, who was with the section headed by Captain James MacCormack, who were to seize Harcourt Street Station, noticed Thomas MacDonagh.   He called MacCormack, and spoke a few words to him.   MacCormack rejoined his section, and told him that MacDonagh had said: " Above all, avoid all unnecessary bloodshed."

Stephen's Green, Harcourt Street Station, Hatch Street, the railway bridge in Harcourt Road commanding the South Circular Road could only be held by a skeleton garrison. It was impossible to occupy the Shelbourne Hotel; fifty Volunteers and Citizen Army men who should have taken it were simply not there. Davy's pub had been taken, and abandoned. Harcourt Street Station post could be held no later than three on Monday afternoon. Frank Robbins had to content himself with three men where he had planned for sixteen. The entire strength of the Stephen's Green garrison and its posts when it surrendered, according to British Army estimates, was no more than 109 men and ten women, excluding Michael Mallin and Madame Markievicz. The Citizen Army estimate was slightly lower, no doubt because the Volunteers who took part were excluded. In the occupation of the Green about fifty men were engaged. Mallin asked Frank Robbins on Monday morning to take over the College of Surgeons on the west side of the Green as a reserve post. The mobilisation had disappointed him and he appealed to MacDonagh for reinforcements. He was in touch with MacDonagh until the end of the fighting.

Mallin advised Robbins to use guile in taking the College. The doorkeeper was a rabid Carsonite who displayed a copy of the Ulster Covenant signed by himself in his room. Mallin suggested that a small party should stroll past and turn swiftly in. Robbins had only three men and three women to assist him. One of the women was Madame Markievicz, very happily for the rabid doorkeeper as it turned out. He was arguing with a holiday drunk as Robbins and his party approached the College. Robbins made a swift rush for the door just as the drunk, after long and maudlin protests, had agreed to call back another day, and reached the door as it was slammed in his face in a panic. At the same minute a shotgun went off, missed Robbins by a few inches of his head and plastered the upper part of the door. The doorkeeper in his hurry could not quite secure the lock, and Robbins wedged his foot inside, followed by his revolver, and a surly surrender accompanied a defiant refusal to show the party where a store of guns in the building were, eighty-nine Army rifles. Robbins and his men were so enraged that they were seriously tempted to shoot him. Madame Markievicz intervened and told them to lock the doorkeeper in his bedroom with his wife and family, and leave him there. This was done, and soon afterwards the doorkeeper was heard sturdily hammering on the bedroom door, but was ignored until the defences had been secured.

Late on Monday night a British machine-gun crew which had arrived from the Curragh and had been busy during the day at the Castle and City Hall was divided into two sections and one dispatched to Stephen's Green with the object of seizing the Shelbourne Hotel. The British occupation of the Telephone Exchange in Crown Alley kept them aware more or less of posts not occupied by the insurgents. This section, however, seems to have had its doubts that the Sinn Féiners might not after all have taken possession of the hotel before them. Strict orders were issued that the men should advance in the dark on tiptoe through Kildare Street. On their way from the Castle they laughed bitterly at this order as they wore hobnailed army boots, and thought that the weight of their burdens and the thunder of their boots must wake every Sinn Féin sniper in Stephen's Green, and all Dublin, and that they could be heard coming miles away.[2] To their relief their march to the Shelbourne and their occupation of it were unobstructed and unchallenged, and they wondered that the rebel sentries kept so easy a watch. From then onwards a continuous and terrible fire from the machine-guns raked Stephen's Green and the roof of the College of Surgeons to which Mallin withdrew his forces, after several Citizen Army casualties and some vigorous sniping which riddled the ground-floor windows of the Shelbourne. Mallin himself had a narrow escape from death as he rushed to one of the gateways of the Green opposite the hotel to drag a wounded Citizen Army man to safety. His hat was perforated by a bullet.

Mallin withdrew to the College of Surgeons early on Tuesday, and the building was under heavy machine-gun fire from the roof of the Shelbourne and continuous sniping from the United Services Club, also on the north side of the Green, throughout the week. Mallin planned several sorties to seize and fire buildings as a cover to attack the United Services Club but had to abandon them so murderous was the machine-gunning in the neighbourhood. He actually had completed arrangements for an attempt to slip through the British cordon with his garrison and adopt guerrilla tactics in the hills when the final order came.

---

[2] *Irish Life* : A Record of the Rebellion of 1916. (Dublin, 1916.)

The fight of the Citizen Army in the City Hall ended on Tuesday morning when the British forces took it after heavy bombing and machine-gun fire.   The *Evening Mail* office and the other Citizen Army posts were by then also in British hands.   All the force possible was hurled against the small band of Citizen Army men who had attacked the Castle.

CHAPTER IX

As noon was striking the column from Liberty Hall turned out of Middle Abbey Street and wheeled to the right across O'Connell Street. Lieutenant Chalmers, 14th Royal Fusiliers, who was entering the Post Office at that moment, turned to a friend, and remarked contemptuously: " Just look at that awful crowd. They must be on a route march." Connolly, in his dark green uniform, marched at the head, Joseph Plunkett at his left, Pearse on his right, and behind them a mixed body of Citizen Army men and Volunteers. Among the Volunteers, under the leadership of George Plunkett, were some fifty men of the Kimmage Garrison armed with pikes and shotguns, and some twenty exiles, under Frank Thornton, from North Frederick Street. In all the column numbered about a hundred and fifty men, all dangerously and incredibly over-loaded with an assortment of weapons and implements. Many carried two rifles, a sledge-hammer and pick; not all wore dark green or grey-green uniforms, their Sunday or workaday clothes were crossed with bandoleer straps and haversacks, while there was a great display of yellow armlets on left sleeves. Brennan Whitmore and Michael Collins were near the front ranks. Somewhere in the rear lumbered two drays, packed with Howth Mausers, shotguns, miniature rifles, Sniders, Martinis, Lee-Enfields, pikes, explosives, boxes of rude bombs made from tin cans or lengths of piping. A closed cab crammed to bursting with war material jolted along, too. Tom Clarke and Sean MacDermott were to the fore, and Winifred Carney, Connolly's secretary, the only woman among them all. The O'Rahilly was speeding in his car, packed with as fine a selection of arms and explosives as he could gather in a hurry, to this muster because, as he phrased it, " I have helped to wind up the clock, and must be there to hear it strike."

When the column reached the G.P.O. portico, white-faced and hostile Chalmers, with his querulous eyes, was still scoffing and gaping. Connolly halted his men with a sudden passionate and strident shout: "Left turn, the G.P.O.,—Charge!" There was a wild cheer, a flourish of the Kimmage pikes, a wilder rush as the ranks broke and hurled themselves through the main entrance in any order at all with a salvo of revolver shots in the air. There were no more than seventy men now. The rest, in sections, were seizing other posts in the area. By Pearse's order, Michael Staines and a party rushed through the main hall and made for the upper storeys at once to overcome the guard. Shots could be heard somewhere upstairs. Staines was challenged by a guard of seven soldiers who covered him with their rifles. Staines fired on the sergeant in charge who fell, not very seriously wounded, merely a grazed forehead which stunned him. The Volunteers rushed on the guard with a determined fury, waving their revolvers and daring them to fire. The guard surrendered at once. It was soon obvious why: they had no ammunition for their rifles.

On the main floor near the entrance there was a wild panic rush of stupefied holiday-makers, indignant old ladies, weeping girls and civil servants tumbling into coats as they were hurried out with red startled faces; a few policemen. Connolly's voice, still harsh and excited, could be heard through the building, calling on all men and women of peace and leisure to leave, and leave at once.

Lieutenant Chalmers bandied indignant words with Plunkett, Brennan Whitmore and Michael Collins outside on the very steps. Abruptly a group of Volunteers seized him. A bayonet in front, a pike behind, a levelled revolver, a laugh from Michael Collins, a rope, and the valiant Chalmers was bound and dumped into a telephone box at the foot of Nelson Pillar for an hour or so. Out through the doors tramped a dozen officials with their hands over their heads, and with a jest from their captors they joined the spectators despite jocose offers from the Volunteers of hospitality and guns and assurances that the insurgent positions were the safest places in the city.

Rifle butts crashed through glass at sides and front as Connolly's voice inside rasped peremptorily: "Smash those windows, and fortify them, and barricade the doors!" The task of building up the interior defences strained the capacity of the small force in the new roomy fortress. The Volunteers were weak in officers, much depleted, eager and enthusiastic, yet inexperienced and confused. Yet even now the plan shaped. Plunkett unrolled a map and showed Brennan Whitmore a circle of positions around the city, already captured, if all had gone as in the headquarters. Over the Post Office floated the flags of the Republic.

High over Prince's Street corner breaks a strange new banner of unmistakable import, inspiration and menace, green, and in the centre, in Celtic letters, half-gold, half-white, IRISH REPUBLIC. In a pause, as order emerges within, Connolly strides out into the yard and looks up at the floating green and gold, at rising barricades, at groups in the windows opposite and on every vital corner, at the coming and going of small armed parties. He smiles genially and says to a friend with simple enthusiasm: " Isn't it grand?"

As good company to Hibernia, Mercury and Fidelity aloft on the pediment, Volunteers hoist Republican tricolours, green, white and orange above the Royal arms then lurking weather-beaten in their triangular tympanum. Down in the vast street dazed, unsympathetic half-hostile crowds ebb and flow before the headquarters of revolt, wildly talking and speculating citizens, sceptical for the most part that there is much in this revolution, some giving it half an hour until the British come, others planning loot, here and there a few onlookers heart and soul with the defiant leap in the dark.

It was just before 3 p.m. as the flags went up. Volunteer and Fianna officers and Kimmage garrison men, led by Joe Gleeson, completed the work. Some cheers came from the street. Stephen MacKenna, for one, watches the flags go up against the clear blue sky. MacKenna, scholar and Republican, friend of Synge and Pearse alike, had fought for the Greeks in 1897, and seen the Russian revolution of 1905 at first-hand as a war correspondent, yet no moment of his life moved him so much as this fulfilment of the dream of years. Half-crippled with rheumatism, he limped along on a stick, cursing the fate that forbade him to dash in and ask for a gun, his two dark volcanic eyes in a trance, a trance that lasted all that day. Five hours later, the poet, Austin Clarke, found him there still with his eyes on the floating tricolours and the armed men seen dimly behind sandbags at the windows. Then all the passion and turmoil of his mind broke out in two words to Clarke, two words only: " At last!"

Later, MacKenna told his friend, Thomas McGreevy, that the vigil broke his patience and he made his way into the building and asked to be taken to Pearse. Wildly he asked to share in the insurrection, and be given any task. Pearse was deeply touched, for

MacKenna was an old and close friend, but he saw that the pallid-faced and helpless man should be at home in bed. He was courteous and evasive until MacKenna's insistence overcame him, and he said: " Well, then, we might seat you on an armchair at one of the upper windows, and then, when the British break in, perhaps you could light the fuses of some of those grenades you see, and drop them on their heads." MacKenna burst out laughing, exclaimed, " Hell!" shook hands with Pearse for the last time, and went home to write one of the most vivid, intimate, and truthful pamphlets ever written on the 1916 leaders.[1]

Yet MacKenna, in his long wait, saw the birth of the insurrection with amazing detachment for so sympathetic an observer. He listened to Pearse read the Proclamation of the Republic, pale and cold of face, to an indifferent crowd and " a few thin, perfunctory cheers." McKenna recorded later that he " felt sad " for Pearse as he read without evoking any popular enthusiasm whatever ; on the contrary " the response was chilling." And yet the Proclamation that Pearse read was one of the great documents of Irish history, and, as he concluded, Connolly clasped his hand and cried out: " Thanks be to God, Pearse, that we have lived to see this day!" The Proclamation was then posted up outside the building, and small groups of Volunteers gathered round another copy in the main hall within, and read the message beneath the deep black capitals:

" POBLACHT NA h-EIREANN.
THE PROVISIONAL GOVERNMENT
OF THE
IRISH REPUBLIC
TO THE PEOPLE OF IRELAND.

IRISHMEN AND IRISHWOMEN : In the name of God and of the dead generations from which she receives her old tradition of nationhood, Ireland, through us, summons her children to her flag and strikes for her freedom.

---

[1] *Memories of the Dead*, published over the pseudonym " Martin Daly." See *Journals and Letters of Stephen MacKenna*. (London, 1936). Ed. E. R. Dodds, pp. 50-2. MacKenna's Pearse interview was described by Thomas McGreevy in a statement to the writer. For eye-witness accounts of the flag incidents, see *Irish Life* Record, and John Higgins, *New Witness*, quoted *Gaelic American*, *July* 29, 1916.

Having organised her manhood through her secret revolutionary organisation, the Irish Republican Brotherhood, and
through her open military organisations, the Irish Volunteers
and the Irish Citizen Army, having patiently perfected her
discipline, having resolutely waited for the right moment to
reveal itself, she now seizes that moment, and supported by
her exiled children in America and by gallant allies in Europe,
but relying in the first on her own strength, she strikes in full
confidence of victory.

We declare the right of the people of Ireland to the owner-
ship of Ireland and to the unfettered control of Irish destinies,
to be sovereign and indefeasible. The long usurpation of that
right by a foreign people and government has not extinguished
the right, nor can it ever be extinguished except by the
destruction of the Irish people. In every generation the Irish
people have asserted their right to national freedom and
sovereignty; six times during the past three hundred years
they have asserted it in arms. Standing on that fundamental
right and again asserting it in arms in the face of the world,
we hereby proclaim the Irish Republic as a Sovereign
Independent State, and we pledge our lives and the lives of
our comrades in arms to the cause of its freedom, of its
welfare and of its exaltation among the nations.

The Irish Republic is entitled to, and hereby claims, the
allegiance of every Irishman and Irishwoman. The Republic
guarantees religious and civil liberty, equal rights and equal
opportunities to all its citizens, and declares its resolve to
pursue the happiness and prosperity of the whole nation and
of all its parts, cherishing all the children of the nation
equally, and oblivious of the differences carefully fostered by
an alien Government, which have divided a minority from the
majority in the past.

Until our arms have brought the opportune moment for
the establishment of a permanent National Government,
representative of the whole people of Ireland and elected by
the suffrages of all her men and women, the Provisional Government, hereby constituted, will administer the civil and
military affairs of the Republic in trust for the people.

We place the cause of the Irish Republic under the protection of the Most High God, Whose blessing we invoke upon

our arms, and we pray that no one who serves that cause will dishonour it by cowardice, inhumanity, or rapine. In this supreme hour the Irish nation must, by its valour and discipline, and by the readiness of its children to sacrifice themselves for the common good, prove itself worthy of the august destiny to which it is called.

Signed on behalf of the Provisional Government:

THOMAS J. CLARKE,
SEÁN MAC DIARMADA,   THOMAS MacDONAGH,
P. H. PEARSE,   EAMONN CEANNT,
JAMES CONNOLLY,   JOSEPH PLUNKETT."

One danger alone threatened the headquarters in the early stages of occupation, a determined attack by the British forces before the Volunteers had completed the work of barricading and defence. There were as yet little more than 700 Volunteers, badly armed and without machine-guns, under arms in all Dublin, nor were they to gain more than another 200 at most before the end. There were 120 British officers and 2,265 men in Dublin and 2,500 arrived from the Curragh the same afternoon; yet, as an official statement said later, these forces, " contrary to expectation," were " insufficient to deal with the situation." The first British move against the insurgent headquarters occurred shortly after the reading of the Proclamation. About 1 o'clock a company of Lancers came at a gallop from the north end of O'Connell Street—the only British force in strength which entered there until the Rising was over. They had been dispatched to the O'Connell Street area from Marlborough Barracks at the same time as the available troops from Portobello, Richmond and Royal Barracks had been ordered to relieve Dublin Castle. As the Lancers reached Nelson Pillar the Volunteers at the upper windows and on the roof of the Post Office fired, killed three of them, and fatally wounded a fourth. In the excitement and panic of the moment, the Volunteer marksmen ignored or failed to understand the order to withhold their fire until the Lancers had travelled the full length of the building, and thus saved the lives of many of the Lancers. As a second volley rolled out the Lancers wheeled and dashed back to the Rotunda so quickly that the wits at once named the

I

speedy retreat "the Leopardstown Races." The Lancers returned almost immediately to their barracks to the joy and surprise of some dispirited Volunteer officers who remarked that if the British charged defended buildings with cavalry there was great hope for Ireland still.

Even while the Volunteers were engaging the Lancers a final detachment of Volunteers rushed out of Middle Abbey Street at the double, in a bee-line to Prince's Street. They were the last men to leave Liberty Hall, which was from then on unoccupied. Their journey into Dublin had been uneventful. Their officers had warned them as they left Rathfarnham to keep their heads if any unusual incident occurred. Eoin MacNeill appeared and questioned their Commandant as they moved off, and added a warning that they were walking into a military trap. With a polite response that they would risk that and obey their orders, the company at half strength marched away through the village to catch the last tram into Dublin. As Jacob's factory was reached the Volunteers were already breaking in, although the only sign of anything astir was a few Volunteer cycle scouts posted at the approaches and a crowd of four or five women hustling a perspiring and indignant policeman in one of the side-streets. Entering Dame Street, the Rathfarnham men saw a long line of empty tramcars near the Castle and City Hall with a crowd of passengers and other sightseers thronging street and pavements, unconcerned, it seemed, although every now and then gunfire could be heard at hand and far off. At College Green the congestion of traffic was even greater. Recruiting posters still flapped unheeded on the walls, soldiers strolled past the Bank with their girls, the sun shone, the holiday crowds even yet had not realised that a revolution had broken out. Through College Street, across Butt Bridge via Tara Street, hurried the Rathfarnham men through an area now desolate to Liberty Hall. The door was locked, armed guards were to be seen at the upper windows, and inside, as the Volunteers trooped in, after a brief challenge, there were many signs that the hour had struck. "Mr. Connolly," broke a voice in excited tones on their ears, "said that from the moment the row started there were to be no longer Volunteers nor Citizen Army men but only the Irish Republican Army." Men stood round in groups and snipers were hurried to the roof with warnings to keep an eye on the railway line. Then a word came from Pearse to proceed to the G.P.O. and away went the Rathfarnham men, and timed their arrival unsuspectingly to the reports of the volleys which drove back the Lancers.

As the windows of the Prince's Street side of the building loomed up, a shout of: "Who are you? Where do you come from?" came from behind sacks and tables in the rudely fortified windows. The reply is satisfactory but the key of the great side door cannot be found. "Mind, mind yourselves! The Lancers!" roars someone, and a volley rolls out from roof and upper storeys. "Line up, line up," drones out a glum Volunteer officer in Prince's Street; "Line up, the Lancers are coming." A Volunteer Commandant cries out sharply: "None of that! Break the windows, and inside with you, you bloody fools!" As he speaks he lifts his rifle and splinters the wood and glass in the window nearest to him. A dozen rifle butts complete the task which even Connolly's order had left but half-completed. Cut and bleeding the men scramble through. A boy of sixteen falls wounded on the pavement, another Volunteer falls beside him, shot in the stomach by his own rifle.

Inside the feverish struggle to build up the defence goes on. Glass still crashes, locks are being blown in with revolvers when a door is obstinate, all hitherto undefended windows are being crammed with sacks, sandbags, boards, typewriters, anything to hand. Connolly barks at Brennan Whitmore as he goes across to Earl Street corner to inspect one barricade: "What good's that? A charge of schoolgirls could knock it over!" Whitmore smiles, and says: "Just try it!" Connolly kicks it vigorously, and breaks into a smile, as it withstands him: "Good!" A priest passes by in biretta and cassock. He wears a worried expression as he hastily adjusts his stole. A florid and dazed policeman, speechless through shock, sits on a barrel, his head buried in his hands. The yard inside behind the great wooden gate is a jumble of carrier bicycles, vans, motor cars, milk churns, baskets, dustbins, vessels from churns to milk jugs filled with water (a needless precaution as it turned out since the water supply was never turned off nor gas nor light). A makeshift barricade covers the side gate. Volunteers are constantly rushed to various positions. Noise and excitement in the streets outside; disorder within—such is the mood of the first hours of the new Republic as seen from its headquarters.

"Hurrah, boys; hurrah, boys!" shouts a young Volunteer

lieutenant as he rushes in and recognises a friend here and another there and hurries past; Lieutenant Liam Clarke in a great hurry, indeed, all laughter and smiles and cheers and gossip, full of the joy of waving flags and barricades at last and a coming battle. Volunteer Red Cross men and Cumann na mBan nurses are attending to several Volunteers suffering from shock. " Damn those windows! " says one Red Cross man, as he bandages up yet another Volunteer: " They have already done more damage than the whole British Army." On the ground rests a man in uniform, his knee cut with cruel gashes, his face twisted in pain. Pearse and his brother Willie arrive, quiet and tense; Willie with a sad look in his eyes. Pearse bends over the wounded man, questions him, cheers him, and turns to watch the inside organisation rapidly proceeding amid a din of orders. Lieutenant Liam Clarke is led past by two men, eyes set, head bent, no longer a cheer or a laugh from him; his face and hands are streaming with blood. His wounds are dressed quickly, and Pearse orders him peremptorily to hospital for he is obstinate and wants to stay and see the fight out. A bomb carelessly handled has burst in his face. " So much for those bloody canisters! " growls a Volunteer. " If poor Clarke's head wasn't blown off, then devil the little else use they'll be— except for moral effect! " And two legends of Easter Week are born: the Sinn Féiner whose head was blown off, and the attempt to blow up Nelson Pillar, for a group of Volunteers hurry out to the base of the monument and test the bombs soon afterwards with fine explosions and clouds of smoke. A sniper on the roof chips Nelson's nose with a neat shot, and thereafter Nelson is left at rest.

The interior grows more orderly every minute. Reinforcements come and go. Some are in trim grey-green Volunteer uniforms, neatly rolled puttees, with rifle and automatic pistol complete, here and there a sabre; the majority are in their everyday clothes, crossed and inter-crossed with bandoleers, water-bottle straps, a yellow armlet on the sleeve, haversacks, and armed often with shot guns or even miniature rifles. On the ground floor, the garrison busies itself with several duties, apart from the constant strengthening of barricades and windows. A munition factory is set up; rifles examined and repaired, and bombs made crudely enough from gelignite, canister and scrap, while others fill empty shotgun cases with leaden pellets. Ammunition is examined and the supply shared out and equalised. Parties depart on commandeering missions for food. There is a good supply of that already. Three lorries arrive laden with cabbages and other vegetables. Cooking has already been resumed where the regular staff left off with the help of the Cumann na mBan and some captured British soldiers under the eyes, none too sympathetic, of Desmond Fitzgerald, who is obdurate to all appeals: "Do you think," he asks one disgruntled Volunteer, "that I am obliged to supply four-course dinners to you all, because some of you never had a decent bite in your lives before? Even if you are going to die for Ireland. Eat that crust and, as for drink, drink water!" A humorous flicker lurks in his eyes as, in the interests of economy and discipline, he firmly refuses other requests; he unbends later, doles out an orange here, a cigar there, and lays down the law on poetry and theology amid the rattle of rifles and the glare of fires.

The occupation of other positions in the O'Connell Street area proceeded even as the Kimmage Garrison and the rest were taking over headquarters. As the column swung into O'Connell Street, Frank Thornton and George Plunkett ordered their sections to about turn and occupied the Ship Tavern in Middle Abbey Street and cleared out the customers. An *Irish Times* paper store was raided and the great printing rolls used to build a barricade across the street. Keating's cycle shop windows were broken and a motor-cycle hauled out and planted on top of the barricade which was also strengthened with furniture and bicycles. A crowd in the rear of the Ship Tavern grew hostile as the Volunteers came out, and laughed at George Plunkett's appeals and warnings. He fired a few rounds from his automatic pistol over their heads and they ran away in terror. He then led his section back to the G.P.O., and said to a friend as he came in: "Did you know anything was on in particular to-day? I didn't, though one must always be prepared." Gerald Crofts, the singer, and a companion peep over mattresses they have placed in the broken windows of a tailor's shop over Noblett's sweet store on Earl Street corner where a tram is being converted into a formidable barricade.

Another section of the Kimmage Garrison swung sharply round towards O'Connell Bridge. Séamus Robinson and five Volunteers make for Hopkins and Hopkins' corner, and begin to break in the door. A policeman comes up. A revolver is stuck into his side without comment. He puts his hands up calmly, and says quietly:

" You boys needn't worry about me. I won't interfere with you.
I have my instructions in case of trouble to return immediately to
barracks, and I proceed forthwith to obey!" He walks away,
leaving his listeners with the belief that some such order " in case
of trouble " had, in fact, been issued to the amiable and unarmed
D.M.P. Another party of Volunteers from the same section crosses
the street and sets up its post over Kapp and Peterson's in " Kelly's
Fort." Both sides of the bridge are now covered by Volunteer
sniping posts. At the same time Arthur Agnew with four other
Volunteers line themselves across O'Connell Bridge, and quietly
wait, with Eden Quay and Bachelors' Walk just behind them. Their
orders are to fire on any troops coming from Westmoreland Street
direction, but to avoid all incidents as far as possible before the
Post Office is taken over definitely: the signal will be a shot from
there, the certain sign that the insurrection has really started. At
noon the shot and several shots are heard. Some time before this
the Volunteer guards saw a British ammunition convoy passing
along Eden Quay with an escort of Lancers. The waggons looked
harmless and innocent enough, and the Volunteer guards on the
bridge, after a short discussion, decided not to interfere with the
convoy which had passed Liberty Hall and the two Volunteer look-
out posts at both corners. Their orders were definite: only armed
British parties approaching from Westmoreland Street.   These
innocent luggage carts were not harming anyone! Still, the guards
were vaguely worried and regretful, although they did not suspect
that ammunition was being flaunted under their noses. The convoy went on towards the Four Courts direction to be held up and
attacked at Church Street Bridge and provoke an action that lasted
the whole week. The Volunteers were afterwards told they had
judged correctly and told to join the Kelly's Fort group where
some Swords Volunteers later joined them. From noon onward
there was the sound of heavy rifle fire all over the city.

Inside the Post Office Connolly put the finishing touches to the
organisation. He laughed impatiently as one of the officers at an
outside post kept up a shower of dispatches on him, and said, with
a droll look: " If that man was standing on his right foot, he would
send me a dispatch to inform me that he was shortly going to put
down his left foot!" He recognises Liam Daly, and remembers
he heard Daly say at a chance meeting in Madame Markievicz's
house that he is a telephone operator. Connolly turns and tells

Pearse: " This is our man to fix that line to the roof." Daly is soon fixing up a telephone from the ground floor to the roof so that movements of troops and movements in the street can be reported at once. A wooden cover has to be fitted round the telephone receiver on the roof to muffle the sound of firing outside.

Daly has a great wrestle with wires and cables. At the instrument room below the roof Michael Collins is in control. J. J. Walsh, who has marched down with some thirty members of the Hibernian Rifles, takes over the trunk telegraphic system and, posing as a superintendent, gets into conversation over the wires with the country offices. He paints a truly terrifying picture of the Dublin revolt, the rebels sweeping all before them. He gains what information he can, and passes it on to Tom Clarke and Pearse. Seán MacGarry watches him with amusement. Liam Daly reports to Connolly by five o'clock that the roof telephone is now working. Connolly sends him across to Captain Breen of the Engineers, in Reis's, " for some sort of a telephone job," with Joe Good and John O'Connor of the Kimmage Garrison. Daly and O'Connor's English accents make the Volunteer on guard suspicious that they are looters and thieves who have come to rifle the jewellers. Daly feels very uncomfortable when the Volunteer hustles him indoors quickly and looks very fierce indeed. Daly's own Captain, Tom Wafer, fortunately is coming downstairs and tells the Volunteer that Daly and O'Connor are respectable Volunteers. Captain Breen tells Daly and O'Connor that their job is to erect an aerial over the Wireless School and D.B.C. after dark, and they will not begin until then. Daly passes the time by breaking down an enormous iron door, with pick and crowbars, leading into Reis's shop. The hours pass and at three in the morning, while Daly and O'Connor worked away at the aerial, a sniper in Amiens Street opened fire on them, and they have to crouch very low to complete the work. But long before then much had happened in the G.P.O., across the street, a very hub of revolt but also of rumour, rumour, rumour. . . .

Rumour, indeed, sped with fantastic tales: MacDonagh had taken the Lower Castle Yard and had been driven out again with machine-gun fire; the Curragh line was held by the Volunteers on both sides; the Archbishop's House in Drumcondra was being attacked by the military; Cork, Kerry and Limerick were in revolt; Irish regiments were coming over to the Republican ranks; strong

Volunteer forces were marching to relieve the capital; Jim Larkin had appeared in Sligo and was fighting his way across Ireland at the head of 50,000 men; Turks had landed at Waterford; submarines had sunk a transport in the Irish Sea; the Germans had landed; the insurrection was sweeping through the country. In fact, British troops were pouring into Dublin; British transports unchallenged were nearing the Irish coast; Maxwell was on his way with plenary powers and planning his cordons and his lime pits and his firing squads; Cork, Limerick and Kerry had made no aggressive move; Galway, Wexford and Louth and Ashe's fighters in County Dublin alone came out; and of the 18,000 Irish Volunteers in all Ireland, little more than 2,000 at most. Yet, as the reports of the actual position in Dublin reached the headquarters, Tom Clarke, his eyes agleam behind his gold-rimmed glasses with a benevolent pride and fire, had good reason to exclaim that he had lived to the greatest hours of Irish history: within inevitable limits the Military Council's plan in the capital had worked well, and a few hundred men were holding their own against an army, at the very Castle gates, in the South Dublin Union, in the College of Surgeons, in a circle of forts, at street corners and along the Quays, at the Four Courts, the Mendicity Institute. The Phœnix Park magazine was ablaze and shots had been fired on Portobello Barracks. Above all, everywhere the spirit of the hitherto untried forces of the Republic, the majority of which had never heard a volley of gunfire or a machine-gun rattle in anger, grew stronger and firmer with every danger, survived the test of death, wounds and fire, and braced itself with a gay stoicism for a resistance to the very end even as ruin mounted and hope died.

Up winding stairs and along winding passages rushed Volunteer detachments, and scrambled up iron ladders to the slates, and occupied the sides and corner of the frontal parapet, along which inside are lined canister bombs and ammunition. Across the narrow space from a neighbouring chemist's shop on Henry Street corner other Volunteers hail them, and later read aloud in derision the Viceroy's proclamation:

" Whereas an attempt, instigated and designed by the foreign enemies of our King and Country to incite rebellion in Ireland, and thus endanger the safety of the United Kingdom, has been made by a reckless, though small body of men, who have been guilty of insurrectionary acts in the City of Dublin:

Now, we, Ivor Churchill, Baron Wimborne, Lord-Lieutenant-General and Governor-General of Ireland, do hereby warn all his Majesty's subjects that the sternest measures are being, and will be taken for the prompt suppression of the existing disturbances, and the restoration of order:

And we do hereby enjoin all loyal and law-abiding citizens to abstain from any acts or conduct which might interfere with the action of the Executive Government, and, in particular, we warn all citizens of the danger of unnecessarily frequenting the streets or public places or of assembling in crowds.

Given under our Seal, on the 24th day of April, 1916.

WIMBORNE."

Loudly the sentences are rolled across to the grinning listeners on the Post Office roof, followed by a request for more grenades. Below the great crowds ebb and flow with the rumours of approaching British forces. Talbot Street is blocked by a barricade and a deserted tramcar, inside which children dance and ring the bell. Boards and sandbags are piled along the roof, and the poles and standard which carry the three waving flags secured. O'Rahilly appears and warns the watching men not to fire without orders. From Amiens Street tower a British officer is seen scanning the scene through field glasses. "Don't fire," says The O'Rahilly as he leaves. "It would give away our position, and you would probably miss him anyway. Nelson will screen you from his fire, too." Down in the street a group of children pass along singing lustily:

"We are the Volunteers, the Volunteers, the Volunteers, we are the Volunteers, and we'll whack the British Army!"

A crowd of looters falls to work. The plate-glass windows of a confectioner's near the Pillar are smashed, and a shower of sweet-stuffs, chocolate boxes, and huge slabs of toffee sprays over and among the crazy mass of shawls, caps, and struggling children. Old women from the slums hurl themselves towards the windows of a shoe store and almost walk through the plate-glass which shivers and breaks among the mob, dealing deep gashes and

bloody hurts which cannot check the greedy and aimless frenzy.
The looting spreads along the shop fronts.   The Volunteers on
Henry Street corner pour down buckets of water and shake their
rifles menacingly.   From the Post Office windows rifles are
levelled, and two volleys of blank-shot are fired over the looters'
heads.   Men dash from the building shouting orders and threats,
revolvers and batons in their hands.   Rifle butts and bayonet
points and cracking batons are soon at work.   Looters rush madly
away, some with their spoils, others dropping them in terror as the
batons tap their skulls, and the pavements are strewn with
shoes, valises, coats, a variety of aimlessly pilfered goods.
Seán MacDermott limps painfully across the street right into the
looters, his hands raised passionately above his head as he appeals
to them not to disgrace this fight for Ireland.   From a toy shop
a crowd of young boys and girls rush with teddy bears and toy
rifles and exploding fireworks; some hours after a fire breaks out
inside the shop, the beginning of the fires which soon are to ring
the area with red skies and leaping flames.   The fire brigade
dashes into the street, and, beneath the eyes of the Volunteer
sentinels in the various posts, battles desperately with the growing
blaze.   The fire engine rests almost against the kerb of Henry
Street, and the Volunteers watch speculating as to whether there
is some military ruse behind the fires as smoke and flame bursts
from yet another looted shop front and the brigade comes and
goes, or whether it is all due to some careless looters.   As yet,
however, the more deadly and most effective cause of fire, which
is to eat out the garrison in the end, heavy cannonade and
artillery, is still hidden.   Away over the D.B.C. building as dark
falls wireless flashes out: IRELAND PROCLAIMS REPUBLIC, followed
by the text of the Proclamation.   Through the night the wireless
still flashes and ships at sea relay the messages so that already
on Tuesday morning in some American papers the news sprawls
across the front pages.   Lieutenant John O'Connor of the Kimmage
garrison has to cower down and adjust the mechanism in the
room below as the operator taps out the messages when British
snipers eventually sweep the roof of the D.B.C. and the Reis
building adjoining where a disused wireless school had been
seized by O'Connor and Fergus Kelly and their comrades.   When
in the end they were driven out by fire and shot, the transmitter
was boldly carried across to the G.P.O., but by then it was

impossible to operate the improvised station any longer. As a group of Red Cross nurses crossed with Volunteer stretcher-bearers the British fire slackened almost to stillness. Volunteers dashed across some minutes later and the British resumed with fury.

To the watching sentinels and the snipers and the men toiling to strengthen the barricades and window defences for the ever-rumoured general assault which, announced every fifteen minutes, never comes, time is dead, and the hour hands of the clocks move like the seconds hand of a watch, dawn, noon, twilight and dark become one with an orchestra of varied din, a smell of smoke, flame, blood and death.   Sandbags, wooden forms, books, were piled compactly behind the empty spaces which had been windows, covering at least three-quarters of the apertures, with the exception of loop-holes, here and there, lower down.   Beside the guards on duty bowls of shotgun ammunition were placed as a reserve supply. At intervals around were spaced buckets full of a liquid preparation with handkerchiefs afloat in readiness for any gas attack.   Pikes and revolvers lay to hand for fighting at close quarters when attackers broke through.

Behind the central counter on the ground floor the leaders, Pearse, Connolly, MacDermott, and Tom Clarke rested in turns on mattresses and later on beds that were brought in; sleep was impossible except in short spells, and, according to the Volunteer Red Cross workers, even then barely possible even with the aid of sleeping draughts.   Early in the week the leaders could be seen seated together in quiet moments on boxes and barrels, chatting in low tones ; calm, pale, tired, sometimes laughing as when Connolly announced that the Citizen Army had captured King George and Kitchener in the Henry Street Waxworks.   Very sure and certain was James Connolly.   " Oh, they are beaten! " he said tersely on Monday night when a Volunteer asked him for his opinion on the chances of the fight.   On Wednesday night as he rested in an un-easy sleep, The O'Rahilly woke him with the report that the British were supposed to be stealing over the roofs in Henry Street, but Connolly merely raised his head and said laconically : " They are *not*," and sank back to rest.   A young boy who had come in began to relate at the top of his voice that there was no food in the shops and the people were afraid of famine.   Connolly roused himself again, patted the boy paternally on the shoulder, and quietly told him not to spread such stories but to go home and help to keep the citizens' spirits up even if food was short here and there.

From Monday night onwards as they heard prolonged and continuous volleying along the quaysides, from the Four Courts and Church Street area to Ringsend and Cabra, the garrison hardened hour by hour to bullets whizzing viciously, to hammering machine-guns, to heavy artillery booming ever nearer while the very foundations vibrated, until the height of the bombardment on Friday, when shrapnel and petrol shell crashed on the roof. On Wednesday morning British machine-gunners on Trinity College, in Westmoreland Street, on the Fire Station, and Custom House, swept Beresford Place and O'Connell Street, backed by snipers. Two eighteen-pounders opened fire on Liberty Hall from Tara Street, across the quays, every window in the side streets was shattered and the nervous gunners imagined that machine-guns and snipers were replying to them from the Labour headquarters, the target they had chosen by preference as " the centre of social anarchy in Ireland, the brain of every riot and disturbance."[2] Connolly had informed the Executive of his union in answer to criticisms of his hoisting the flag on the hall on Palm Sunday that the Citizen Army would leave the premises within a fortnight and not return. In the spirit of this promise orders were given that the hall should be evacuated on Easter Monday and all arms and war stores removed. This was carried out under the supervision of Seamus McGowan of the Citizen Army on Monday afternoon and the hall left in sole charge of the caretaker, Peter Ennis, who remained until artillery fire drove him out. No positions were held by the insurgents nearer than Hopkins & Hopkins' corner in O'Connell Street. Shell after shell from the 18-pounders was hurled towards the hall without serious result. On Wednesday the machine-guns on the Custom House, the Tivoli Theatre in Burgh Quay, and the Fire Station tower were supported by the Admiralty gunboat, *Helga*. At eight o'clock in the morning the first attack was made on Liberty Hall and shells were fired over the loop-line railway bridge at the target for more than an hour, accompanied by heavy machine-gun fire. Northumberland House nearby was reduced to ruin, the outer walls of Liberty Hall were little damaged although

---

[2] *Weekly Irish Times*, April 29, May 13, 1916; *Irish Times* Handbook, p. 23.

the interior lay in ruin and every window was shattered. The *Helga* withdrew, and sailed away to attack de Valera's headquarters at Boland's Mills, where it scored some good hits on the unoccupied distillery which de Valera had ordered to be decorated with flags, and a solitary Volunteer signaller on the roof to tempt the gunners.

Threatened by encircling British troops, Oscar Traynor, Seán Russell, and 60 Volunteers at Fairview, on Connolly's orders, withdrew with all their stores, and strengthened the Hotel Metropole, Middle Abbey Street, and other outposts in the O'Connell Street area.

"Don't be alarmed," said James Connolly, as he listened to the bombardment on Wednesday morning. "When the British Government is using artillery in the City of Dublin it shows that they must be in a hurry to finish the job, but there are probably some forces coming up to help us." And what those forces were he left in no doubt when he informed William Pearse that the British evidently believed that the Germans had landed or were about to land.[3]

Bullets sing past the ears of the roof watchers, rattle against the frontal pillars, and cut grooves in the cobblestones of the roadway. Duels are waged across the slates between the Volunteer snipers and the hostile machine-gunners on Trinity. From the D.B.C. restaurant near Middle Abbey Street corner comes a constant rattle of Volunteer snipers' rifles, and later news that Captain Wafer who leads them has been killed there. A cruel wound through liver and kidneys. He lingers in agony for an hour, and flames are his shroud.

A priest visits the G.P.O. roof, an old man who looks weary, and with an air of incredulous compassion for all the mad young men facing immediate death. A wild boy of twelve years, a bloodthirsty, whitefaced and voluble little scamp had casually wandered in from the street and made his way to the roof just before. He cheers at each burst of gunfire and reply from the Volunteer guns with

---

[3] This version of Connolly's words is also given, *Gaelic American*, "Inside Story of the Easter Week Rebellion," July 29, 1916. All the *Gaelic American* reports of the Rising were based on contemporary accounts of actual participants. The statement in this article that Connolly spoke the words to the men on the roof is improbable although he certainly so expressed his views at the time. Other members of the G.P.O. garrison believe that Connolly made the same statement to Michael Collins in the instrument room. It is also possible that Connolly visited the roof somewhat later, as the *Gaelic American* account states, when the roof was swept with shrapnel.

Rabelaisianisms, very confident that every Volunteer bullet finds its billet while the British shots are but sound and fury: " Janey, what don't I wish the so-and-so's!" The Volunteers order him away, but he ignores them, shouting: " Do you hear that one now? They'll all be wiped out before yous are done with them! Janey, there goes another of them. I'd see them all in Hell!" In turn the priest appeals to the young firebrand to leave fighting to the Volunteers and go home, or at least downstairs. The boy is offended and refuses.

The priest tells the Volunteers that as there is danger of an immediate attack he will give them all conditional absolution, and asks each man whether he is sorry for past sins, and man by man agrees that he is in fact sorry. One Volunteer, dreaming away to himself, indignantly retorts with impatient emphasis: " Of course, why not?" when the priest thinking he has not heard, repeats the question. Having given the absolution, the priest goes away. A sailor man from the Citizen Army who has collected in his travels on land and sea a truly shattering and magnificent vocabulary, arrives. He carries a load of canister bombs which he distributes with very direct though scabrous instructions. The contrast between the priest who has left the whole roof in a state of grace and this tornado of colourful blasphemy overcomes some of the Volunteers who roll on the slates, helpless with laughter. The sailor, with a parting word, leaves them. (Downstairs, the sailor man's language terrifies one Volunteer who protests: " Heaven help us all! Do you want the ground to open under us?" He organises public opinion to drive the sailor man to confession. The sailor man defiantly asserts that he has not gone to confession for fifteen years, and expresses himself with even greater colour and heat until a priest intervenes, waves aside the accusers and assures him that time is no obstacle. The sailor man sits down, pensively lights his pipe, and unburdens his soul.)

Pearse and his brother pass along the roof after their return from a tour of the O'Connell Street positions, where they both had some close escapes from flying bullets. As they arrive a Volunteer officer, Lieutenant Michael Boland, has just issued an order for the hundredth time in genial tone to his men to keep under the cover of planks and sandbags. He is an ex-British soldier who had fought through the South African War, and to a friend beside him he has said in a whisper: " What do I think of it? A mad business. Shut in here with our leaders, and the flags over our heads to tell the enemy just where to find us when they want us. We should have taken to the hills like the Boers, but we're here now and we'll just have to stick it." He refrains from giving this advice to Pearse, who has already said that Robert Emmet's two-hour revolt was already in the shade. Pearse, impassive and confident, in his green uniform, grows so absorbed with a survey of the Volunteers visible on guard in the Imperial and Metropole and adjoining houses, at the hostile and noisy nests of snipers and machine-guns beyond the Liffey, at mounting flame and débris from the Parnell Monument to O'Connell Bridge that Boland in alarm raps out a special appeal to Pearse himself to keep under cover. Pearse smiles, thanks him, promises the men on the roof who had been on duty without sleep since Monday afternoon that they will be relieved shortly, and passes on. "A curious business," comments William Pearse in his slow, lisping voice as he looks in passing at the fires and chaos in view, "I wonder how it will end? I know a lot of good work has been done but there is a great deal more to do." There is a melancholy and patient look in his sensitive dark brown eyes.

The fires spread slowly down the blocks of building facing the Post Office, and the fire brigade chiefs had long since given up hope of controlling the flames which curved in a circle round the G.P.O. area. Nearer and nearer came the thunder of the great guns which battered down the Volunteer positions near the O'Connell monument, Kelly's fort and Hopkins' corner. An over-wrought Volunteer suddenly brandishes a gun, uttering wild threats, raving. Pearse intervenes quickly, the man is locked up until his frenzy passes. The garrison in the Imperial signalled across the street. Fire at last drives them to retreat and they dash across, escaping the bullets by a miracle. The fire steals on and on. Boom! Boom! Boom! The great building shakes while the defenders stand behind the barricades of coal sacks improvised within. Pearse watches it all calmly, moving from place to place. When rumours are related to him of German ships and transports in the bay, he shrugs his shoulders and maintains silence, a look of pity in his eyes. There is a constant call to arms and rumours of the coming British attack, of armoured cars, and an advance through the cloak of the burning Imperial's ruins.

On Thursday afternoon Connolly numbers off his men and

waits while Pearse addresses the garrison.   His speech is full of
fire and promise, and praise for the men who have held out for
four magnificent days, making Dublin's name splendid among the
names of cities, the same phrasing and spirit which he later writes
in his last dispatch the next day, behind the rhetoric a plain hint
that the end is near:

> " Headquarters, Army of the Irish Republic,
> General Post Office, Dublin.
> 28th April, 1916 (9.30 a.m.).

The Forces of the Irish Republic, which was proclaimed in
Dublin on Easter Monday, 24th April, have been in possession of
the central part of the capital since 12 noon on that day. Up to
yesterday afternoon Headquarters was in touch with all the main
outlying positions, and despite furious and almost continuous
assaults by the British Forces all these positions were then still
being held, and the Commandants in charge were confident of
their ability to hold them for a long time.

During the course of yesterday afternoon and evening, the enemy
succeeded in cutting our communications with our other positions
in the city, and Headquarters is to-day isolated.

The enemy has burnt down whole blocks of houses, apparently
with the object of giving themselves a clear field for the play of
artillery and field guns against us. We have been bombarded during the evening and night by shrapnel and machine-gun fire, but
without material damage to our position, which is of great strength.

We are busy completing arrangements for the final defence of
Headquarters, and are determined to hold it while the buildings
last.

I desire now, lest I may not have an opportunity later, to pay
homage to the gallantry of the soldiers of Irish freedom who have
during the past four days been writing with fire and steel the most
glorious chapter in the later history of Ireland. Justice can never
be done to their heroism, to their discipline, to their gay and un-
conquerable spirit in the midst of peril and death.

Let me, who have led them into this, speak in my own name,
and in my fellow-commandants' names, and in the name of Ireland
present and to come, their praise, and ask those who come after
them to remember them.

For four days they have fought and toiled, almost without cessation, almost without sleep, and in the intervals of fighting they have sung songs of the freedom of Ireland. No man has complained, no man has asked 'Why?' Each individual has spent himself, happy to pour out his strength for Ireland and for freedom. If they do not win this fight, they will at least deserve to win it. But win it they will although they may win it in death. Already they have done a great thing. They have redeemed Dublin from many shames, and made her name splendid among the names of cities.

If I were to mention the names of individuals, my list would be a long one.

I will name only that of Commandant-General James Connolly, Commanding the Dublin Division. He lies wounded but is still the guiding brain of our resistance.

If we accomplish no more than we have accomplished, I am satisfied. I am satisfied that we have saved Ireland's honour. I am satisfied that we should have accomplished more, that we should have accomplished the task of enthroning, as well as proclaiming the Irish Republic as a Sovereign State, had our arrangements for a simultaneous Rising of the whole country, with a combined plan as sound as the Dublin plan has proved to be, been allowed to go through on Easter Sunday. Of the fatal countermanding order which prevented those plans being carried out, I shall not speak further. Both Eoin MacNeill and we have acted in the best interests of Ireland.

For my part, as to anything I have done in this, I am not afraid to face the judgment of God, or the judgment of posterity.

> (Signed) P. H. PEARSE,
> Commandant-General,
> Commander-in-Chief, the Army of the
> Irish Republic and President of the
> Provisional Government."

In private Pearse had said so early as Wednesday night: "When we are all wiped out, people will blame us for everything, condemn us. But for this the war would have ended and nothing have been done. In a few years they will see the meaning of what we tried to do."

On Thursday afternoon Connolly was wounded twice by British

K

snipers. Pearse indeed had good reason, in his reference to this in the dispatch just quoted, to describe him as "the guiding brain of our resistance." His force, authority, and determination to keep the morale of the defenders to the highest point in spite of the terrific pressure on them was evident as he periodically called the garrison to arms; as he sharply and tersely numbered off his men at the fire-lit counters, on the long ground floor, in corners near the exits. He went briefly through the formulas of drill and barked routine commands at his followers. He cheered them with a jest or a prophecy of victory. He joked with the depressed and praised the bold. The facts of his final sortie were afterwards related by Seán McLoughlin, who accompanied him, and also by Connolly himself to his daughter. After McLoughlin had reported to Connolly the situation in the Mendicity Institute, as already noted, this Fianna officer was given on Thursday charge of a section of Volunteers and Citizen Army men for an expedition against the British cordon pressing in closer and closer around the head-quarters. Connolly's orders to him were, according to his own account, that an attempt should be made to check the British movement from the south side of the river. McLoughlin states that he was ordered to take over the *Irish Independent* offices at the corner of Liffey Street. The firing was very heavy as the party dashed into Abbey Street through a narrow alleyway which led from Prince's Street, and moved still under intense rifle fire towards their position. Connolly watched the men for a while and turned back towards the G.P.O. His own account agrees in general, though adding final details, with McLoughlin's story.[4] A bullet

[4] *Irish Worker*, April 19, 1924; *Portrait of a Rebel Father*, Nora Connolly O'Brien, p. 318; *Capuchin Annual*, p. 223, "The G.P.O.," Dr. James Ryan. The contemporary account given by Seamus O'Brien in *The Irish Rebellion of 1916 and its Martyrs* (New York, 1916), quotes from Joseph Plunkett's journal for that Thursday: "Commandant Connolly was wounded in the left arm and ten minutes later in the left leg (by a sniper). The leg wound is serious as it caused a compound fracture of the shin-bone." O'Brien states that Connolly received his first wound while inspecting a barricade, returned, ordered his men to the windows to distract their attention from himself, had his wound dressed, and returned to the street where he received his second and more serious wound. An article by M. Staines-M. W. O'Reilly, "The Defence of the G.P.O.," *An t-Oglách*, January 23, 1926, states: "The first serious blow our garrison received was when General Connolly was wounded. He was dispatching a squad to Abbey Street and went boldly out into O'Connell Street and was almost at once picked off by a sniper. He was essentially a man of action, great personal daring and quick decision. Despite the seriousness of his wound he insisted on being brought round on a stretcher to superintend and to help in every way he could."

struck him above the ankle, he fainted and lay unconscious on the cobblestones for some time. He was then too far from the men he had placed and from the headquarters alike to be seen. Eventually he crawled back, and was carried inside. His wounds were dressed by Dr. James Ryan (who had also dressed his first minor wound under a promise of secrecy in case his men's confidence should be shaken), and an immediate operation decided upon. It was performed behind a screen on the ground floor by Dr. O'Mahony, R.A.M.C., who was held prisoner by the Volunteers, and working overtime cheerfully on his captors; a medical student, Dan McLoughlin, then put Connolly's leg in splints. Dr. Ryan had no other anæsthetic except chloroform. "Nothing could break the will of this man," is Dr. Ryan's judgment on Connolly's conduct after his terrible injury, a severe and badly lacerated ankle wound resulting, in Dr. Ryan's opinion, "probably from a rifle bullet at comparatively close range." While the bullet was being extracted, one of his constant bodyguard since his kidnapping, Harry Walpole, heard him cry out in extreme agony: "Oh, God, did ever a man suffer more for his country!" Connolly suffered great pain, and was given injections of morphia later; even then the pain was dulled for intervals only and Connolly remained restless and slept very little. Weak from loss of blood and wounds as he was, Connolly refused to be moved from the building or to accompany the rest of the wounded to Jervis Street Hospital where they were sent by Seán MacDermott's directions with the Cumann na mBan early on Friday morning.

Connolly passed a very uneasy night but by Thursday morning he had recovered sufficiently to insist that he should be wheeled into the front hall on a bed with castors from which he could direct the fight and remain with the garrison. Some time later, Harry Walpole came up to Connolly and noticed that he was reading an exciting detective story. Connolly smiled and said: "A book like this, rest, and an insurrection at the same time! Why this is revolution *de luxe*!" This restful interlude did not last very long because Connolly in spite of his fitful sleep, his weakness, and the pain of his wound, sent for his secretary, Winifred Carney, who arrived with typewriter and Webley revolver. He then dictated and issued a dispatch to the G.P.O. garrison, phrased in the most defiant and hopeful terms. His description was aimed at maintaining the morale of the fighters. His summary of the situation was at variance with even the known facts, and with Pearse's more outspoken and candid dispatch of the same day, previously quoted:

"Army of the Irish Republic,
Headquarters (Dublin Command),
28th April, 1916.

TO SOLDIERS:

This is the fifth day of the establishment of the Irish Republic, and the flag of our country still floats from the most important buildings in Dublin, and is gallantly protected by the officers and Irish soldiers in arms throughout the country. Not a day passes without seeing fresh postings of Irish soldiers eager to do battle for the old cause. Despite the utmost vigilance of the enemy we have been able to get information telling us how the manhood of Ireland, inspired by our splendid action, are gathering to offer up their lives if necessary in the same holy cause. We are here hemmed in because the enemy feels that in this building is to be found the heart and inspiration of our great movement.

Let us remind you what you have done. For the first time in 700 years the flag of a free Ireland floats triumphantly in Dublin City. The British Army, whose exploits we are for ever having dinned into our ears, which boasts of having stormed the Dardanelles and the German lines on the Marne, behind their artillery and machine-guns are afraid to advance to the attack or storm any positions held by our forces. The slaughter they suffered in the first few days has totally unnerved them and they dare not attempt again an infantry attack on our positions.

Our Commandants around us are holding their own.

Commandant Daly's splendid exploit in capturing Linen Hall Barracks we all know. You must know also that the whole population, both clergy and laity, of this district are united in his praises.

Commandant MacDonagh is established in an impregnable position reaching from the walls of Dublin Castle to Redmond's Hill, and from Bishop Street to Stephen's Green.

(In Stephen's Green, Commandant Mallin holds the College of Surgeons, one side of the square, a portion of the other side, and dominates the whole Green, and all its entrances and exits.)

Commandant de Valera stretches in a position from the Gas Works to Westland Row, holding Boland's Bakery, Boland's Mills,

Dublin South-Eastern Railway Works and dominating Merrion Square.

Commandant Kent holds the South Dublin Union and Guinness's Buildings to Marrowbone Lane, and controls James's Street and district. On two occasions the enemy effected a lodgment and were driven out with great loss.

The men of North County Dublin are in the field, having occupied all the Police Barracks in the district, destroyed all the telegraph system on the Great Northern Railway up to Dundalk, and are operating against the trains of the Midland and Great Western.

Dundalk has sent 200 men to march on Dublin and in other parts of the North our forces are active and growing.

In Galway Captain Mellows, fresh after his escape from an Irish prison, is in the field with his men. Wexford and Wicklow are strong and Cork and Kerry are acquitting themselves creditably. (We have every confidence that our allies in Germany and kinsmen in America are straining every nerve to hasten matters on our behalf.)

As you know, I was wounded twice yesterday, and am unable to move about, but have got my bed moved into the firing line and, with the assistance of your officers, will be as useful to you as ever.

Courage, boys, we are winning, and in the hour of our victory let us not forget the splendid women who have everywhere stood by us and cheered us on. Never had man or woman a grander cause, never was a cause more grandly served.

(Signed) JAMES CONNOLLY,
Commandant-General, Dublin Division."

On Friday morning there was a brief lull, and so strange was the short absence of noise even amid the ruin of the blazing buildings outside that a rumour went round that there was a truce and that there would be arbitration, and there was a persistent opinion among many of the Volunteers that having fought for more than three days according to international law the insurgents were entitled to be recognised as belligerents, and that Ireland would be admitted to the Peace Conference. According to the report of Pearse's speech to the garrison on Wednesday given by The O'Rahilly's nephew, Risteard MacAmhlaoibh, a St. Enda's student, Pearse concluded by saying " that we have successfully held out as a Republic against the might of England for three full days. Wherefore, according to international law, we are legally entitled to the status of belligerents, and the presence of a delegate in that Peace Conference which must inevitably follow the war."[5]

The relief was short, and suddenly the artillery and the snipers reopened the attack.   In the meantime the defences had been strengthened.   Early that morning the leaders insisted that the Cumann na mBan must leave the Headquarters.   The wounded were also removed to Jervis Street Hospital by MacDermott's orders.   Connolly's secretary, Winifred Carney, refused to leave and insisted on remaining with him.   It needed a strong personal appeal from Pearse to persuade the members of Cumann na mBan to leave the G.P.O. They accompanied the wounded—some sixteen in number—under white flags to Jervis Street Hospital.   Pearse spoke briefly and warmly to the thirty-four girls and women who made up the Cumann na mBan contingent, and shook hands with each, saying that they had inspired the Volunteers by their courage to resist to the end, and had won by their own bravery a sure place in the record of the fight for freedom.   Winifred Carney, Julia Grenan, and Elizabeth O'Farrell remained with the G.P.O. garrison.[6]   Pearse regarded the activities of the women in Easter

---

[5] *The Belvederian*, IV. (Dublin, 1917; also quoted in *Banba*, " A Retrospect," by M. J. Lennon, May, 1922.)   Others who heard Pearse's speech do not recall that he made so explicit a reference to the alleged right under international law and the Peace Conference, though certainly in private conversation Pearse seemed to suggest that he believed a revolt in Ireland during the war would assure German support for Ireland at the Peace Conference.   In his courtmartial speech he advanced no such claim, and stated that he understood his life was "forfeit" to British law, and appealed for an amnesty for his colleagues and followers in exchange.   A bogus version of the surrender terms current after 1916 included a reference to belligerent status after 72 hours' fighting and the Peace Conference.   Maxwell's own version of the final negotiations, as well as the Irish Volunteer accounts, however, make it clear that while the surrender was unconditional there was an implied promise that the lives of the rank and file would be spared.   The MacAmhlaoibh account in every other respect is remarkably accurate, and it may well be that the recollections of others, including the writer's, are at fault.

[6] The part played by the Cumann na mBan in Easter Week is dealt with in articles by Eithne Coyle, " The History of Cumann na mBan, *An Phoblacht*, April 8–15, 1933; Elizabeth O'Farrell, *Catholic Bulletin*, April–May, 1917; Julia Grenan, *Catholic Bulletin*, June, 1917; Miss M. Reynolds, "Cumann na mBan in the G.P.O.," *An t-Oglách*, April 2, 1926; Mary Donnelly, "With the Citizen Army in Stephen's Green," *An Phoblacht*, April 19, 1930; May Murray, "A Girl's Experience in the G.P.O.," *Poblacht na hEireann*, April 20, 1922.   Winifred Carney's account of Easter Week is given in R. M. Fox's *Green Banners*, pp. 288–92.

Week with intense admiration. It was due to his influence as much as MacDonagh's and Connolly's that the Proclamation formally recognised the right of woman's suffrage in a free Ireland. Until almost the end the Cumann na mBan shared the dangers, the fire, the bullets, all the ordeals of the fighters, in the most dangerous areas, on the barricades, through the bullet-swept streets and quaysides, carrying dispatches, explosives, and ammunition through the thick of the fray, assisting in the hospital, cooking, and in some cases, approaching the British military posts to deliver warnings from Pearse that the Red Cross posts of the insurgents had been fired on by British snipers while in the end it was a woman who marched out to initiate the final negotiations. So Winifred Carney's sharp retort to Pearse when he suggested she should leave the G.P.O. was somewhat mistaken. Not that Pearse alone provoked her criticism, Joseph Plunkett's artistic display of a bangled wrist and fingers sporting antique rings offended her austerity, and in spite of his dangling Mauser automatic pistol and military sabre, led her to express some doubts of such an unsoldierly combination to Connolly who merely smiled and said Joseph Plunkett could please himself, for at all events Plunkett needed no lessons and could teach them all in military science, clear-minded, a man of his word.

Plunkett was an unforgettable figure as the end drew nearer. Brennan Whitmore who, with Michael Collins accompanied him from Liberty Hall to the Post Office, depicts him on that morning as frail and ailing, a veritable personification of mental power prevailing over great physical weakness yet in the crisis this weakness was not apparent. During the worst stages of the shelling no one was more assiduous in keeping up the spirits of the defenders. He walked past the long line of men at the front windows, smiling carelessly, his sabre and pistol dancing merrily, and calling out at intervals: "One of the enemy's barracks is on fire!" He looked out at the raging conflagration which swept closer and closer in glaring circles, laughed, and announced: "It is the first time it has happened since Moscow, the first time that a capital has been burned since then!" On he sauntered, the Mauser ever dangling at his heels, some Volunteers smiling a mocking Dublin smile, others puzzled for the sanity of this strange apparition in pleated uniform with cool and peering stare, many impressed at the man romance was soon to carry into the street ballads linking him for his midnight marriage in a condemned cell inevitably with Emmet, and sooner to march to surrender with a white flag fluttering like birds fluttered in his own dark verse; so dignified for all his exotic glitter that it may well be believed that a British officer solemnly saluted him at his courtmartial.

A message suddenly speeded round that the defenders were to be held in readiness to retire as the roof was on fire. The order was conveyed quietly to the officers. Pearse hastened to the upper storeys where parties of Volunteers were rushed quickly. A petrol shell had struck a glass and wood erection over the upper rooms and the British snipers were making the spot very dangerous. Twice a bullet crashed into the wall behind within an inch of Pearse's head as he watched and superintended the Volunteers at work with axe and hosepipe toiling up the numerous ladders that led to the roof. There was a din of axes, a sea of water, Volunteer snipers crouched and replied to their enemies with constant volleys. Downstairs men dashed into the cellars to remove explosives stored there even as flames swept down the liftshafts; and some further to explore if there was any chance of escape for the garrison through the sewers, only to totter back dazed and retching with the stench and glimpse of a sea of filth along which two narrow pathways ran.

The destruction of the Headquarters had begun when a shell first crashed on the roof at one o'clock and caused a fire which was mastered. Two hours later the fatal incendiary shell burst over the portico, and caused another fire. Although this, too, was partially checked, the flames spread from above and roared down the liftshafts to the very cellars. The British artillery had now made sure of its target and shells burst and caused fires in various places while the British sniping became more and more effective. Five hours more the hopeless fight went on while débris crashed with the giving floors and thick columns of flame and smoke rose steadily and increased in volume with every minute. At last the snipers on the roof were called down. Some remained an hour and a half, after emphatic orders to descend, battling with the flames. At last The O'Rahilly prevailed on the fire-fighters to recognise that the work was in vain, and in turn with even greater difficulty to persuade the snipers to leave their posts, and in one case at least The O'Rahilly had to win his point only at the point of his own revolver.

Towards eight o'clock on Friday evening all was ready for the evacuation.   Pearse and Plunkett went round calling the men to attention, and marched them into the yard by the great side gate.   The floors were thundering down in ruin, and through the waves of fire outside and within great cracks in the walls showed the ruined Imperial and the desolate streets.   Pearse directs the distribution of food and gives orders that as much as possible should be packed in haversacks, and cheese and bread are served out.   He tells the men that the plan now is that the building is to be abandoned and an effort made to reach William & Woods' factory so that eventually a junction can be made with Daly's men in the Four Courts.   In the sombre and flaming house of fire the men begin to file slowly to Henry Street exits.   There is the sound of a shot, and a tall, dark, handsome man, one of the Kimmage Garrison, an exile, falls, his face pallid, his eyes closing, and groaning in pain.   Accidentally a shotgun held by a man nearby has been discharged into his back.   Within two minutes other shots are heard, and men fall groaning on the floor.   " Unload, and hold the muzzles of your guns up! " comes in chorus.

The O'Rahilly releases the prisoners, some thirteen British soldiers, a D.M.P. man, British officers with apologies for the grim choice that faces them: their only hope of safety is to dash for safety with the garrison.   He goes out and surveys the street briefly, returns and orders some men who are still playing hoses on the flames to retire.   Dermott Lynch descends to the cellars where he hears some prisoners have been held.   Through the roaring flames he makes his way, and reappears with a British officer whom he sets free.   Patrick Pearse goes quickly towards the Henry Street exit with a party of forty men headed by The O'Rahilly. When the men line up in the street Pearse briefly addresses them, telling them that as the H.Q. must be evacuated they are the advance party to establish a new H.Q. in William & Woods' factory in Parnell Street, that Captain Liam Breen of the Engineers, would supervise the establishment of the new defences there, and that they were under The O'Rahilly's command.   Pearse watched the party make their way over barricades and returned to the building.

Some three hundred yards further on as The O'Rahilly's men turned into Moore Street a terrific fire from rifles and machine-guns was opened on them.   Hats were knocked off and several of the Volunteers felt the bullets cut their clothes. The O'Rahilly and Patrick Shortis were shot dead by machine-gun fire as they reached Moore Lane. Liam Daly and a companion when the first burst of firing struck the main body ran along the left side of the street to escape. They could hear the whine of bullets and the rattle of machine-guns down the dark alleyways. Daly was shot through the left arm and made his way to some stables.

Clarke informed his wife at their final interview that he was the last man out. Others believed that Pearse returned alone after several visits to the street, and this was the impression amid that indescribable confusion, spatter of bullets on the roadway and the rattling British machine-guns down the dark lanes through which the men dashed for the cover of the Moore Street houses, via Henry Place and Moore Lane. Clarke, MacDermott and Plunkett rallied them on and past the deadly machine-guns and rifles which lighted and cracked and spat death and wounds through the gathering dusk. Far ahead Connolly was borne on a stretcher. He noticed a Fianna boy who was one of his stretcher-bearers interposing himself as a shield for Connolly at every flash and report, and said later to his daughter: "We can't fail now. Such lads will never forget." Plunkett orders a van to be dragged across one of the lanes down which the machine-guns rattled, a feeble screen enough, but it served its turn while Plunkett stood there shouting: "Don't be afraid, don't be cowards any of you, on, on, on!" About a dozen Volunteers were seriously wounded by the rifle and machine-guns; some scattered, some broke through stores and stables and then across roofs towards the main body, and all eventually reached the Moore Street headquarters, a grocery store. Walls were bored, windows barricaded, and pick, poker, and crowbar tunnelled ahead. Guards were placed, and the garrison snatched what sleep it might until morning. Nelson Pillar rose impassive above the blazing Post Office. Hour by hour Connolly groaned in agony. Afar off snipers still were at work. Over the derelict Headquarters two Tricolours flew high above the flames. The green standard sank slowly across the parapet, and hung limply over the burning street.

CHAPTER X

AT THE MENDICITY INSTITUTION

On Wednesday morning, April 20, 1916, two Volunteer dispatch carriers hurried from the Mendicity Institution near Usher's Island on the Liffey's southern quays through barricades and dangerous streets and lanes past the Four Courts and the duels of British and Republican snipers with a very urgent message from Seán Heuston, Commandant of their post, to James Connolly at headquarters, informing him that Heuston and some twenty men were still holding out after a terrific fight against some hundreds of British troops who had then nearly completely surrounded them, and were raking their fortress with machine-gun fire on all sides. Moreover, an all-out assault was expected almost immediately; food supplies were exhausted and ammunition was almost spent.

The dispatch carriers were members of Fianna Eireann and Volunteers like Heuston himself, P. J. Stephenson and Seán McLoughlin. They reached the General Post Office, and noticed at once that Connolly grew unusually animated and excited as he read Heuston's dispatch. He strode across the ground floor of the Post Office to Pearse, and in short, terse, vivid words told him an amazing story. Pearse listened with eagerness and said that all possible aid, and a word of encouragement must be sent at once to the fighters. Stephenson waited while Winifred Carney, Connolly's secretary, typed the reply. But aid was already impossible. Almost immediately it was learned that the Mendicity had been captured with its Commandant and garrison, and that the lost position was invested by a powerful British cordon through which even the most daring Volunteer scouts could not penetrate.

There was an immediate and obvious reason for Connolly's emotion: his orders to Heuston had been to hold up any troops moving towards the Four Courts for three or four hours, and by this delay give the garrisons there and in the headquarters itself time to establish their defences.

Connolly then heard from Stephenson and McLoughlin that

Seán Heuston had not only held his fort for the few hours specified, but was still there, a very hornets' nest for the enemy after nearly fifty hours.   There was a second reason, away back in Connolly's memory why the tale of Heuston's stand in that particular place moved him deeply.   He knew the history of that wide quadrangular building with the obscure name in black letters across its front, not only one of the oldest charitable institutions in Dublin, but also a house with great and tragic history in its very stones.   In its way the very name of the Mendicity must have stirred him nearly as much as the Citizen Army flag, the Plough and the Stars, floating over the Imperial Hotel opposite moved him.   The Imperial Hotel was the property of his antagonist of 1913, William Martin Murphy, and there had been baton charges under its windows when Larkin spoke from its balcony one bloody August Sunday.   So over the Imperial Hotel Connolly flew the Plough and the Stars.   That the Tricolour flew over the Mendicity sent his mind back to a grim story he had written for his *Workers' Republic* so long ago as another August—an August in 1899—a description of Dublin out-casts and down-and-outs as they gathered after dawn in Island Street, once named, and always deserving in his opinion, the name of Dirty Lane, at the rear of the Institution.   Curious old rules bound the lease of the house from the time the philanthropists of the Association for the Suppression of Mendicancy in Dublin, in 1826, had taken it over.   Mendicants were forbidden to enter by the front door inside which there is a charming hallway to this day with cupids and busts to the philanthropists who did their best even if Connolly gave them little credit, and Sir John Gilbert before him snarled at them for turning a great mansion into " a fitting receptacle for the most wretched paupers."   Gilbert was fired by a historic fury, Connolly by a social one, though the philanthropists had good intentions, in spite of their somewhat rigid rules, running balls, having sermons preached in all the churches, and even threatening to march the poor mendicants in one great procession through the Dublin streets to shame the hard-hearted.   Even to this day the Mendicity Institution's work goes on: 9,000 people every month were aided in the year 1948.   No questions are asked, no one is turned away; the hungry must be fed—such was the principle laid down by the sixty gentlemen who drew up the rules.   Two meals a day are served as when Connolly wrote, a breakfast of milk, porridge and bread; a dinner of meat, vegetable and potatoes. Eighty per cent. of those who come are men and women, old and past work, who live on relief.

Connolly is believed to have visited the Institution, and filed in with the outcasts and hungry. His sketch of this experience was centred on a tale of two starving men, one a young man who had tramped from Ulster to seek his fortune: mad with hunger, he upsets a boiler of soup over himself and is scalded to death. Yet Connolly knew enough to know that the Mendicity Institution had in the past been the very seat of wit, beauty, art, and more: a mansion which in its day had sheltered Michael Dwyer's men, Lord Edward Fitzgerald, the United Irishmen. Before a bell tolled to summon the hungry to wooden benches and plain fare the Mendicity had been Moira House, set amid handsome grounds. John Wesley, on a visit there in 1775, saw a more elegant room than any he had seen in England, the very window inlaid from floor to ceiling with mother of pearl, and asked: " Must this, too, pass away like a dream?" It passed when the Council of the Association for the Suppression of Mendicancy took it over, shore off an upper storey and dismantled the internal decorations, although even yet something of the 18th century haunts it. History was busy around Moira House. A few doors away, Francis Magan, betrayer of Lord Edward Fitzgerald, born a year before Wesley's visit, lived twenty years later: Magan stayed there half a century, and watched Wesley's dream change to a nightmare of decay, even as his own 20 Usher's Island changed while he lived there with an eccentric sister and a haunted conscience.

Moira House in its time was the town residence of Lord Moira, opponent of the Union and later Governor-General of India, friend and protector of the United Irishmen and friend of Emmet. There Pamela Fitzgerald heard of her husband's arrest and death. There had come Wolfe Tone, William Sampson, Thomas Russell, Grattan, Curran, and every famous figure of the day. There Thomas Moore had found in the library translations of Irish legends to inspire his songs, the library which was removed with haste to England when General Lake, stung by Moira's denunciations, in the Irish and the British Parliaments alike, in 1797, of political corruption and military tyranny in Ireland, breathed the most outrageous menaces of arson and violence. It was merely by a very slight chance that Francis Magan had not staged the capture of Lord Edward in Moira House one night in May, 1798: there was a clash in the lane nearby between Lord Edward's escort and Major Sirr's men, and the Major himself even more narrowly escaped a too-hasty dagger thrust and some very badly aimed bullets.[1]

Thus Seán Heuston's fort was on the apt historic site although the marksmanship of his garrison was far better than that of Lord Edward's escort in the same neighbourhood more than 100 years before.

Seán Heuston's own path to leadership, in one of the most hardly fought fights in all Easter Week, had been a very short one. Three years before he had come to Dublin from Limerick.   He became very busy indeed in the Fianna headquarters in Hardwicke Street with the details of training and organisation.   He drilled in the Dublin halls in secret with the I.R.B. men before the Volunteers were founded.   He was very active in the Volunteers as one of their first officers; very clever in obtaining armaments at Howth, and under fire as the gun-runners marched back to Clontarf with the rifles in July, 1914.   He was a man of few words; in appearance, thick-set with broad forehead and fierce eyebrows above dark and thoughtful eyes.   Even on his march to Usher's Island on Easter Monday at the head of a dozen men, Seán Heuston had no words to waste.   He met a Volunteer of his own company on the way who asked him what was afoot so early, and merely answered: "Fall in!"   Heuston as promptly sent the Volunteer on his way when informed that he had an urgent summons from Seán MacDermott to Major MacBride in his pocket.[2]

Marching on, Heuston occupied the Mendicity at noon, and ordered the occupants out.   He placed his garrison at their posts, few enough for the task in hand.[3]   After he had supervised the

---

[1] This account of the Mendicity is based on: *Workers' Republic*, August 27, 1899, "The Mendicity and Its Guests," by "Setanta" (James Connolly); Gilbert, *History of Dublin*, Vol. I, pp. 392-400; Lewis, Topographical Dictionary of Ireland, Vol I, p. 550; Fitzpatrick, *Secret Service Under Pitt*; Annual Report, Mendicity Institution, 1946, and some information supplied by an official of the institute.

[2] *Dublin Brigade Review*, 1939, "A Diary of Easter Week," Ignatius Callender, p. 87.   This diary contains one of the most comprehensive descriptions of feelings and events behind the Volunteer positions and among the citizens outside.

[3] A first-hand contemporary account quoted by a member of the Cumann na mBan, "A Dublin Woman's Story of the Rebellion," *Gaelic American*, November 11-18, 1916, gives the strength of the Mendicity Garrison as about thirty at full strength, and twenty-six, including two killed and two seriously wounded at the surrender.   Several Volunteers

securing of the defences inside, he asked three Volunteers to come into the street with him and build a barricade on the quayside. Returning very quickly, he again inspected the defences and insisted that the doors and windows must be more thoroughly barricaded. Sacks were filled with clay and clothing and other useful makeshifts; heavy furniture was placed against the outside doors. Then the best marksmen were placed at the windows, which commanded a view of the quays for a considerable distance, and most significantly, of the Royal (now Collins Barracks) away on the northern quays opposite.

At about 1 o'clock, Heuston's snipers noticed a regiment leave the barracks and march along the quays and across the river. They were four deep, the head of the column rested on Blackhall Place and stretched along the northern quayside back to Watling Street, and around the corner into the Royal Barracks itself.[4] This body of troops had almost passed the Mendicity, quite unsuspecting that the grim building on the southern bank beyond held such a menace, when the Volunteers opened fire, and followed up with such effective volleys that there was a panic and immediate dash for the nearest refuge. The soldiers scattered wildly and sheltered themselves anywhere cover was available: in deserted tramcars standing emptied of passengers on the tracks; behind quay walls; in side streets. Others took cover in houses and streets facing the Mendicity and fired across the river before Heuston's attack slackened. This was no retreat after the first shock of surprise but the opening of one of the hardest-fought and most persistent sieges of Easter Week. Soon the entire immediate area was overrun by the British, intent on overcoming and investing the danger to their operations against the Four Courts and General Post Office alike. Benburb Street, Blackhall Street, Blackhall Place, both sides of Queen Street, Watling Street—where a strong barricade was erected—were thick

---

were sent away with dispatches before the end; the garrison was reinforced from the G.P.O., mostly by Swords Volunteers. Later estimates give the final strength as about twenty or say merely "a small number." See *Capuchin Annual*, 1942, p. 232; *Dublin Brigade Review*, p. 16. Other estimates are given above. *Wolfe Tone Annual*, 1946, p. 47, also deals with the Mendicity fight.

[4] P. J. Stephenson in a statement to the writer, after consultation with other members of the Mendicity garrison, including James Brennan and Dick Balfe, who were present at the surrender. These accounts agree, for the most part, with the contemporary account in the *Gaelic American*, already quoted.

with the khaki besiegers, sitting and lying close, all in such numbers that the contemporary estimate of some 300 to 400 British troops cannot be exaggerated: a force powerful enough, at all events, to strain Heuston's small force to the limit of endurance from the outset. And very small for the task that force was: fifteen in all at the first volley, as two of the seventeen had been sent out on dispatch and other missions, were caught up in the Church Street area fighting, and could not return.

As evening advanced the firing slackened and died away. Heuston sent a dispatch to Connolly asking for reinforcements, and on Tuesday afternoon—or late on Monday night, according to other versions—a force of from thirteen to seventeen Volunteers from the Swords Company arrived in charge of Richard Coleman. They had survived some brisk and dangerous skirmishing on their way. There was sporadic firing all through Monday night. On Tuesday afternoon the British intensified their attack, and the fight grew hotter and fiercer as they closed in. Machine-gun fire from Queen's Street Bridge was opened as soon as the British swept over Queen's Street corner and Arran Quay, a sea of soldiery, a hurricane of bullets. From this point, fortunately for the defenders, an adjoining house projected into the roadway directly in the line of fire and hampered accuracy of aim very much as the Loop Line Bridge had diverted the *Helga's* shells from direct hits on Liberty Hall. It was at this point that the British headquarters were finally established. Tuesday night—with the exception of occasional outbursts of sniping and the sounds of the Four Courts and Church Street areas near at hand—was in general peaceful for the Mendicity garrison; some, indeed, managed to snatch a few hours of sleep. The quiet was merely a surface one, which kept Heuston and his guards all the more on the alert, as it was only too clear that the British were slowly surrounding the Mendicity for final isolation and an all-out attack. Busy as they were with their own defences, the Volunteers outside this cordon made some attempt to relieve Heuston by preventing the extension of the attack towards Church Street: to effect this four houses on the southern quays at Lower Bridge Street corner were set on fire and burned down.[5] The end, however, was near.

By Tuesday night, Heuston had indeed abandoned all hope, if he ever had much after the almost immediate investment of his

---

[5] *Capuchin Annual*, 1942, "The Four Courts Area." P. Holohan, p. 234.

position by such strong British forces, of falling back and joining the Volunteers in the Four Courts and Church Street areas. Almost up to the last hours, however, he managed to send through some of his men with dispatches to the G.P.O. His state was very critical. Food was practically exhausted, ammunition was running low, his men were tired, and there had been several casualties.

Early on Wednesday morning, the British ordered the occupants of the houses on both sides of the Mendicity to leave. Soldiers took up sniping posts on the roofs of several houses in Thomas Street, which is on a height overlooking the quays and the back of the building. A lane at the rear was also occupied. The Mendicity, in fact, was by then completely encircled. Heavy machine-gun fire and continuous rifle volleys were concentrated on the position, and the garrison felt trapped indeed as every street corner became alive with the singing bullets and the rattle-rattle-rattle of the barking, hammering, persistent machine-guns. Heuston constantly visited the posts and cheered everyone with brief and genial words.

Towards noon a new and decisive terror came. A party of soldiers crept under cover along a wall in front of the Mendicity and hurled in grenade after grenade. The Volunteers defied the new weapon as best they could by catching the bombs and hurling them back. Sometimes the catch was a good one; sometimes a bomb burst. This deadly game seemed to the men inside to last for hours although few of the bombs burst inside the house. Two Volunteers were killed and two badly wounded, Liam Staines and Dick Balfe, both close friends of Seán Heuston. This was almost the last incident of the fight. The bomb burst in Staines's hand as he rushed towards a window to hurl it back. He collapsed on the floor. Dick Balfe, who was behind him, was also severely injured by the explosion. The two men lay in agony on the floor, half-dying, and their companions knew that within the Mendicity there was no hope of saving their lives. Apart from this, the garrison were spent with hunger and fatigue, surrounded without chance of retreat, so hopelessly trapped that they could not even fight their way out so dominated was every exit and point by the British snipers and machine-gunners, badly shattered in nerve by the din of bomb, rifle and machine-gun together. Heuston knew that the one hope of saving wounded and uninjured alike was to surrender. Nor was even this a clear alternative. It had been

L

impossible for the last few hours for even a single dispatch carrier to leave. Human endurance and courage had reached their limit. After a brief consultation with his men, Heuston ordered the white flag to be hoisted from the windows, and marched out, with little more than a score of Volunteers—twenty to twenty-six in all, according to the reckoning of contemporary accounts and the memories of the survivors.

It was indeed a pygmy troop. The British were angered and amazed that so small a force had made such a resistance and inflicted such heavy casualties. Raging and panicky officers, red in the face and nerves a-tingle, screamed at Heuston and his men, and hustled them roughly. As the Mendicity garrison lined up in the yard, a shot came from the direction of Roe's Distillery in Thomas Street, where a party of British soldiers overlooked the back of the Mendicity building. Peter Wilson of Swords was hit and dropped dead. The Thomas Street party of British soldiers were not in close touch with the investing party, and at that moment had not realised that the garrison had in fact laid down their arms. The precise facts of the shooting remain dark: it was probably an accident common in street fighting, and helped by the extreme inexperience of the young British soldiers, who impressed the Volunteers, and less hostile observers, there as elsewhere, as raw recruits who hardly knew how to load a rifle; in the Church Street area in particular their tendency to lose their heads became a by-word, and a grim menace to the civilian population. As the flag of truce was visible, some present believed that the shooting was wanton and deliberate, and not due to panic or misunderstanding.[6]

---

[6] A British naval officer who was on leave in Dublin during the Rising, told the writer that in the Stephen's Green area he had to intervene and inform a number of British soldiers how to load their rifles in a house where they entered. He discovered in conversation that they were recent recruits, hurriedly instructed and as hurriedly rushed into the midst of the Easter Week fighting. In Guinness's Brewery a sergeant and a party of soldiers shot two British officers in mistake for insurgent spies. In the adjacent North King Street area during the heavy fighting at Church Street soldiers ran amok, shot fifteen civilians out of hand, and buried some of them in cellars: "We then heard a voice cry, 'Are there any men in this house?' About thirty soldiers rushed upon us. They ran like infuriated wild beasts or things possessed. They looked ghastly and seemed in a panic. There was terrible fighting going on outside in the street and an armoured car at the door." *A Fragment of 1916 History*, J. J. Reynolds, p. 15. Maxwell admitted that there were " deplorable incidents " and that the majority of the troops who fought had less than three months' service. His attitude towards the " deplorable incidents " brought on him the contempt of Sir Francis Vane.

It was estimated at the time, certainly with inevitable exaggeration, that the British losses during the siege of the Mendicity amounted to 180; they as certainly were very heavy. With the exception of one Volunteer aged about forty, the ages of Heuston's garrison ranged from eighteen to twenty-three. All received sentences of imprisonment running from one year to penal servitude for life. Heuston was both a company leader of D. Company, First Battalion, and a Captain of Fianna Eireann. Seán Heuston—then about nineteen years of age—was courtmartialled, condemned to death, and executed in Kilmainham on May 8, 1916.

On the day before his execution a friend asked him if he had heard the result of his courtmartial, and he replied quite calmly that he had not, adding: " There is no hope for me. I expect to be shot." As soon as he heard the sentence, he wrote from his prison cell: "Whatever I have done, I have done as a soldier of Ireland, and I have no vain regrets." It was in the spirit of the other fighters from Fianna Eireann in Easter Week, one of whom led his party from behind a Church Street barricade, and shouted to his companions to the great astonishment of the British officer who took their surrender: " We have fired our last shot. We obey our leaders' orders to hand in our arms, and we expect only the treatment of the men of Ninety-Eight!"

When Seán Heuston fell to the last volley in Kilmainham, the Franciscan, Father Albert, who attended him, looked down on the dead man's face, and found it " transformed, and lit with a grandeur and brightness I had never before noticed."[7]

---

[7] *Capuchin Annual*, 1942, " How Seán Heuston Died." Fr. Albert, O.F.M.Cap., p 342; another version of Father Albert's interview with Heuston in Kilmainham is quoted, *War by the Irish*, John McCann, pp. 64-5.

CHAPTER XI

MACDONAGH AND MACBRIDE AT JACOBS'

MAXWELL noted in his first dispatch that by midnight of the first day of the outbreak all approaches to Dublin Castle were held by the Volunteers with the exception of the Ship Street entrance. In this the Jacobs' factory garrison under Thomas MacDonagh and Major John MacBride played a leading part. This factory is a powerful and well-situated building in a network of streets and lanes, a dominating position across the route to the city and Dublin Castle by Camden and Aungier Streets, well-stocked with food, and very difficult to take by direct assault. Its surroundings were in fact a death-trap for all forces which might have the task of attacking it, and its strength made it formidable even against artillery. Jacobs' factory commands the neighbourhood and the many windows in its vast triangular frontage overlook Portobello Bridge, the roofs of Ship Street Barracks and Dublin Castle—whose Birmingham Tower lay under the control of the Volunteer snipers from the two high towers of the factory from which, in addition, there was a bird's-eye view of the city in general. The impression that MacDonagh's men were isolated and pined in comparative peace until the fight finished is untrue, although their casualties were no more than one killed and several wounded. Their main activity, however, was sniping, varied by some frequent and important sorties, one excursion indeed probably diverting a dangerous attack from Boland's Mills at a very critical stage.

The total strength of the garrison was 150 Volunteers of the Second Battalion, assisted by some members of Fianna Eireann, and a party of the Cumann na mBan.

MacDonagh's force mobilised on Easter Monday morning in Stephen's Green and set up a temporary headquarters in a shop known as the " Byon " where MacDonagh announced the coming Proclamation of the Republic, and issued orders for the seizure of the main position at Jacobs' factory and the various outposts. They marched off just as the Citizen Army contingent arrived to take over the Green. The main body halted at Bishop Street just outside the factory, and some forty Volunteers went through Malpas Street to Barmack's in Fumbally Lane. Little's public-house in Cuffe Street and Delahunt's in Camden Street were also taken over. Four Volunteers seized a house opposite Kevin Street police station. Some of these posts were evacuated about six o'clock the same evening after attacks in force by the British who used hand grenades and fired repeated volleys as they advanced.

The majority of MacDonagh's force went on to occupy Jacobs'. Four policemen were arrested and made prisoners en route. The factory was entered from two points. The main gate in Bishop Street (near Bride Street) was forced with axes and hammers. Near Peter's Row at Bishop Street, a ladder was chained to a lamp standard and swung against the factory windows which were soon opened. A police sergeant and constable who rushed up scandalised by the noise of axes, hammers and an uproar of lusty strokes and lusty cheers cut short their protests when six riflemen covered them and curtly told them to mind their own business if they valued their lives.

Inside the defences were rapidly built up. Windows were barricaded with flour bags, and the walls were loopholed at various convenient points. Observation was kept all the week from the two high factory towers through glasses and the sniping from here was said to be very effective for a wide area around as the marksmen were supplied with range finders. MacDonagh was joined by Major MacBride who came straight into Dublin, and joined in the fight which broke out as he happened to pass Jacobs' as it was being taken over. He was not in uniform, and, according to one version of his speech just before the surrender, the insurrection, apparently, took him by surprise. It is known, however, that Seán MacDermott had sent a messenger to try and get in touch with him. At all events, the occasion found the man, and MacBride threw himself enthusiastically into the fray as MacDonagh's ablest auxiliary, and led in addition several dangerous raiding parties during the week.

Volunteer patrols and pickets were continuously dispatched by MacDonagh as opportunity and need demanded. As the days passed, and to the men and women in Jacobs', as elsewhere, all the days of Easter week seemed one long, sleepless, fantastic space of time fused into one, the increasing British military grip made the

work of these patrols and pickets very dangerous so that their work
had to be carried out at early dawn and during the hours of darkness. The heavy firing from the City Hall, Portobello, G.P.O. and
Four Courts areas, the great fires and artillery activity were clearly
seen and heard by the Jacobs' garrison, although their own comparatively immune stronghold prevented them from fully realising
the terrific pressure and devastation prevailing elsewhere. This did
not prevent them from very actively taking the offensive within the
first hour of hostilities. About one o'clock on Monday it was made
known by scouts that a party of British soldiers were marching
through Camden Street, and that some distance to their rear a
larger force were stationed with a machine-gun. Ten Volunteers
immediately prepared to ambush the advancing soldiers, and took
up their stand on the roadway and sidepath at Bishop Street and
Redmond's Hill. An advance guard of two soldiers with an officer
and twenty-five men soon came in sight and were fired upon at
once at short range. The officer and six men fell wounded and
the rest of the party rushed away. The Stephen's Green garrison
came into action, and Citizen Army men in Cuffe Street also
assisted this attack. Later the British wounded were carried away
by military Red Cross stretcher bearers. The Volunteer snipers
at once ceased fire when the Red Cross men arrived, and this truce
lasted until the wounded were removed.

Early on Monday afternoon dispatches reached MacDonagh and
MacBride with copies of the Proclamation from Headquarters. The
dispatches outlined the general position so far as it was then known
in the Post Office, and the story of the Lancers attack in O'Connell
Street was mentioned in particular. Twelve members of the
Cumann na mBan also arrived and remained on duty until the
surrender. MacDonagh sent a report to the Post Office and
Connolly later noted that MacDonagh was established in " an
impregnable position from the walls of Dublin Castle to Stephen's
Green." MacDonagh is supposed to have sent a message to Pearse
referring to his own poem, " The Yellow Bittern."[1] Donagh
MacDonagh surmises that this cryptic message referred to some
difficulty with the water supply. The opening lines, however, may
have struck MacDonagh as a humorous description of his own

---

[1] *An Cosantóir*, " Thomas MacDonagh," Donagh MacDonagh, October,
1945. The sources of this chapter are *Dublin Brigade Review*, *Catholic
Bulletin*, September, 1918, and the personal accounts of several participants.

position as a poet and wit who, for the first time in his life, found himself as the leader of a revolution:

> The yellow bittern that never broke out
> In a drinking bout might as well have drunk;
> His bones are thrown on a naked stone
> Where he lived alone like a hermit monk. . . .

In reply to an appeal from Michael Mallin at midnight, MacDonagh at one o'clock sent twenty Volunteers to relieve the Citizen Army men in the Portobello area, and after a second message, twenty more to Stephen's Green where they occupied a Turkish Baths which they held until heavy British sniping and machine-gun fire from the Shelbourne Hotel drove them out the following day when Mallin fell back from the Green and withdrew his entire force to his Headquarters already set up on Monday at the College of Surgeons.

All through the week small parties of Volunteers left Jacobs' late at night or very early in the morning with food, arms and messages to the College of Surgeons, where Mallin and Madame Markievicz were in control. These parties returned from their dangerous missions, foraging and reconnoitring *en route,* with the din of the battle ever near them and the flame-lit skies over their heads. And very near to them lurked ever death, dismay, and the panic-stricken Portobello barracks and the British cordons closing slowly nearer. Sometimes MacBride dropped quietly from a window in Jacobs' and went off to guide and place Volunteers in new positions.

On the very fringe of MacDonagh's fortress and within sight of the observers in the towers overhead, Colthurst raged and ranted. On Tuesday evening, Francis Sheehy Skeffington passed over Portobello Bridge, and was challenged and arrested by a military patrol. He was unarmed and carrying a walking stick. From the outbreak of the Rising he had busied himself to prevent looting. He tried to organise a civic police force and protested to the looters. As fear and death gripped the city streets his efforts became futile, but he went on with his thankless task. On Easter Monday, while the Citizen Army attack on the Castle approaches was in progress and volleys and counter volleys swept Cork Hill, Skeffington was among the spectators. A British officer fell dangerously wounded near the Castle gate and lay there apparently bleeding to death.

Skeffington, in spite of the heavy fire which hindered the bystanders from helping the injured officer, persuaded a chemist to come with him, and they went through the hail of bullets up to the Castle gate. As they arrived some British soldiers had succeeded in dragging the captain into the Castle, and there was only a great pool of blood. When Mrs. Skeffington later reproached her husband for taking such a grave risk, he replied quietly: " I could not let anyone bleed to death while I could help."

Skeffington was taken to Portobello Barracks with some other prisoners, searched, and detained without charge while those arrested with him were released. He had led a militant anti-recruiting and anti-war campaign in Ireland from the day the war started, had hunger-struck himself out of a Dublin prison, and his name was very much on the black books of Dublin Castle. At midnight on Tuesday, Captain Bowen-Colthurst ordered the captain of the guard to hand over Skeffington to him. This was done entirely against the regulations which forbade the captain of the guard to hand over his prisoners without a written order from the commanding officer. Skeffington was taken by Colthurst and another officer in charge of a raiding party along the Rathmines Road. Shots were fired at windows whenever a head appeared. Outside Rathmines Catholic Church, Colthurst held up two boys who were leaving the church after attending their sodality. Colthurst roared at them that martial law was in force and that they could be shot like dogs. According to one account given afterwards by Mrs. Sheehy Skeffington, Colthurst ordered one of his officers to " bash " one of the boys, who was thereupon knocked senseless with a rifle butt. Colthurst whipped out a revolver and shot the senseless lad. The Simon Commission Report declared that there was no suggestion that " either of the young men showed violence, and it was clearly established before us that Captain Bowen-Colthurst shot young Coade, who fell mortally wounded and was subsequently taken by an ambulance to the hospital in the barracks. . . . The evidence of the different witnesses can only be reconciled by inferring that more than one case of shooting occurred during the progress of Captain Bowen-Colthurst's party."

Colthurst's extraordinary raiding methods included the bombing of several houses and the shooting of Councillor O'Carroll in Camden Street on April 26, after his capture in an evacuated Volunteer post. Colthurst asked O'Carroll whether he was a Sinn

Féiner, received the reply, "From the backbone out!" marched
him into a backyard and shot him through the lungs. The same
day, April 26, Colthurst took Skeffington and two other prisoners
from their cells, and ordered a party of soldiers to shoot them in
Portobello Barracks.[2]

That Colthurst was insane with fear, religious mania, and political rancour, was the opinion of Tim Healy who first doubted his
madness but changed his view as he watched him at his trial.   One
of Colthurst's own letters quoted in the Simon Report certainly
conveys a sense of the panic which had seized the Portobello
garrison, which so far as the numbers in the building went, was
four times the strength of MacDonagh's at Jacobs':

> "On Tuesday, and up to Wednesday morning, rumours of
> massacres of police and soldiers from all parts of Dublin were
> constantly sent to me from different sources.   Among others
> the rumour reached me that 600 German prisoners at Old-
> castle had been released and armed and were marching on
> Dublin.   I also heard that the rebels in the city had opened
> up depots for the supply and issue of arms, and that a large
> force of rebels intended to attack Portobello Barracks, which
> was held only by a few troops, many of whom were recruits
> ignorant as to how to use their rifles, and a number of the
> others were soldiers and sailors who had taken refuge in the
> barracks.   We had also in the barracks a considerable number
> of officers and men who had been wounded by the rebels and
> whose protection was a source of great concern to me.   I
> believed that it was known that these leaders were confined
> in the barracks and that possibly the proposed attack on the
> barracks was with a view to their release.   Rumours of risings
> all over Ireland and of a large German-American and Irish-
> American landing in Galway were prevalent.   I had no know-
> ledge of any reinforcements arriving from England, and did
> not believe it possible for troops from England to arrive in
> time to prevent a general massacre.   I knew of the sedition

---

[2] The Simon Report of the Inquiry into the Skeffington murder, and
Colthurst's courtmartial, which found him " guilty but insane," are given
in the *Irish Times* 1916 *Handbook*.   Mrs. Skeffington's *British Militarism
As I Have Known It*; Sir Francis Vane's *Agin the Governments*; Tim
Healy, *Letters and Leaders of My Day*, are also important first-hand
accounts.

which had been preached in Ireland for years past and of the popular sympathy with rebellion."

Human reason snapped behind the British strong walls and behind the Volunteer positions alike. In Boland's Mill a crazed Volunteer shot a comrade dead and ran amok; in the Post Office an unstrung Volunteer had to be disarmed; more harmlessly an exhausted guard on a Volunteer barricade fell asleep, awoke with a start, and as a harmless cat strolled towards the planks and over-turned cart, shouted wildly: "Merciful Heavens! They have loosed the lions of the Zoo against us!"

On Thursday a message reached MacDonagh from de Valera that the situation was somewhat critical. Food was plentiful but ammunition was running low and an attack by the British was expected. Boland's Mill was by then in fact harassed by incessant sniping, the outposts had fallen, and all communication with the Dublin Headquarters had been broken. Reports reached Mac-Donagh at the same time that British military pickets were in force in Merrion Square. He decided to dispatch fifteen cyclist scouts armed with Howth Mausers to attack the pickets, and if possible reach de Valera's position. The party went along the south side of Stephen's Green, Leeson Street, Fitzwilliam Square and in Merrion Square sighted a British sentry outside a house occupied by a number of soldiers. They at once fired on the sentry and wounded him, and next attacked the house from the meagre shelter of doorways, lamp standards and the roadway. After some fierce exchanges between the two parties, the Volunteers had to give up hope of getting through to de Valera and retreated along the west side of Stephen's Green. There they came under machine-gun fire from the Shelbourne Hotel and the United Services Club. John O'Grady, one of the Volunteer party, was fatally shot in the stomach, and carried back to Jacobs' by his companions. The Merrion Square attack coincided with some heavy sniping by some of de Valera's men near the Loop Line Bridge at Westland Row. MacDonagh's picket gave the British the impression that an attack in their rear was a real danger, and the measures they took to meet it relieved the pressure on the Boland's Mill garrison. The attack there was diverted to elaborate trench digging and barricading to prevent further threats to the rear.

The last shots from Jacobs' were fired on Sunday at a large

party of military in St. Patrick's Park who dispersed.   By that
time the garrison had lost their outposts in the neighbourhood.
There was fierce fighting on Wednesday when some of these outposts taken over on the previous morning were attacked by a small
party of fourteen soldiers led by a naval officer, supported by a
force of 100 soldiers, in Harcourt Street nearer to Portobello. They
bombed and raked the Volunteer posts so heavily that the Volunteers were driven out.   MacDonagh maintained communications
with Mallin practically without interruption.   He was reported as
very confident and cheerful, and as expressing optimistic hopes of
an early end of the European war.   One captured dispatch of his
read:

> " Army of the Irish Republic,
>   Dublin Command,
>   Battalion IV (*sic*).
>   30/4/16.   5.30 a.m.

To COMMANDANT MALLON (*sic*).

(1) Dispatch received.   I do not understand it.   I have
received no order from H.Q. *re* evacuation, and do not think
it advisable or practicable.   I have received an order of a
personal nature but have been unable to obey.   I have notified this to H.Q.   I do not know where H.Q. is.

(2) I have been in touch with Batt. IV at Thom's, Love
Lane, Cork Street.   They are very strong in numbers and
food.   They have beaten off every attack with loss, and have
lost no men.

(3) Good news of international situation.   England is down
and out.   Enemy officers are uttering proclamations full of
falsehoods.   Small actions seem to be developing against my
right (Bride Street).   Thank God, as we are tired of sniping.

(4 and 5) Torn in original and illegible).

> THOMAS MACDONAGH,
>   Commandant."[3]

---

[3] Quoted *Irish Life*: " A Record of the Irish Rebellion of 1916."   Máire
Níc Shiubhlaigh (Mrs. Eamonn Price), who was with the Cumann na
mBan in Jacobs', noted that MacDonagh showed only one trace of depression throughout the week, and that was when the surrender was
announced.

CHAPTER XII

CEANNT AND BRUGHA AT THE SOUTH DUBLIN UNION

WHEN Eamonn Ceannt had issued his sudden mobilisation call to the Fourth Battalion at Emerald Square near Dolphin's Barn for an hour before noon, on Easter Monday, he discovered in due course that Sunday's countermand had indeed dispersed his men: of the battalion roll of 1,000 Volunteers less than 200 took part in the Rising in various positions, and of these less than 100 appeared at Emerald Square while Ceannt had little more than sixty Volunteers under him in the South Dublin Union. One account of the surrender suggests indeed he had less, for when Sir Francis Vane asked him in amazement whether the main buildings had been held with only forty men, Ceannt replied quietly: " No, forty-two."

The task set Ceannt and his Vice-Commandant, Cathal Brugha, required, in fact, for its success something more than the skeleton strength they succeeded in mustering. His lieutenants had done their best. As one of them, who received his orders at 10 o'clock, gathered a handful by a wild three-quarter hour dash over a wide and scattered area in South County Dublin, arrived at Emerald Square just before noon, he found the battalion preparing to march off. Near Harold's Cross Bridge he had passed the men of the Kimmage garrison, exiles all, swinging along with a determined tread, headed by their commanding officer, George Plunkett, armed with an extraordinary variety of weapons, pikes, shotguns and rifles, some wearing gaily-coloured scarfs and wide hats, all tramping resolutely and briskly with an anticipation of adventure in their eyes, if not that day, some day anyway.

The Kimmage men, some fifty-four strong, were in fact halted by George Plunkett as soon as they reached Harold's Cross Bridge with the quip: " Why walk when we can ride? Let us travel in comfort." A tram was stopped, to the indignation and terror of some passengers who objected not only to fifty-four men boarding the car but in particular to pikes, firearms, and an uncomfortable variety of luggage.   The conductor protested and the tram was promptly commandeered, and the driver told to go ahead to Dublin without any further stops.   George Plunkett then insisted on paying full fares for all although the conductor said with bitter resignation: "Yous have captured the tram anyway, so why pay?" Plunkett, with great courtesy replied: "It may indeed be the last fares I'll ever pay you or anyone else, but we are honest men and not hooligans, and always pay our way."

In the meantime, John Joyce and his band reached Emerald Square little suspecting that bullets would be whistling round their ears before an hour had passed, and some of them lying dead or wounded in the open fields at Mount Brown, and British soldiers advancing on them to a din of rifles and machine-guns.   Yet Ceannt's first words were a very plain statement of what faced them.[1]

Ceannt told his men tersely: "You are in action to-day!" and then briefly of the proclamation of the Republic, and the positions assigned to them, and that their objective was the South Dublin Union, which lay between Rialto Bridge and James's Street.   It was one of the most important links in the Volunteer chain of positions, a great fifty-two-acre cluster of buildings, a position of high strategic value, near at once to Richmond and Islandbridge Barracks, to Kingsbridge Railway Station and, above all, to the British military headquarters in Ireland, the Royal Hospital.   On its James's street side, its frontage was modest but on the south a wall ran nearly half a mile beside the Grand Canal.   " Ramified by streets, alleys and courtyards, and studded with residences, halls, dormitories, churches, sheds," notes the contemporary description in the *Catholic Bulletin*, March, 1918, " the interior presents the appearance of a good-sized town; and, during Easter Week, the inmates, exclusive of officials, numbered 3,282 souls."

As noon struck, Ceannt, Brugha and their staff entered at Rialto Gate.   An angry and surprised porter seized a telephone and called the police, yelling: "Those scoundrels, the Sinn Féiners, are

---

[1] This account of the S.D.U. fighting is based on the personal statements of Colonel John Joyce, David Sears: *The Dublin Brigade Review*, pp. 35-37; *Catholic Bulletin*, March-July, 1918; *An Cosantóir*, October, 1946, "Eamonn Ceannt," Donagh MacDonagh; June, 1947, "We Surrender," Lily M. Brennan; *An t-Oglách*, June 12, 1926; *Cathal Brugha*, "Sgeilg;" *Agin the Governments*, Sir Francis Vane.

here!" The instrument was dead as the wires were already cut. He surrendered and handed over his keys. At the same time another party of Volunteers entered by the James's Street Gate. In the distance sounded the music of a military band in Richmond Barracks. "They don't know yet," said Ceannt, smiling. Suddenly and ominously the music stopped. Leaving an officer and nine Volunteers to guard Rialto Gate, Ceannt sent his main body forward to the James's Street entrance to join up with the men there. He warned them that a very loud explosion might be expected from Phœnix Park direction where the Magazine was to be seized and fired. The deafening explosion he prepared them for did not in fact take place though the Magazine by then was well ablaze. The British were even then learning that the revolt was in progress and hastening to repel it. Dublin police phone messages had already warned the Royal Hospital and the military chiefs there were aware that the Four Courts, Jacobs' Factory and other positions had been seized or attacked. Feverish preparations were being made within rifle shot of the S.D.U. to hurry troops to the Magazine and, above all, to relieve the Castle. Within an hour a wireless message was to be flashed from Kingstown to London for immediate help. The mobile column from the Curragh had been summoned. Panic and confusion still reigned in British military circles. Luckily for them the Dublin Telephone Exchange had not been occupied as the full number of Volunteers detailed to seize and take it had been scattered by the countermand and failed to appear in time. A small party which hurried to that task found to their chagrin that they were too late and that there at least the British had not been caught unawares. It was a dear miss, for if the exchange had been captured, the Royal Hospital orders would have been very much delayed and dismay and demoralisation would have aided the insurgents.

Forty minutes after Ceannt had taken over the Union the first shots were fired by his sentries on the 3rd Royal Irish Regiment on its way citywards to the Castle. Their advance guard of thirty men halted about 300 yards away on the slope of Mount Brown *en route* for James's Street. Fire was opened on them from the positions which had been taken over by the remainder of Ceannt's men, by those in Marrowbone Lane, under Séamus Murphy, by the small party under Colbert in Watkins's Brewery, Ardee Street, from Roe's Distillery in James's Street, and from the main Union

building itself.   The snipers at the Union windows fired first and
general volleys followed quickly from the three other posts.   One
British officer fell wounded and the soldiers rushed in panic for
safety, dashing into neighbouring houses, crouching under the
shelter of walls, or retreating.   Almost immediately machine-gun
and rifle fire opened up from the Royal Hospital and other points,
and so fiercely that some Volunteer outposts in the open fields had
to withdraw with the loss of three killed and a number wounded.
The brunt of the fighting was soon to fall on the Union garrison
as the Roe's Distillery men, some twenty in all, were isolated by
the following day and disbanded.   Colbert's men in Watkins's
Brewery left that position at dawn on Wednesday and joined the
Marrowbone Lane garrison, which included seven Fianna boys
and twenty-three members of Cumann na mBan, and about 100
Volunteers or more towards the end of the fighting through various
additions, although the original party which took over the place
on Monday numbered only twenty.

The procedure in the South Dublin Union after occupation was
as in the other positions.   James's Street gate was closed and a
barricade built inside.   Windows and passages in the various
buildings were made secure, and snipers were posted in a number
of offices overlooking the main street, and guards and look-out men
posted.   The night nurses' home was converted into headquarters.
Red Cross flags were flown from all buildings not used by the
Volunteers.   Throughout the fighting the work of the institution
went on.

The main Volunteer stronghold was in the James's Street block
of buildings and the snipers there dominated the area.   Most
of the Volunteer casualties were suffered in the open fields within,
then known as the McCaffray Estate, the Orchard Fields, and the
Master's Fields, stretching southwards from H.Q. to the Grand
Canal.   The Volunteers were exposed to the British fire from the
Rialto buildings on the Canal and from the Royal Hospital which
overlooked the Union grounds, and with many windows at which
expert snipers made themselves a constant nest of deadly and
maddening scorpions.   The James's Street post marksmen, however, also made themselves masters of the open spaces in turn,
and were supported by the Volunteers at Roe's Distillery and
Cromwell's Quarter, which commanded the area laterally.   What
handicapped the defenders of the Union was their weakness in

numbers which ruined all plans prepared beforehand since the great area could not be manned effectively nor communication maintained with the advance posts, and these inevitably were carried by the superior British forces. The dilemma of the Mount Street Bridge fighters also presented itself very forcibly in the S.D.U. Five, eight, or even one man had to defend an entire building. This desperate bluff, however, misled the attackers as elsewhere as to the real numbers of the Volunteers, of whom many afterwards shuddered to recall the audacious risks they had taken under the dashing leadership of Ceannt and Brugha. A Volunteer officer and five men were posted at the inner side of the canal wall; in the fields near Rialto a solitary Volunteer dug himself in; Hospitals Two and Three in the fields were held by eight men, two on the ground floor, six on the top.

The Marrowbone Lane Distillery garrison covered or protected the approaches on the outer side of the canal wall, as the distillery was only a few hundred yards distant on the far side of the canal itself. High walls made the east or city side immune, inaccessible and dangerous in the extreme with the exception of one vulnerable spot at the Basin end, lower than the rest. Here five Volunteer guards were on duty, and were finally detected by the British, and driven back by an attack from the rear.

The first attack after entry was the signal for continuous fighting. The troops who retreated at James's Street reformed, sent for reinforcements and attacked again in the rear at Rialto. Cathal Brugha, as soon as he entered, had posted Joyce and his party in fields on the south of the road at Mount Brown where the first Volunteer casualties occurred. When the attack from Rialto came Ceannt's outpost of nine men at Rialto Gate were in a corrugated iron shed just inside. The shed was divided into dormitories and corridors, the only possible position from which the gate and entrance could be held. Hasty barricades of mattresses and bedding and furniture were erected at the windows even while the sound of the volleys at James's Street end came to warn them that the fight had begun in earnest. There was a lull as the retreating British reformed and planned and finally swept round to the rear. There was constant firing as the headquarters at James's Street was sniped and machine-gunned at intervals for nearly two hours, and Ceannt's own party fell back to the Nurses' Home, the strongest position. The military had in fact entered the grounds and driven

in the outlying Volunteer posts. The attack on the Rialto end
lasted some fierce and terrible two hours.

Fusillade after fusillade was fired by the British on the Rialto
sheds at close range. Half an hour after the attack started the
walls of the sheds were like a sieve, and one of the Volunteers, John
Traynor was killed. The remaining defenders had many near
escapes as the thin walls offered no real protection, and the bullets
whizzed through the thin tin walls and pierced the partitions and
the iron tubing of the beds. The British had attacked from two
sides. A small gate beside the entrance was forced open and one
party dashed in firing repeated volleys. Other parties made their
way along the canal bank under heavy fire from the Marrowbone
Lane garrison on the opposite bank. Another gate in the rear of
the sheds was forced while some of the soldiers scaled the walls,
some nine feet high. The Volunteers in the sheds fired on them,
and several fell including an officer. One Volunteer was sent out
for instructions to Ceannt as the post was becoming untenable.
Ceannt ordered the Volunteers to fall back but the messenger who
had with difficulty reached Ceannt could not return as Rialto was
now under heavy fire and the intervening fields and spaces as well.
Several British officers were killed in the attack. Very soon the
Rialto position was hopeless though the defenders fought on, from
room to room, removed a wounded companion to hospital and
returned defiantly to fight it out.   Eventually the British surrounded the sheds and fought their way in, the Volunteers retiring
with sharp volleys until the last partition was broken down by a
lawn mower used as battering ram, and they surrendered.

From then onwards the weakness of the Volunteers compelled
them to concentrate on their headquarters which they, nevertheless,
held by hard fighting and with unbroken spirits until the Sunday
following the general surrender.   The British had first divided
their positions at Rialto and James's Street and then cleared away
the Volunteer posts and outposts between. The Volunteers, besides
being weak, were not familiar with the Union grounds.   Some
fourteen of them who held a line of communications between
Rialto and James's Street in several posts were soon isolated and
out of touch with each other.

This was not achieved without some very hot fighting in which
the Volunteers lost at least three men, with several wounded
severely. Post after post was taken with weight of numbers and a

M

terrific concentration of rifle fire aided by machine-guns which kept up a constant fire from the Royal Hospital and posts in Rialto and James's Street. Two dead Volunteers lay in the open all Monday on a pathway in front of Hospital Two and Three. This building was surrounded by a party of fifty soldiers who burst into the grounds from Rialto and there was a vigorous exchange of shots between the Volunteer party of six in the upper storey and the soldiers. The trapped Volunteers fired from window after window in turn. The soldiers entered and found two other Volunteers on the ground floor who at once fired on them and retreated firing at their pursuers as they fled down a network of dormitories and passages. Finally, both Volunteers escaped by a lower window —one gravely wounded in the stomach, the second uninjured. They lay still, and evaded the pursuers for a moment. The unwounded man trained his rifle on the corner of the building round which they heard the soldiers approaching. The first soldier who turned the corner dashed back hastily. The Volunteer rose and dashed away in his turn for the main group of buildings at the James's Street end some distance away. A second party of British soldiers rushed round from the other side of the hospital and tried to bar his escape. He fired right into them and they dashed for cover into the hospital. As he ran past some of the other buildings he saw Eamonn Ceannt in front of an infirmary tending a badly wounded Volunteer. The sound of soldiers running towards them drove Ceannt and the Volunteer to seek a place where they could make a stand. They escaped by a ladder provided by an inmate across a large wooden gate which closed an alley, and took up positions to fire on the pursuers. Ceannt also sent word by the inmate who had rescued them to the matron of the infirmary that one of his men was lying wounded outside the infirmary. Two inmates and a nurse at once brought the Volunteer inside and, as he appeared to be dying, sent a messenger for a priest. Ceannt and his companion after further adventures regained a safer position.

Shortly afterwards the British pressed home the attack on the six Volunteers in the upper part of Hospital Two and Three. The six men were stationed in the east wing. The noise of the firing brought Nurse Keogh, who was in the west wing, down the stairs to look after the inmates on the ground floor. As she reached the foot of the wide stone stairs she reached a doorway at right angles

to a corridor where two British soldiers were kneeling with rifles
trained on the doorway.   They mistook her in spite of her white
uniform for a Sinn Féiner or fired in panic at the sound of her
approach, and she dropped dead, the bullets from both rifles entering her body.   As a second nurse rushed down the stairs in turn,
she heard an officer shouting: " Are there any Sinn Féiners
upstairs?"   She placed the dead body of Nurse Keogh on a table
in the corridor.   An inmate next carried in the wounded Volunteer
who had been lying in front of the building since the earlier fight
on the ground floor; apparently dying, the Volunteer was laid on
the floor.   A large party of military next dashed to the top storey
yelling: " Hands up, surrender!"   They smashed down a partition, overpowered the six Volunteers by main force, clubbed
them with rifle butts and carried them off prisoners.   Most of the
positions not occupied by Volunteers were distinctly marked by
Red Cross flags, and the tragic incidents at Hospital Two and
Three were not repeated.   There they were due to the Volunteers
—who were acting as scouts and trying to maintain communications
—being surprised by the appearance of the military and the panic
of these in turn.   During the fighting one of the kitchen staff was
also killed by a bullet during the exchange of shots.

The battle went on with retreats and advances by the
invaders.   On Monday and Tuesday the British had occupied the
southern part of the Union grounds and advanced on the main
group of buildings, and then retired confused and uncertain on
the Wednesday.   Over the wide spaces of the South Dublin Union
and through the many buildings the bloody game of hide-and-seek
went aimlessly on.   There was tunnelling and counter-tunnelling
through walls, and unexpected meetings, with hand-to-hand
encounters of the British and the Volunteers.   Ceannt, Mauser
pistol in hand, took part in several of these fights.   Sometimes
both sides occupied the same building with only a partition wall
between them.   Fatal shots lurked round every corner of the many
intersecting passages.   Sometimes the advancing British soldiers
lost their way and ran into a burst of rifle fire from Volunteer
guards at some window beneath which they passed unsuspectingly.

The spirit of Ceannt and Cathal Brugha dominated the determined Volunteer defence, which was not broken at headquarters
until circumstances gave the British on Thursday an unusually
capable commander who hemmed in the Volunteers and held them

until the surrender. Of Ceannt it was remarked that he asked no one to carry out any order that he would not readily have obeyed himself from the moment he raised the Tricolour over the Union until the moment he surrendered. His Vice-Commandant, Cathal Brugha, had had such a spirit and indifference to danger that those who shared his risks said of him that he walked into death-traps with a jest, and a force radiated from him that scorched up the very fear of death. "He was as full of fight," said William Cosgrave, one of his officers in the Union, "going into the fray as when he lay with the life ebbing out of him."

It was a curious fate that sent Sir Francis Vane from Portobello Barracks, where panic had reigned since the Rising began, to fight two such leaders. In Portobello were Sir Francis Vane and Captain Bowen-Colthurst, the two deep contrasts of the reaction of the British military mind to the revolt: Vane, the chivalrous and courageous soldier, who fought Ceannt and Brugha to a standstill with a cool brain and a warm heart; Colthurst, the crazed Irish neurotic, whose mad fear ran amok with Bible texts and murder, a tool, in Vane's opinion, of a vicious anti-Irish militarist clique in Dublin Castle. Colthurst was to murder Sheehy-Skeffington, shoot down civilians in a frenzy, and dominate his dithering sub-ordinates to such a degree that a London paper remarked caustically that if he had ordered them to shoot themselves they would have obeyed. It was Vane who unmasked the Skeffington murder at the cost of his own career, even if he first wrung from Kitchener himself the comment: "This Colthurst ought to be shot!"

On the night of April 24, Vane himself relates, Portobello Barracks was a panic-stricken garrison, a heart-breaking but inevitable state of affairs with military and civilian refugees pouring in; small parties from many regiments with innumerable young officers, inexperienced and unknown to each other, so that in his view even worse tragedy than occurred might well have been expected. Vane strove hard to fit the crazy pieces into some coherent pattern and use for the best the material to his hand.

The largest military unit was the Royal Irish Rifles, an Ulster regiment under Major Rossborough, numbering some 300 men. Wild rumours were rife among the British troops in the barracks of huge rebel armies marching on Dublin and of German troops having landed to help the insurgents. Vane later commented that it was lucky indeed that these tales were merely camp gossip, and untrue, because he had only 600 men to hold a barracks that normally housed two battalions, and the perimeter was an almost impossible one.   He set himself to reduce the area to be held by securing all buildings in the vicinity, by sending out pickets, and by establishing observation posts with secure lines of retreat to the main body in case of attacks in force.   He personally conducted raids in the vicinity and in a search of seventy houses in Grove Park immediately behind Portobello found only a few revolvers and antiquated Sniders.   He established an observation post in the high clock tower of Rathmines Town Hall.   It was not, however, until Thursday, April 27, that Vane took charge of the attack on the S.D.U., and much had been endured by the attackers and attacked before then.   He was informed on that day that an important ammunition convoy two miles away, in a locality very vaguely described, was held up by a strong insurgent force.   He gathered all the available men not on duty, some fifty in all, with six officers from five different regiments.   At length, he arrived outside the S.D.U. where he found the convoy in difficulties and unable to pass until the Volunteer fortress was taken.   He noted that the soldiers, mainly raw recruits, were badly shaken by the Volunteer handling of them on Wednesday.   The column was being vigorously attacked in front and on both flanks.   Colonel Oates, the officer in charge of the convoy, asked him to take charge of the attack.   Vane threw his men, mostly war-hardened soldiers, into the thick of the fray, throwing out flanking parties to mask the fire.

The rear of the Volunteer headquarters in the Nurses' Home was raked by a terrible concentration of rifle fire, and at the same time the attackers swept into the grounds from Rialto and several other points and, covered by repeated volleys, converged rapidly on the insurgent H.Q.   There was also a very brisk exchange of shots with the Marrowbone Lane Distillery garrison which opened a murderous and heavy fire on the party advancing along the opposite canal bank where the stretchers were soon busy carrying off the many casualties.   There were many casualties, too, as the attackers advanced, for the Volunteer snipers at the windows fired repeatedly, perforce recklessly exposing themselves, so terrific and constant was the concentration of British rifle fire on their position. The volume of fire poured into the rear of the Nurses' Home was almost overwhelming, the din was ear-shattering and unnerving, and no man felt his chance of survival could be estimated in more than minutes.   Even behind the Volunteer defences it was difficult to maintain proper contact between the defenders as the hurricane of bullets howled in through the windows at all angles.   Even to pass up and down the stairs meant taking a dangerous risk, a risk which could be only taken by making a desperate dash for it.   In these circumstances the Volunteers made a mistake which almost handed over the position to the British, which indeed would have handed it over except for the lucky accident that one man of iron will and incredible courage passed a certain spot at the moment when, although the British did not know it, their attack had succeeded and they had really captured the Union, and Ceannt and his men waited grimly determined on one last and bloody stand.

The man who smashed the British attack and saved the Union was Cathal Brugha, and this is what happened: an exploit even more desperate in its way than the defence of Mount Street Bridge. Ceannt, seeing that the British fire was wearing down the Volunteer snipers in the Nurses' Home, decided to send for reinforcements to the men who were holding the James's Street frontage. He dispatched messages for help, and then went towards James's Street himself shortly afterwards.   The frontage was not then under attack, and Ceannt's call to them was an obvious measure to take.   Unfortunately, some misunderstanding arose as to which garrison Ceannt had ordered to be evacuated.   In his absence an order was issued for the evacuation of the Nurses' Home.   There was no panic.   David Sears was firing away at a window when he and other marksmen on the same floor were called away quietly and calmly, and told to get back to the James's Street position, and they all felt they were obeying orders.   How the mistake originated is not clear but in the sequel both the James's Street men and the H.Q. party then evacuated their posts.   Sears and his comrades met the other garrison coming to their assistance on a ground floor dormitory half-way between the two positions.   It was now about four o'clock.   The building over the main gate at the James's Street frontage had been connected by tunnels through various buildings with H.Q. and there was great freedom of communication between them.   The actual strength of the two garrisons was from Monday night, twenty-seven officers and men at H.Q., and sixteen at James's Street, some forty-three in all.   (When Ceannt informed Vane that his defence numbered forty-two, Cathal Brugha was out of action.)

The strain on these small forces had been almost unbearable, so hopelessly undermanned were the vital posts. From the Monday night nine sentry posts had to be maintained continuously. Excluding the five officers, Ceannt, Brugha, William Cosgrave (who acted as Adjutant), Alderman P. S. Doyle, one Red Cross man, one cook, and one Volunteer who had a nervous breakdown, this left twenty Volunteers to man the nine posts. Two of the posts had to be withdrawn during the hours of darkness towards the end of the week owing to the exhaustion of the sentries through lack of sleep. Even on the Thursday night the sentries had to be doubled because none could be trusted to keep awake alone. They talked together in whispers, one falling asleep in the middle of a remark to be awakened with difficulty by his companion who then fell asleep to be wakened himself in turn. Cathal Brugha patrolled the posts paternally and silently, congratulating the sentries with a brief word when challenged. David Sears, who was the youngest member of the Union garrison, regarded these battles against sleep as the most haunting experiences of the whole fight. After the heavy Thursday's fighting, he spent the entire night on sentry duty. On Friday morning, Ceannt promptly and peremptorily ordered him to bed.

The evacuation of the Nurses' Home H.Q. occurred at the most dangerous time it could possibly have occurred since it coincided with the very moment that the British had finished a tunnel through which they penetrated one of the walls of that building. The front door of the Nurses' Home opened into a hall with an arch opposite facing on a hallway. From there the stairs led straight up to a small landing about six feet high, and then turned parallel with the front of the house. The British incursion was into a room to the left of the hall-door as it was entered. A room also flanked the right of the hall door. A powerful barricade, five feet high, had been built across the archway. It was made with stout plank hoardings, a foot apart, the space between tightly packed with clay, and over it, and covering it, was a barricade about a foot high, on the landing behind as a cover from which the defenders could fire over the main barricade. These works were intended as a second line of defence if the front door were carried, though this door, in fact, was well covered from a window above it in the first storey where Volunteer guards were on the watch with revolvers and repeating rifles. There was little chance of attacking with a battering-ram, and one attempt to advance there had been driven off with loss. From the time the barricade was erected the Volunteers were more or less cut off from the hall and the two ground floor rooms opening off it. The British learned that the left ground floor room was never used and under the cover of the heavy rifle fire they completed the tunnel at their ease, and arrived in the hall with loud shouts of " Surrender!" They were answered with a defiant shout and a rapid series of shots across the barricade, and replied with a volley and hand grenades.

If they had timed their entry a few minutes later the victory was theirs. Cathal Brugha was the last of the men retiring in obedience to the mistaken order. He was passing the barricade or had arrived in the kitchen which was to the right of the hall from which the stairs led. Brugha fell badly wounded with at least five bullets and several bomb splinters in him. He dragged himself across the kitchen and into a small yard at the back. Both the back door and the door of the kitchen were open. Brugha could see through both doors and enfilade the barricade at an angle of forty-five degrees. He had a " Peter the Painter " automatic, fitted with a wooden stock, and he used it with effect although badly wounded. It was learned later that in this fight before the finish he suffered twenty-five wounds in all: five dangerous ones which cut arteries, nine serious wounds, and eleven more. He sat on the ground with his back propped against the wall of the small yard, and prevented the British from crossing the barricade for something near to two hours alone, and unaided. The men who had gone in front of him believed that he had been killed as the British burst through. They also thought, and with them the main body which they had joined, that the British had seized the Nurses' Home. Only the will and courage of one man then held the attack at bay.

One of the many tunnels the defenders had driven through the walls as they prepared their defences led through from their new position to the small yard where Brugha was, but it was considered impossible to attack the British by this route. A prepared enemy could have shot down the attackers one by one as they climbed through the small hole in the wall into the yard. The new position in itself was nearly as bad. The Volunteers could only train two rifles on the probable route by which the British assault must come.

The best snipers were placed in these positions, and the rest of the Volunteers sat round and waited for the end.

Eamonn Ceannt again addressed them very briefly, and told them that they had made a good fight, that there would be no surrender, and they were all to fight to the last. A decade of the Rosary was said. Those who had cigarettes left shared them and prepared for a last smoke. The invading British would rake them with fire at their ease, and there would be very little opportunity to reply in the maddening death-trap into which they had blundered so unluckily after all their tough resistance.

As they waited, away in the distance a defiant voice was heard singing:

" *God save Ireland, say we proudly, God save Ireland say we all, Whether on the scaffold high or the battlefield we die. . . .*"

A scout was sent back towards the singer, and returned with the news that Cathal Brugha was in the yard and still alive. The Volunteers, headed by Ceannt, rushed back. He was sitting in a pool of his own blood, which, David Sears thought as he looked at that unforgettable scene, must have covered some four square yards. Brugha's uniform was splashed with blood around his many wounds and he was still singing in a weak but defiant voice, stopping at intervals to challenge the British to come on, promising them he would always find a bullet for them no matter how wounded he was, demanding to know whether there was any British officer brave enough to come out and fight a Volunteer officer.

There were in fact no British there. So long as Brugha covered the barricade they could not cross it, and for the time being they had retreated. Single-handed he had driven them back. For the first and last time during the fight Ceannt showed emotion. He knelt beside Brugha, tears came into his eyes, and for a minute it seemed that he was losing control of himself. Brugha, in a voice so weak that it appeared the life was ebbing out of him, asked the Volunteers to all sing *God Save Ireland* while he died, and then go back to the fighting. *God Save Ireland* was then sung with deep feeling by all present. (It was the second song in which Ceannt had joined that week. On Monday he had hoisted the Tricolour on a long gas pipe over the Union, and all had joined in singing the *Soldiers' Song*. Two minutes later the British had shot away one of the cords supporting the flag which floated then only on one cord.)   Brugha was carried away, his wounds still bleeding, still speaking bold words of encouragement to his comrades.   (On Friday he was removed to the Union hospital on a stretcher, and later arrested by the British, taken to Dublin Castle hospital from which he was released uncharged as his captors imagined his wounds were incurable.)

After dark the British returned and again stormed the fatal barricade with grenades.   From 7.30 to 9.30 the final battle for the Union raged across this barrier.   There was bombing and volleying, and counter bombing and volleying in the darkness between the British and the Volunteers, and the combatants could not see each other.   Volunteers lay flat on the landing of the stairs blazing away with revolvers at the top of the barricade in a continuous barrage to keep the storming party from crossing. Canister bomb after canister bomb was hurled towards the spot from which the British alone could enter.   In the end the Volunteers were the victors and the British once again withdrew.

From Thursday night until the general surrender Ceannt and his men remained in the South Dublin Union in comparative peace. There was no further general attack nor was it until Sunday morning that the garrison knew that the insurrection was over.

CHAPTER XIII

DE VALERA AT BOLAND'S MILLS

ON Easter Monday Eamon de Valera and the officers of the Third Battalion realised only too well that if the G.H.Q. had set them a hard task for Easter Sunday, the countermanding order and the "critical situation" had set them an almost impossible one. Originally the plans they had to carry out assigned 400 men, their full strength at the beginning of the year, to defend two miles of railway line from Dublin to Dun Laoghaire, railway workshops, a long stretch of the canal, the gas works, Boland's Bakery, Boland's Mills, railway bridges, canal bridges, and all the approaches to these. Doubt and confusion dispersed and demoralised all but 120 men. The mobilisation failed completely in Dun Laoghaire, Blackrock and the outlying areas. Yet so audacious and spirited a bluff was played by less than half the battalion in these bewildering circumstances that when the fight was over, some British critics declared that if every position had been defended with such skill and determination the insurrection would have lasted three times as long. It was in this area that the outstanding action of the week, Mount Street Bridge, was fought, that more than half the British casualties were incurred, and that de Valera first gripped the imagination of Ireland.

Shortly before noon, Westland Row Station was seized by some dozen men of B. Company who cleared the station, seized signal boxes, built barricades, cut telephone wires, and placed guards at the main gate. Other sections occupied the railway line towards Merrion at various points from Westland Row onwards. Simon Donnelly and thirty-four men of C. Company marched off from Earlsfort Terrace where Captain Joseph O'Connor also mobilised A. Company which later occupied positions and trenches along the railway, took over the railway works and sheds, as well as several posts in Grand Canal Street, South Lotts Road, and elsewhere.

Simon Donnelly and his men stopped at Upper Mount Street while Lieutenant Michael Malone, George Reynolds, and a dozen

187

men, cycled along the canal and halted at Mount Street Bridge. There Reynolds and four men took over Clanwilliam House which lay on the city side, and dominated the bridge, three more Volunteers occupied St. Stephen's Parochial Hall, on the other side of the bridge, three Volunteers the schools on the opposite side of Northumberland Road, and Malone and three Volunteers No. 25 Northumberland Road. Simon Donnelly and the rest of C. Company then marched to Boland's Bakery in Grand Canal Street and entered it. The staff at first thought they were victims of a misguided sense of humour until a display of guns and some eloquence undeceived them, and there was a rapid clearance. De Valera, Captain Joseph O'Connor and other officers of the battalion, were present while the occupation was completed, and little more than 100 men posted themselves across the main route of the inevitable British invasion from Dun Laoghaire.

Boland's Mills, on the canal basin, were held by a small force, and the real headquarters were set up in the bakery in Grand Canal Street, which was defended by a force of some twenty Volunteers divided into security posts, inside and out. The bakery wall in the rear was breached and a gangway made to the railway line fifteen feet above the building's level. Trenches were dug across the line, at points which covered Westland Row Station and Lansdowne Road. Snipers occupied several of the bridges, and, at Haddington Road Bridge in particular, made themselves a menace to the garrison of Beggars' Bush Barracks from the first, and took their own part in the fighting around Northumberland Road during the fight for the approaches to the city. Many positions were taken over temporarily, and rumours spread of the strength of de Valera's forces. The gas works on the city side of the canal and a disused distillery near by, Guinness's granary were among the buildings which surrounded the low flat sheds of the bakery, and of which a partial or pretended temporary occupation was made. The seizure of the gas works lasted long enough to effect the dismantlement of essential parts of the plant in order to confuse British military movements by plunging a large part of the city into darkness.

George A. Lyon's tribute to de Valera as a leader sums up the strategy which was employed and the spirit in which the fight in the Ringsend-Boland's Mills area was waged: " De Valera certainly knew every inch of the area under his command with mathematical accuracy. He knew to a nicety the altitude of any building one could mention to him, the positions it governed and the possibilities it afforded for successful occupation. He may have appeared weak on the point of organising faculty and to lack a sense of control over his own spirits, but it must be considered that he was a lone figure in a position of intense responsibility. . . . It was characteristic of de Valera to attempt the impossible and he made no reduction in the scale of his operations notwithstanding the fact that less than one-fifth of the men allotted to his command had responded to the mobilisation order. He might have sat down in Boland's and waited to be dug out of it, but that was not his way."

Certainly it was not de Valera's way. His restless movement from place to place, from the bakery to the railway line, his plans for sorties, his commands and countermands, an occasional oath, and many pot shots at snipers with his double-barrelled sporting rifle, his refusal to rest, his ruses—all build up the picture and confirm this judgment. Like Connolly and Ashe, de Valera is depicted as a scorner of danger almost to recklessness, much to the concern of his officers who knew that with his death the defence would collapse, so deeply had his personality won the confidence of his men as a leader capable of the unexpected stroke that would extricate them from the gravest strait.

That the Boland's Mills garrison was in the gravest strait slowly impressed itself on the defenders in spite of the rumours that had spread of 30,000 Germans marching down the Naas Road, 30,000 Germans landing in Kerry, thousands of Germans swarming ashore at Howth, thousands of Clan na Gael men on the seas from America. Simon Donnelly noted these and some contrary ones, and issued an order that all strangers who came along with information and tall stories were to be stopped from communicating with the Volunteers but should give the tale to the section commander in charge of the post. There was much individual initiative and isolation in this battle in Boland's Mills area.

The guns of the *Helga*, which sent one shell crashing into the bakery itself, and a naval gun mounted on a lorry on the canal banks near Mount Street Bridge, were deflected from more damaging activity by a green flag with harp, hoisted proudly over the disused distillery, and a courageous semaphore signaller on the roof who sent out many orders not to fire on aeroplanes, and other fictitious messages. The building was a very high one, with a lofty tower. De Valera feared that the British might occupy it, which would have meant they dominated the Volunteer positions. He caused rumours to spread that it was strongly held by the Volunteers and took particular care to obtain the green flag and harp which was more familiar to the British as an Irish emblem than the Tricolour. The Volunteers who ascended the tower were hotly peppered with rifle and machine-gun fire as the flag was erected. Then the shells crashed into the building and played round the tower and shook the flag staff but did not dislodge it. The tower and building were shattered, and there was a great din of gun-fire and crashing masonry, while the nerves of the Volunteers inside were so badly shaken that when they came out their hearing was temporarily gone. They looked blankly at Donnelly and George A. Lyons, and could not hear what they said, nor understand that there was no need to remain at all after the first shell had been drawn. The guns hammered away at the distillery for some time and then turned on Boland's Mills and sent a few shells through the walls without doing very much real damage.

This was on Thursday, while the Mount Street Bridge area fighting was at its height, and the British forces had already entered the city by several routes, although their main body had halted at Ballsbridge and their advance section of 800 men were still held at Mount Street Bridge—the story of which is told in the next chapter.

Throughout the week the Boland's Mills garrison were severely sniped by the British who were gradually closing in on them. The Volunteer snipers kept up a constant fire from Haddington Road Bridge on Beggars' Bush barracks, and there had been hand-to-hand fighting and a British party which invaded the railway line after creeping out of the rear gate of the barracks was routed and driven back with several casualties by Captain Joseph O'Connor, Simon Donnolly, Seán Guilfoyle and seven Volunteers who surprised them near Bath Avenue and attacked with grim determination. The first Volunteer section was supported by a second party of Volunteers who were concealed near Shelbourne Road. Two British N.C.O.s were killed and several Volunteers wounded in this fight.

With the fall of the Mount Street Bridge positions the position in Boland's Bakery grew steadily worse. De Valera found that the British had secured sniping posts in Mount Street and Volunteer

snipers who ventured to establish posts in Grand Canal and
Clarence Streets were driven back with casualties by a terrific out-
burst of machine-guns and rifles from many of the lower Mount
Street back windows.   A courier was sent to MacDonagh in
Jacobs', as an attack from Westland Row was expected from the
British troops who had reached Lincoln Place through Baggot
Street and Kildare Street while their main body had been held up
on the main Dun Laoghaire-Dublin road. MacDonagh, as related
before, sent out the party which diverted the attention of the British
to the danger of an attack to their rear, and the expected frontal
attack on Boland's Mills and Bakery never came. De Valera was
not at all dispirited, but on this most critical day planned several
sorties, and flew his flag of green over the distillery and invited
the dramatic but harmless shelling of the positions he had decided
had better be shelled rather than his real headquarters.

The strain on the small and scattered garrison, however, hourly
increased. Nightly they could see the glare of the huge fires in the
city and the noise of the distant fighting, the snipers' battles over
the O'Connell Street roofs, the rattling machine-guns, the crash of
buildings falling afar off, and the shells bursting.   George A.
Lyons noticed one Volunteer growing more and more strange as
they kept guard at one of the bakery gates. When Lyons advised
him to rest he refused and talked louder and louder although a
night attack was expected and silence had been ordered. Lyons
was ordered elsewhere soon after, and went away after taking leave
of his friend Peadar Macken who was in charge. Macken several
times appealed to the Volunteer with the strangely bright eyes and
loud rambling tongue to go away and sleep. The man suddenly
ran amok, shot Macken through the heart, and attacked a sentry
who shot him dead.

De Valera late on Friday decided to evacuate the bakery and
Simon Donnelly led the men up on to the railway line where they
saw an amazing sea of flame over the city, the central positions in
O'Connell Street on fire. The sight, especially after the depressing
experiences of the day, and the evacuation of their own position
unnerved some of the Volunteers. One man's nerves gave way
completely and he fired wildly around him with a small revolver,
slightly wounding a man near him. Simon Donnelly, much to
his regret, but with a humane presence of mind, saved the over-
wrought man's life by promptly knocking him down with the

butt of a revolver. An order came soon after from de Valera to reoccupy the bakery which was held till the surrender.[1]

The most remarkable struggle in the Boland's Mills area remains to be told.

---

[1] The story of Boland's Mills area has been told in great detail by George A. Lyons in *An t-Oglách,* April 10-24, 1926; Michael J. Lennon, *Banba,* " A Retrospect," April, 1922, and " Easter Week Diary," *Irish Times,* March 29—April 3, 1948; Simon Donnelly, " With the 3rd Battalion," *Poblacht na hEireann,* April 20, 1922, and a lecture, " Mount Street Bridge "; *Catholic Bulletin,* October, 1917.

CHAPTER XIV

ON Wednesday, April 26, the British reinforcements landed at Kingstown (Dun Laoghaire) and began to march on Dublin in three separate columns. The mobilisation of the Volunteers at Dun Laoghaire and at Blackrock had been a complete failure, and therefore no opposition or even hint of any hostility, not even a solitary rifle crack disturbed the British forces. Indeed the first demonstration of any feeling towards them was a friendly one, cheers and even bouquets of flowers greeted the soldiers. One column marched into Dublin along the Stillorgan route and reached the Royal Hospital without incident, the second marched along the main Dublin road via Ballsbridge and proceeded by Pembroke Road over Baggot Street Bridge, and then reached Trinity College through Kildare Street and Lincoln Place, the third marched straight along the main route, passed Ballsbridge, and came under the fire of the Volunteer outposts. The second column in fact remained at Ballsbridge and took the Pembroke Road-Baggot Street route after the third column had been attacked, and the British realised the dangers entrenched at Northumberland Road, Haddington Road, and Mount Street Bridge—the only one of the city bridges held by the Volunteers, Baggot Street, Charlemont Street, and Leeson Street bridges being free.

De Valera's forces were engaged in an audacious bluff to mask their small numbers. They extended their outposts along Northumberland, Lansdowne and Shelbourne Roads, often occupying positions with a token force, and spreading rumours of their great strength in the hope that the enemy would be deceived. There was, however, also something more than bluff in reserve. On Easter Monday, Lieutenant Michael Malone, de Valera's aide-de-camp, led a party of 14 men, which included some cyclists, along the canal to Mount Street Bridge. He sent George Reynolds and four men to Clanwilliam House which overlooked the bridge on the city side, three Volunteers into the Parochial Hall across the bridge, three others into the schools on the opposite side of Northumberland Road, while Malone himself and three others took over the corner house, No. 25 Northumberland Road. Early on Tuesday Malone rearranged his forces. He sent home two Volunteers on account of their age, merely telling them to leave their rifles behind as he fully realised that few, if any man of these posts could survive. James Grace and Malone then remained to defend the position. On Monday evening they and Volunteer snipers on Haddington Road railway bridge fired on a body of uniformed men marching towards Beggars' Bush Barracks, killed five and wounded seven. This was the " G.R.s," or the 1st Dublin Battalion Associated Volunteer Corps, a body of professional men over military age, who were returning from manœuvres at Ticknock among the Dublin hills. They carried rifles but no ammunition. They rushed in panic to Beggars' Bush Barracks a short distance away, and assisted the British garrison there, which was receiving considerable attention from the Volunteer snipers, in the defence until the Rising was over. The Volunteers had no means of knowing that the Veterans' Corps were really unarmed. The attack, however, and the constant sniping of Beggars' Bush Barracks disposes of the charge that the later attacks from the Volunteer posts on British troops were unexpected and cowardly ambushes.

At nine o'clock on Wednesday morning information reached the Volunteer officers in the 3rd Battalion area that there were very large-scale landings of British troops at Kingstown (Dun Laoghaire) with war equipment. This was confirmed soon afterwards when a Volunteer scout who had been sent out towards the coast to check the information returned with the news that thousands of troops had been disembarked, and were marching towards Dublin, and had already passed Williamstown.

Some 2,000 Sherwood Foresters were seen advancing along the Blackrock Road. The officers in charge frequently consulted maps and distrusted and disregarded both the warnings of trouble ahead and the information given to them by the generally friendly spectators. The march forward was slow and the column often halted and rested. Eight hundred troops marched ahead with the main body some distance behind. At Ballsbridge the majority of the Sherwood Foresters encamped. A second section halted near the junction of Lansdowne and Pembroke Roads, lying on the ground, smoking, eating fruit and chatting with civilians who gathered round. Some Volunteer snipers fired several volleys of revolver shots in their direction, threw them into panic and withdrew. The soldiers suspected that Carrisbrooke House near-by was a Volunteer outpost and fired on it. The Volunteers had indeed held it on Monday but withdrew after an hour— " immediately they found there was no back lane ", according to the hostile contemporary report in the *Irish Times*. Carrisbrooke House showed marks of British rifle fire on its brickwork and window-panes, several local residents were detained but soon released, and the scattered soldiers reassembled. In the meantime the advancing 800 Sherwood Foresters had encountered something more serious than puckish snipers, and the most famous struggle of the whole insurrection had begun just after noon.

The Sherwood Foresters trudged with due precautions along Northumberland Road, a line of troops in Indian file flanked both footpaths at six foot intervals followed by soldiers four deep who periodically dropped flat on footpaths and roadway, advanced with bayonets fixed, observing the houses closely as they passed, entering gardens and examining all walls, bushes and available cover.

The Volunteer posts in the meantime had been overhauled and the entire strength of the garrisons at 25 Northumberland Road, Clanwilliam House and the Parochial Hall numbered thirteen men. The three Volunteers in the schools had been withdrawn to Boland's Bakery. Michael Malone and James Grace held No. 25, which they had barricaded as strongly as they could although Malone scrupulously kept his over-chivalrous promise to the occupants before they left that the house should be unharmed to the extent of not breaking loopholes in the walls and hesitating to use the furniture ruthlessly for barricades. (This, observed George A. Lyons subsequently, was all too scrupulous a practice among too many of the Volunteers, the very ghost of William Smith O'Brien, " gentlemanly revolutionist of Ballingary," flaunting itself abroad too conspicuously during the entire week. Yet this was the general spirit. " It is a pity," said some of the G.P.O. garrison, tunnelling for their lives in Moore Street, " that we have to break up the poor people's homes. They won't thank us for that.") Four men held the Parochial Hall: Patrick J. Doyle, who was in charge; Joseph Clarke, William Christian, and a Volunteer named McGrath. This position was the most exposed of all, and the defenders were practically face to face with the British troops behind barricades separated from the many assaults by a few yards only. Clanwilliam House had seven Volunteers to defend it. One Volunteer had returned to Boland's Bakery for reinforcements, he was sent away on another mission, and four men with food and supplies sent in his place. The names of these men who had eventually to bear the full weight of an attack from hundreds of British troops were: George Reynolds, Patrick Doyle, Richard Murphy, the brothers, Tom and James Walsh, James Doyle and William Ronan.

As the head of the British column passed No. 25 fire was opened on the advance guard. In the panic the soldiers scattered, and believing that the attack came only from No. 25, owing to the heavy volleys which Malone and Grace concentrated on them, very rapid fire with a high-power automatic Mauser pistol and Lee-Enfield rifles, as soon as the ranks were reformed, attempted to rush the house at the point of the bayonet. Officers waved their swords. Riflemen knelt in the middle of the roadway and poured a quick fusillade into all the windows of the house. There were several desperate charges, and the soldiers washed over the front steps, firing wildly, and almost at once hurling grenades into the house while another party rushed to the rear along a lane at the back. British snipers ascended the belfry of Haddington Road Church, which overlooked both Malone's post and Clanwilliam House, and sheltered behind stonework and a leaden trapdoor, kept up a dangerous and persistent attack on both positions. Malone and Grace shot down the soldiers as they hammered on the door with the butts of their rifles. The Clanwilliam House garrison joined in the fight almost as soon as the first volley was fired, and this intervention exposed the British to a devastating cross-fire before they realised the presence of Reynolds and his men in the first-floor windows of their fort. Moreover, Malone and Grace were proving such formidable marksmen that the British could not pass, or determined not to pass, No. 25 until it was taken once and for all. This problem was to occupy them for some five hours, and long before that Clanwilliam House was very much an objective. The ordeal of Malone and Grace was a terrible one. They were bombed heavily with grenades, the snipers on Haddington Road Church swept the stairways, every window in the house was riddled with volleys, side, front and rear. Bomb after bomb exploded in the basement, which was also swept by rifle fire. The two men were dazed by the constant explosions and reports of rifles. They found very little cover. They were driven from the basement. They remained in the hall and repelled one attack, when the soldiers entered the parlour on the first floor after a shower of grenades, by firing through the locked door. A loud explosion in one of the back rooms followed a bout of bomb-throwing in the rear: 500 rounds of "Howth" rifle and revolver cartridges lying on a bed blew up.

Hour after hour passed and amid the din of bomb, rifle, and finally the rattle of machine-guns playing away towards Mount Street Bridge, where the attack on Clanwilliam House was in full progress, with minor waves of soldiers washing against No. 25, the main body rushed past towards the bridge, cheering loudly, led by their officers flourishing swords. And still Malone and Grace held out by some marvel amid the hellish uproar, the bursting bombs, and the volleys which had turned the post into a wreckage of wood, glass and riddled doors. They decided they would wait and fight it out on the stair-head with rifle and bayonet. The British burst in at last, screened by preparatory bombing of front and rear. The two defenders were separated in this rush: the invaders had broken in on the middle floor. Malone was on the stairs above it, Grace in the kitchen, in the darkness, at that time. The kitchen door was heavily barricaded with two iron garden seats and a table. Grace was then guarding the rear. Malone was keeping what watch he could in the confusion from upstairs. The plan was that they were to unite at the stair-head as soon as the windows and back door were forced. The sudden entry of the soldiers destroyed this plan. Even as Malone called out, "I am coming down," the stairs were swept by a second volley, and he fell dead.[1]

Grace escaped although the soldiers closely searched the house. They visited every room except the kitchen. A slight noise drew a further volley into the basement through a bomb hole in the ceiling. Grace waited for hours in the dark with a revolver and

---

[1] The sources on which this chapter are based are: the *Catholic Bulletin*, October, 1917; November, 1917; December, 1917; the published accounts by George A. Lyons, *An t-Oglách*, April 10-24, 1926; "Mount Street Bridge," "With the Third Battalion," Simon Donnelly, *Poblacht na h-Eireann*, April 20, 1922; personal statement by Joseph Clarke to the writer.

his four last cartridges. The soldiers never came, perhaps because they thought that nothing could remain alive after the heavy bombing of the lower part of the house. Grace finally removed the kitchen barricade, slipped into the garden, and locked himself into a tool shed. He heard soldiers in the garden listening for sounds inside the house, grunting, " they must all be finished now," and going away. He thought over his long watch with Malone on Easter Monday night when the two men by turns listened to the heavy firing from Portobello area and saw the flashes of snipers away over in Fairview, and military searchlights sweeping the skies. Even as he waited with his revolver ready, he could hear heavy firing still close at hand. At last a stillness. He crept out into Percy Lane at the back, which led towards the canal. He had a crazy idea that he might swim across and enter the city As he crossed the wall he saw sentries, and slipped back into the garden. He crossed the wall and hid in a garden on the other side of the lane. He saw the sky red with a great blaze towards Mount Street. Grace was fired on by sentries the following night, and escaped to a wooden shed in another garden. Eventually, a rounding-up party captured him, and he was taken to the comparative peace of an English internment camp.

The red glare Grace saw in the sky on Wednesday night was the funeral pyre of Reynolds and two of his comrades in the ruins of Clanwilliam House.

The struggle for that post had been even more severe than the struggle for No. 25, and Mount Street Bridge and the neighbourhood were littered with hundreds of dead and dying troops. For hours the defenders of Clanwilliam House had beaten back wave after wave of British troops. As Reynolds and his comrades watched this advance it reminded them of some great khaki serpent creeping slowly and inevitably towards them, hundreds of khaki uniforms, men on all-fours crawling pertinaciously along the street, the gutters, snatching whatever slight cover was to be found. Gradually there was a new horror to this advance, the living avoiding the dead-still khaki forms and moving on themselves to death. The men in the Parochial Hall were in the midst of this slow, crawling, roaring, cursing, death-dealing advance, yet as the Hall was set back from the footpath in a deep recess they had not the wide view that Reynolds and his men had from the upper and middle windows of their post. The four men in the Hall were in the thick of the fight, firing steadily into the soldiers as party after party dashed, crawled, and rushed frantically on to the bridge. The steady fire of the men in the windows halted every attempt, and whatever soldiers actually crossed were shot down by the Clanwilliam garrison's revolvers discharged on their heads.

Only very gradually the British strength told against the seven unshaken men. Opposite Clanwilliam House, across the canal, the British seized every point of vantage, and from the windows of many houses there poured out a deadly raking fire which turned the interior of Clanwilliam House into a ruin of shattered ceilings, burst water pipes, falling masonry, and fires which broke out again and again. Machine-guns rattled against the walls, and from the tower of Haddington Road Church speeded many a shot through the picturesque stone tracery dead on that menacing target which for hours defied the onslaught. Hour after hour went by with the storm of noise, and death and wounds, and cheering British troops who could not pass the bridge.

The men in the Parochial Hall held out until nearly six o'clock. They could see the faces of their foes as they fired revolver and rifle across the barricades. Bomb after bomb was thrown against them. Like Malone and Grace, like the Clanwilliam House garrison, too, the Parochial Hall had been isolated since early on Tuesday. No message and no aid reached them from Boland's Bakery. The weak garrison in this area had now dissolved into so many independent posts, each on its own, each fighting for its life. At one stage, however, the Volunteer snipers on the railway line below Beggars' Bush Barracks, on the wall of Robert's Yard in the rear of Clanwilliam House, and in the water tanks of the Dublin and South Eastern Railway's locomotive works near Boland's Mills made themselves very much felt during the attack on No. 25 and on Clanwilliam House—especially just after the first shots at noon, and, later, when there was a flank movement against Clanwilliam House from both sides of the canal bank on the east.

The men in the Parochial Hall fired their last shot, and retreated through the back to Percy Place. Their retreat was intercepted by British troops, who, by that time, 6 p.m., had completely occupied Percy Place on the country side of the canal and Warrington Place on the city side, from which they advanced constantly, a second crawling khaki serpent intent, in spite of many a wound, on strangling the life out of the seven intrepid marksmen who still defied machine-gun, flank attack, bursting grenades, and the perpetual rushes which came nearer and nearer.

The captured men from the Parochial Hall met with a very abrupt reception. Joseph Clarke was seized and searched by several soldiers. A revolver was found in one of his pockets. He was placed against a door in Percy Place, with his hands above his head. A soldier fired at him with his own revolver. He gave a slight start as the bullet struck the door just above him. The door was thrown open almost immediately, and a doctor in a white coat came out and cursed the soldiers roundly. A yard behind was full of wounded British soldiers. The shot had missed the doctor by a fraction, and the wounded man he was treating. The doctor protested angrily when he learned the truth. Joseph Clarke was led away, his hands tied behind his back with a rifle pull-through, and there was no further attempt on his life.

Doctors and spectators, indeed, throughout the fight played a mediating or rather a merciful part, and in this they were seconded by George Reynolds and his men. After the first few bloody charges of British troops the bridge was strewn with soldiers, victims of bungled orders, stupidly sacrificed, groaning in agony, fumbling with water bottles, seeking cover behind the dead, suffering from ghastly injuries at so close a range, torn bodies, shattered skulls, broiling in a burning haze. For the most part the British troops were as new to the wars as the Volunteers, and Maxwell noted in his first dispatch that at Mount Street "the battalions charging in successive waves, carried all before them, but, I regret to say, suffered severe casualties in doing so. Four officers were killed, fourteen wounded, and, of other ranks, 216 were killed and wounded. The steadiness shown by these two battalions is deserving of special mention, as I understand the majority of the men have less than three months' service."

Maxwell's dispatches were invariably starred with libels against the Volunteers and a petty and vindictive spirit. He accused the insurgents, in general, of arming the looters and the Mount Street Bridge fighters of firing on the Fire Brigade and ambulances as well as on the nurses, ambulance men, and doctors at Mount Street. The Volunteers withheld their fire to allow the doctors and nurses to treat the wounded on the bridge, and even when the attack was resumed, while the wounded were being treated, took every precaution to avoid hitting the ambulance men and the nurses.

Reynolds, who exposed himself fearlessly to direct the fire of the Volunteers in the very thick of flying bullets, issued order after order to the marksmen to avoid the doctors, stretcher bearers and nurses.[2] In spite of Red Cross heroism, the British wounded, in some cases, lay untended for many hours.

Keener and more deadly grew the British marksmanship. James Doyle's rifle was shot out of his hands. Richard Murphy was shot dead as he fired from the middle windows, partially reclining on an armchair. Tom Walsh and his brother were fighting beside him, firing away from the centre windows of the drawing-room with Howth Mausers. Showers of bullets poured through the windows. Some of them were incendiary ones which caused small fires that had to be extinguished. One of the Volunteers passed a soda siphon to quench one of these fires; it was shattered in his hands as he held it. Patrick Doyle, at another window, suddenly stopped firing and spoke no more. The Walshs were astonished as Doyle had kept shouting encouraging remarks above the awful uproar. They spoke to him, and when he did not answer shook him gently. He dropped to the floor, dead. Overhead, James Doyle and Ronan kept up their fire hour by hour, in separate rooms. Smoke rolls through the house. The roof catches fire. At last ammunition gives out. Reynolds some time before had extinguished a fire in one of the upper rooms where he had stored the valuables of the family which had left Clanwilliam House after the Volunteers commandeered it. He then handed Doyle and Ronan their last ten rounds, and assured them that soon there would be reinforcements with plenty of ammunition. Whether he really believed this is very doubtful as Clanwilliam House had been isolated from the Third Battalion H.Q. from the start of the fight.

The next time they saw Reynolds he was lying stretched dead on a landing. The Walshs called them as he fell. Reynolds had issued orders for a retreat as ammunition was gone, and the British were already bombing the lower part of the house. The roof was one crackling, howling, lurid blaze. The stairs were unsafe. Reynolds had been killed as he took a last look at the bridge he and

---

[2] Dr. C. M. O'Brien, who was present throughout the fight at Mount Street, flatly contradicted Maxwell's charge in a letter to the Press, adding a tribute to the Volunteers' strict observance " of the laws of open battle." See also *Irish Life*, May 26, 1916, pp. 243-4, " Red Cross Work and Stretcher-Bearing During Irish Republic," J. Crampton Walker.

his men had held against Maxwell's " successive waves " for nine hours.

The bombing of the house drove the survivors, William Ronan, James Doyle, Thomas and James Walsh, to the basement. They discovered that their barricading of the rear had been too thoroughly done. Reynolds' plans for retreat had included a way through the roof which was then impossible through the leaping flames. Explosions were shaking the building and they could hear the British advancing with loud cheers. The atmosphere was stifling and emetic with fumes from the explosives. They dashed into a back room, and broke through a small barred window in the back door into the garden. They crossed wall after wall until they reached safety.

The British troops did not cross Mount Street Bridge that night, Maxwell's dispatch explained, " as, in view of the opposition met with, it was not considered advisable to push on to Trinity College that night, so, at 11 p.m., the 5th South Staffordshire Regiment, from the 176th Infantry Brigade, reinforced this column and, by occupying the positions gained, allowed the two battalions of Sherwood Foresters to be concentrated at Ballsbridge."

Volunteer snipers were still at work near Mount Street Bridge late that evening. The only news that reached the Third Battalion headquarters of the greatest fight of Easter Week was the flames roaring high above Clanwilliam House.

CHAPTER XV

WHEN Edward Daly mobilised the First Battalion on Easter Monday at Colmcille Hall, Blackhall Place, he found, as all the other Volunteer leaders had found elsewhere, that his ranks were seriously depleted. Some estimates of his strength that morning are as high as three hundred men, others as low as one hundred and fifty. Piaras Beaslai, his Vice-Commandant, declares that at first less than a third of the men turned up at Blackhall Place, although many, assisted by members from other units, appeared before the fighting was over, while those who were unable to join the Four Courts garrison joined up at other positions. The first Battalion had been assigned a line running from the Mendicity Institution on the south bank of the Liffey, through the Four Courts on the north bank to Cabra where it was to contact Thomas Ashe and his Fifth Battalion. The North Dublin Union was to be used as the headquarters and Broadstone railway terminus occupied. These plans could not be fully carried out, yet the fighting in the Four Courts-Church Street area was so fierce, sustained, and determined that it prolonged the life of the insurrection, demoralised the British troops sent to break it, and made Maxwell's efforts to strangle the Rising in his cordons a bloody and costly venture.

The Volunteers who assembled in the Colmcille Hall thought, in many cases, that the special mobilisation was nothing more than an ordinary route march; others had their doubts, some knew. At a quarter to twelve, Edward Daly called them to attention, and watched them in silence for some seconds. Long afterwards they remembered him as he stood then, a slight spare figure in his grey-green uniform, dark eyes alight in the pallor of his thin face, the glint on the metal badge of his military cap, his fingers tapping the gun at his side. When he spoke at last, in a level tone which rose quickly to a shout, the words were almost prosaic, yet they shook all who listened, some with alarm, a few with anger, the majority to an enthusiastic disobedience, for they cheered him: " Men of the First Battalion, I want you to listen to me for a few minutes, and no applause must follow my statement. To-day at noon, an Irish Republic will be declared, and the Flag of the Republic hoisted. I look to every man to do his duty, with courage and discipline. The Irish Volunteers are now the Irish Republican Army. Communications with our other posts in the city may be precarious, and in less than an hour we may be in action."

Some of the First Battalion were even then very much in action. Seán Heuston was already nearing the Mendicity Institution across the river. There was, moreover, a side show in progress in the Phœnix Park, where a party of Fianna Eireann and Volunteers had arrived outside the Magazine Fort kicking a football before them and romping gaily nearer and nearer the main gate of the Fort. They intended to get in and send the Fort, high explosives and all, sky-high as an unmistakable signal to all positions that the war had begun beyond all doubt.

The majority of the Volunteers who listened to Daly were in high spirits, some, staggered by the shock, asked to see a priest, one or two, with a brief protest that they had not joined the ranks for such adventures, went away. The call to arms had been sudden, and the action that Daly spoke of came almost at once. The various units marched off from the hall and took up positions in Church Street area where barricades were thrown up at North Dublin Union and Constitution Hill, Mary's Lane, North King Street, and Brunswick Street. Houses were also taken over in these districts. It was in North King Street that the hottest fighting of the closing days of the Rising took place.

The main party of Volunteers which took over the Four Courts was led by Joseph McGuinness. After an attempt to enter by blowing the lock of a side door, the party marched round Chancery Place, overcame the protests of the policeman on duty at the gate, and swept through the building, which was rapidly barricaded, and snipers posted at strategic points. As a barricade was being completed at the end of Church Street, a troop of Lancers, escorting an ammunition waggon, passed along the quays towards Phœnix Park. The Volunteers at the barricade, believing the Lancers were coming to attack them, opened fire, killed one Lancer, and dispersed the troops in a panic. Some of the Lancers dashed up Church Street firing volleys, and, in an exchange of shots, another Lancer was killed. The Lancers then retreated to a building in Charles

Street, to the east of the Fourt Courts, where they were sealed in by Volunteer snipers, after an unsuccessful attempt to storm the position, and remained there until the fight was nearly over.

The Volunteer and Fianna raiders in Phœnix Park had, in the meantime, retreated to the Four Courts after a partially successful attack on the Magazine Fort. They kicked the football through the gate and suddenly overpowered the sentry on duty outside. The raiders rushed in, and surprised the soldiers in the guardroom. A second sentry, who was parading the parapet of the fort, appeared sometime later, refused to surrender, and raised his rifle to fire on the raiders. There was a sharp tussle, and an exchange of shots, in which he was badly wounded, and disarmed. He died of his wounds later; according to one account because his companions either did not, or could not, bandage his severe leg wound.

The Fianna members of the party, P. Daly, L. Marie, Patrick and Garry Holohan, Eamonn Martin, and Barney Mellows, had attended a course of instruction under Thomas MacDonagh for some weeks before in the Father Mathew Park, Fairview, in preparation for the raid; they had been told how to handle explosives, given directions how and where to set to work in the fort, and MacDonagh impressed upon them particularly that the place must be taken, if possible, without loss of life,—a view of warfare which somewhat disconcerted some of his listeners.[1] The keys of the storerooms, they were told, were to be found hanging on a board in the guardroom. The key of the high explosives store, however, was not there. It was decided to lay fuses under ammunition boxes in the ammunition stores and other rooms, light them, collect all the arms and ammunition available, release the prisoners, and make off on bicycles and an outside car, waiting outside the Park. The rifles, bayonets, and ammunition were loaded on to the car, which was covered by a cyclist scout behind. As the party were leaving the Park, a lad named Playfair, the younger son of the Fort caretaker, was seen making for Island Bridge Barracks to raise the alarm. He was overtaken and shot fatally as he entered one of the officer's houses at the bend of Island Bridge Road. The cyclist who fired the shots had challenged him to halt and told him to turn back. " Poor lad," said one of the party later, " we had no choice, he had to pay the penalty."

---

[1] *Capuchin Annual*, 1942, " The Four Courts Area," P. Holohan.

The Fort Magazine was soon shaken by a number of small explosions and a serious fire broke out which lasted until Tuesday morning in spite of the efforts of the Fire Brigade and the military to master it. The high explosives store was saved from the flames, and so far the raid had missed its real aim of totally destroying the Fort. Yet, as the raiding party made their way towards the Four Courts, they saw that no starting signal was then needed for insurrection. Seán Heuston and his snipers were very busy. Soldiers were lying on the streets, and stretcher parties were carrying away the wounded. Soldiers were lined up on the parade ground of the Royal Barracks and ammunition was being served out. The party turned off the quays and soon were busy among the barricades in Red Cow Lane and North Brunswick Street, and ventures before the end as dangerous as their wild twenty minutes near the Fifteen Acres.

Daly's headquarters during most of the week were in the Father Mathew Hall, Church Street. He used the Four Courts as a headquarters only late on Friday night some short time before the surrender order reached him. From Tuesday until Daly was compelled to leave it, the Hall was also a first-aid post where the Cumann na mBan attended to the wounded. Monday and Tuesday were taken up for the most part in the seizure of houses and strengthening of barricades across the streets. These barricades were made from commandeered cars and vehicles of all descriptions, porter barrels, building materials, boilers, planks, and anything to hand from poles and barbed wire to furniture. In the middle of some of these barricades a way through was kept clear, though well guarded. A cab or motor car door in the centre of a barricade was found extremely useful. The Church Street area fighting centred, in general, round these barricades. Early on Monday railway bridges and railway lines were attacked by small parties. On Tuesday positions on the North Circular Road and Cabra were attacked by British soldiers, backed by field guns. The houses were cleared and barricades blown away. Some Volunteers were captured but the majority escaped.

On Tuesday evening a small party from the Four Courts area, under Denis O'Callaghan, including Eamonn Martin and Garry Holahan, who had been busy since the Park Magazine raid at the Church Street barricades, marched off towards Broadstone Station. It had been intended to attack this station earlier, and occupy it.

The incomplete mobilisation postponed any effective move to take and hold Broadstone. As soon as the garrison had been increased somewhat by the Volunteers who had arrived that evening the attempt was made. It was not known that the British had already taken the station over, and placed a strong force there. While the shelling of the North Circular Road barricades was in progress, the British established communication with the Broadstone Station, and dispatched a company of Dublin Fusiliers there. They entered unknown to the Volunteer scouts and established a strong position. It was dusk as the Volunteers arrived at Constitution Hill, and went towards the station. They noticed some uniformed men near the gate, and thought that other Volunteers must have anticipated them. As Eamonn Martin, who was near the front, advanced into the open, rifle and machine-gun fire was opened on the Volunteers. Eamonn Martin was hit by a rifle bullet which pierced one of his lungs. He insisted on returning to Daly to report. Daly at once sent him to hospital, and orders to the party to fall back on North Brunswick Street. They established sniping posts there, and kept up continuous fire on Broadstone Station for the rest of the day.

Throughout these exciting incidents, Seán Heuston and the Mendicity garrison and the O'Connell Street fighting, with the sounds of the South Dublin Union fray, added to the turmoil outside the Four Courts and the network of Daly's barricades. His men moved round freely, and gradually the population, at first frightened, suspicious and hostile, became friendly. Daly and his officers issued many warnings of danger to the people and Volunteers helped those who had to evacuate their possessions to store them in safety. A bakery was still at work within the Volunteer cordon, and food queues were organised and Dubliners from other districts were admitted through the barricades and allowed to take away two loaves each. Shops still functioned and looters were unknown. The Bridewell, beside the Four Courts, was taken over, and some twenty policemen found hiding in the cellars placed in the cells until Daly came on the scene, set them free, and filled the cells with his R.I.C. and military prisoners.

On Wednesday, Linenhall Barracks, near the Volunteer posts in Lisburn Street, was still held by some forty unarmed members of the Army Pay Corps. A small Volunteer party called on them to surrender, and when they refused blew up one of the walls, and smashed down the main door with sledge-hammers. The soldiers then surrendered and were made prisoners. A large quantity of military stores were taken from the barracks which was fired some hours later to prevent its reoccupation by the British forces which were pressing forward. The barracks was burned down but the fire spread to other premises, and blazed until Friday night, in spite of efforts by the Volunteers to confine it. All the adjoining houses were burned down, including a druggists', where barrels of oil were hurled into the air to explode with dark and foul-smelling clouds of smoke. There was an exodus from the North King Street tenements but many remained to face a new horror which crept nearer and nearer as the barricade fighting there became fiercer and the British and the Volunteers fought stubbornly from house to house and from barricade to barricade.

Friday was a day of bloody and savage terror in the Church Street and North King Street areas. Sir John Maxwell arrived in the early hours of that April 28. His official biographer, Sir George Arthur, reveals that Lord Kitchener, having experienced Maxwell's merits in dealing with Egypt " in the hour of danger," was certain that Maxwell's Scottish blood and " strong common sense flavoured with an imperturbable good humour marked him out as the man to deal promptly with Ireland." [2] (G. K. Chesterton thought that Maxwell's actions in Ireland were, " in a strictly serious sense," those of " a bloody fool," while Lloyd George dubbed him not only a fool but a brute.) So Maxwell, with full powers from the British Cabinet to act as he thought fit, duly landed at the North Wall, Dublin, to tackle promptly " the occasion fraught with danger to Ireland herself, and, unless quickly checked, not unlikely to have sinister effects on the conduct of the war." His imperturbability was shaken somewhat by his affectionate concern for his wife, who was on the point of a serious operation, although this did not in any way arrest his own imminent exploits in the way of political surgery. He showed his insight and sympathy with racial characteristics by ordering a pit to be dug for a hundred corpses, and imperturbable is the very word to describe the tone of the letter he wrote to Lady Maxwell as soon as he landed: " We arrived at 2 a.m. From the sea it looked as if the entire city of Dublin was in flames. These infernal rebels have got a lot of rifles with, appar-

---

[2] General Sir John Maxwell, Sir George Arthur (London, 1932). Chapters XXVII-XXIX deal with Maxwell in Ireland, and quote Maxwell's reports and letters to Asquith and Kitchener.

ently a fair supply of ammunition. Everything is hung up, no food or supplies of any sort can be got. It is not safe to walk into the town. Grafton Street and all the shop part have to be cleared of these infernal fellows who have occupied a certain number of houses and snipe anyone who passes." [3]

In a dispatch to Asquith later, Maxwell admitted that the Rising had grave potentialities within it: " There can be no doubt that had there been more capable leaders, and had the assistance from Germany been fulfilled, the insurrection would have been more formidable and on a larger scale." [4] Or, in plainer language, Maxwell knew very well that he was not grappling with a German attempt at invasion, and his own biographer echoes the belief that " Germany was not out to risk very much except a tolerably large sum of money on the Irish adventure, and was perhaps fairly well satisfied with the flutter she caused in the United Kingdom." [5] Maxwell's first report to Kitchener, however, betrayed panic and misunderstanding of the actual situation and the state of public opinion: " I do not like the temper of the people, all reports tend to show that a general rising could easily occur if outside support is forthcoming." [6] Of Casement, Maxwell wrote: " If his adventure had not misfired we would have been up against a much more serious affair." Maxwell—supported by heavy artillery and reinforcements hurried in by thousands—gave orders to close in on the O'Connell Street positions from east and west, to form a cordon along the Grand Canal, thus enclosing the southern part of the city, and encircling Dublin completely. His first proclamation read:

" Most vigorous measures will be taken by me to stop the loss of life and damage to property which certain misguided persons are causing by their armed resistance to the law. *If necessary, I shall not hesitate to destroy all buildings within any area occupied by rebels, and I warn all persons within the area specified below, and now surrounded by His Majesty's troops, forthwith to leave such areas* under the following conditions:—(a) Women and children may leave the area from any of the examining posts set up for the purpose, and will

---

[3] *Maxwell*, Arthur, p. 248.
[4] *Ibid.* p. 261.
[5] *Ibid.* p. 276.
[6] *Ibid.* p. 261.

O

be allowed to go away free; (b) men may leave by the same examining posts, and will be allowed to go away free, provided the examining officer is satisfied they have taken no part whatever in the present disturbance; (c) all other men who present themselves at the said examining posts must surrender unconditionally, together with any arms and ammunition in their possession." (*Weekly Irish Times*, April 29—May 13, 1916. No italics in the original.)

There is no mealy-mouthed ambiguity about this. Maxwell in his dispatches is quite clear and definite on the British use of heavy artillery. (Quoted in full, *Irish Times* 1916 Handbook, pp. 92-97.) All this proved the readiness to be prompt and assume responsibility which endeared him to Kitchener. His biographer for some reason attempts to minimise the British use of artillery by the evasive assurance that " artillery fire was only used to reduce the barricades or against a particular base known to be strongly held. . . . Except for the bombardment of Liberty Hall, the headquarters of the Citizen Army, guns were scarcely used, and only when sniping could not be mastered by machine guns or rifle fire was a round of shell called into requisition."[7] There is, perhaps, an uneasy consciousness in this quibbling that Connolly's argument that the use of artillery implied a dangerous admission of insurgent strength and status had some force.

One base strongly held, in which many barricades required to be reduced, and which certainly called for artillery, was the Church Street-Four Courts area. Armoured cars to hold parties of fourteen men were improvised from G.S.R. boilers mounted on lorries. Under the cover of these, which were hotly sniped by the Volunteers, the Lancers who had been held up in Charles Street were relieved, and artillery brought into position near the junction of Essex Quay, Wood Quay and Exchange Street, and four hits registered on the Four Courts on the eastern wing. Much heroism and daring were displayed by the Volunteers in a series of minor actions

---

[7] *Maxwell*, Arthur, p. 250. Bases " strongly held " included the G.P.O., the Four Courts, Boland's Mills, Mount Street Bridge, and the O'Connell Street areas. Liberty Hall was unoccupied although the hostile gunners saw snipers and machine-guns replying from every stone and window. The Rising in Cork was largely checkmated by the threat of heavy artillery, and although only one shell fell five miles away from the Galway positions, there was much pride expressed at the time in pro-British circles for the destroyer in Galway Bay. (See *Irish Press*, " Galway in Easter Week," April 5, 1934. Ailbhe O Monachain.)

at barricades and attacks on houses occupied by the advancing British.   One such house at Bridge Street corner was attacked single-handed by Peadar Clancy who directed it should be sniped heavily from all corners of the Four Courts.   He then walked across Church Street Bridge from his barricade with the utmost coolness, carrying tins of petrol while British snipers made the earth quiver under his feet.   He walked on until he reached the British post, hurled the petrol tins into the building, set it alight, and completely burned out the enemy.[8]

One storm centre of the street fighting was " Reilly's Fort," a public-house at the corner of Church Street and North King Street. The British took over Bolton Street Technical Schools, and, aided by the iron screen of cars, made a fierce attack on the Volunteer posts at Reilly's Fort, the Blanchardstown Mill premises and Monks's bakery.   This attack was made by the South Staffords who greatly outnumbered the Volunteers.   In their advance they tunnelled through houses or fired into them as they passed.   At some stages of the fight, the British and the Volunteers faced each other across one narrow street and fired on each other from barricaded windows.   As they pressed on the British also threw up barricades.   Some of the Volunteer barricades and posts unknown to the British lay outside their cordon.   Machine guns, bombs, and rifles hammering, bursting, and volleying became familiar sounds from daylight to dark.   Under the long strain the nerves of the British troops broke, they saw red, ran amok, and through panic and rage murdered civilians, dragging them from the houses, shooting them and throwing them into attics or burying them in cellars.

The length and fury of the North King Street battle is told in a statement, read at the inquest on some of the North King Street victims, from Lieutenant-Colonel H. Taylor, who commanded the South Staffords :

" The operations in the portion of King Street between Linenhall Street and Church Street were conducted under circumstances of the greatest difficulty and danger for the troops engaged, who were subjected to severe fire, not only from behind several rebel barricades which had been constructed across King Street, and other barricades in Church Street and side streets, but from prac-

---

[8] Peadar Clancy was afterwards Vice-Commandant of the Dublin Brigade.   He was murdered by Black and Tans in Dublin Castle in November, 1920.

tically every house in that portion of King Street and other buildings overlooking it.

"Strong evidence of these difficulties and dangers is afforded by the fact that it took the troops from 10 a.m. on the 28th of April until 2 p.m. on the 29th of April to force their way along King Street from Linenhall Street to Church Street, a distance of some 150 yards only, and that the casualties sustained by the regiment (the great majority of which occurred at this spot), numbered five officers (including two captains) wounded, fourteen N.C.O.'s and men killed, and twenty-eight wounded."

At least fifteen civilians were shot out of hand and bayoneted by the British soldiers during this fight. Maxwell admitted that . . . "possibly some unfortunate incidents, which we should regret now may have occurred . . . it is even possible that under the horrors of this attack some of them 'saw red,' that is the inevitable consequence of a rebellion of this kind. It was allowed to come into being among these people and could not be suppressed by kid-glove methods, where troops were so desperately opposed and attacked. . . ."

A quotation from the statement of an old woman, Mrs. Kate Kelly, who was an eye-witness of the shooting of three men taken out and shot from a house in North King Street will give the atmosphere of these "unfortunate incidents."[9]

"I used to do the housework for the Hickeys and was in their house in Easter Week. When the military came in on Friday evening after Mrs. Hickey went across the street, Mr. Hickey and Mr. Connolly were sitting together in the street outside. Mr. Connolly was a carrier and had come over about the moving of two mirrors from Hickeys. As the military rushed up about 6.45 on Friday night, Mr. Hickey and Mr. Connolly ran into the house for safety. Connolly, although he lived only a few doors away, was never able to get back home. Connolly remained in the house with us all Friday night and was killed with Mr. Hickey and his son Christy next morning.

"That night Mr. Hickey and his son were lying on a mattress stretched on the floor. I was in another room close-by. About 6 a.m. on Saturday morning I heard a noise of picking at the walls.

---

[9] *A Fragment of 1916 History*, John J. Reynolds, pp. 11-12. The Taylor and Maxwell quotations above are given in *Irish Times 1916 Handbook*, pp. 27-29.

I shouted to Mr. Hickey: 'Somebody is breaking into the house.'
He got up and soon after several soldiers dashed through a hole
which they made in the wall from next door. They had broken
into Mr. Hughes's four doors away and made holes in the wall all
the way up to us. The soldiers had drawn bayonets and crowbars
and picks. They rushed at us and shouted: 'Hands up.' We were
terribly frightened, and soon after an officer put his head through
the hole in the wall and shouted: 'How many prisoners have you
there?' One of the soldiers replied: 'Three males and one female.'
The officer then called out: 'Mind those prisoners till I
return.'

"We were kept prisoners for four hours while the officer was
away. Mr. Hickey and Mr. Connolly gave every explanation to
the soldiers, and said they were not in the Volunteers at all. But
it was no use. The officer returned. I remember well, the bell
was just ringing for 10 o'clock Mass. We were then led in through
the hole in the wall through the rooms of Mrs. Connolly next
door (who lodges over Mr. O'Toole, tobacconist). Passing through
her rooms the military, which consisted of an officer and four
soldiers, made us enter through another hole into the disused empty
house next door—No. 170—where the men were to be slaughtered
without mercy. The officer said: 'March on the female first.'
Mr. and Mrs. Carroll and her daughter were in their room, and
as they knew their neighbour Mr. Hickey well, they spoke to him.
Mr. Hickey as he passed, said to Mrs. Carroll: 'Isn't it too bad,
Mrs. Carroll?' 'Yes, indeed, Mr. Hickey,' she said, and the last
thing he said to her was: 'Very often the innocent suffer for the
guilty.' As I came to the hole in the wall I stumbled, was
frightened, and nearly fell down. Mr. Hickey stepped forward
and said: 'Well, Kate, I'll help you,' and assisted me through.
Then the child passed next [Christopher Hickey, aged 16] and
then Connolly. I fell down on the floor of the empty house when
I got inside and called out: 'I hope they are not going to kill us.'
The soldier replied with a laugh: 'You are a bally woman, you're
all right.' I was left lying in the front room and the men were
brought into the back. Both Mrs. Carroll and I heard poor Christy
pleading for his father's life: 'Oh, don't kill father.' The shots
then rang out, and I shouted: 'Oh, my God,' and overcome with
horror, I threw myself on my knees and began to pray."

Mrs. Hickey had crossed the street to a dairy on Friday night, and was warned as she passed a barricade on her return by the Volunteers to hurry home as the military were turning Capel Street corner and would arrive soon. The firing broke out while she went into a second shop, Corcoran's, just opposite her own house, and she stayed there as the fighting continued all night and she thought the place would be blown to pieces.

" Next morning I was terribly anxious to get home, and Mr. Corcoran at great risk, went to the door, and got an officer to pass me over the street. This was 10.30 on Saturday morning. There were five or six soldiers round our shop under cover and the firing was still going on. I said to one of the soldiers: 'I want to go into my home.' 'You can if you like,' he said, 'but there are a few dead bodies lying round over there, you can cross them if you wish.' I was too terrified to venture and returned to Mr. Corcoran's until Sunday morning. On Sunday morning I saw people passing, returning from Mass and from the Technical School where they had been held by the military. I asked everyone I knew: 'Where is Mr. Hickey?' I went about all day searching the hospitals, etc., until I was nearly worn out, little thinking that my husband and son were lying murdered in the house a few yards across the street.

" About 5 p.m. on Sunday evening I again went round to our house at the corner of Beresford Street. Two soldiers were on guard outside. I said: 'This is my house. I left my husband and child here. I must go in.' He replied: 'No, you can't, you had better see an officer.' I went round to the front hall door in King Street where I met Mrs. Carroll, the tenant in the next house. She said in a very solemn manner: "I want to speak to you.' She then stopped and just said: 'Oh, poor Christy.' I knew then they were gone. I then rushed upstairs, the two soldiers following me and shouting: 'You can't be here; come on.' When I rushed into the room, there I saw my poor angel, my darling son. He was lying on the ground, his face darkened, and his two hands raised above his head as if in silent supplication. I kissed him and put his little cap under his head and settled his hands for death. Then I turned and in another place close-by I saw poor Tom lying on the ground. 'O Jesus,' I cried, 'my husband, too,' and not far off lay the corpse of poor Connolly. I reeled round and remember no more as the soldiers hustled me down the stairs and into the street. . . . I was brought for examination to the Castle, and several times addressed the officers there asking them why they had killed my son, a young lad, not sixteen years of age."

Mrs. Connolly heard nothing of her husband until Sunday evening, " when I heard that he had been murdered by the military, and I was brought over to the empty disused house this side of Dunn's the butchers. The three bodies were lying in the back room of the first floor upstairs. My poor husband was greatly marked and had several great gashes about the neck and head which appeared to be bayonet wounds."

The climax of the North King Street slaughter of civilians by the military was at the " Louth Dairy " where Peadar Lawless, a young man of twenty-one, and three older men were shot on Saturday morning. The house was raided between eight and nine o'clock. The sergeant in charge refused to accept their assurances of non-complicity in the insurrection, that they were well-known citizens who could be identified, that there were no arms or ammunition in the house, that no Volunteers could have escaped from the house which was surrounded by the troops, that they could not have fired shots from the roof to which there was no access. The sergeant pointed to a bullet rip in his hat, sent off all the women under escort to a neighbouring cottage in Linenhall Street. When Mrs. Lawless returned that evening and insisted on entering: " And then a scene of horror met my eyes. My son lay dead in the same spot I had left him—on the landing of the top-back room, his body half in and half out of the doorway. Poor Mr. McCartney lay dead against the wall in a sitting position. Their brains had bespattered the curtains. Poor Finnegan was in the same relative sitting position, but had fallen dead across the bed. Patrick Hoey was out of his old place where I had left him, but he must have received fearful treatment as his head was burst open and macerated."

Mrs. McCartney described the soldiers who burst in as " a savage brutal crew, a disgrace to mankind," led by " an ignorant sergeant, who seemed particularly cruel and would listen to no explanation." Things were then quiet in the district, and the fighting nearly over : " I can never for one moment believe that any of these soldiers really thought that the men had fired on them." Her husband's body was looted, his watch, and other valuables stolen. A diamond pin escaped notice because it was blotted out with his blood. A soldier later said of McCartney, a Dame

Street tobacconist of 36 years: "The little man made a great struggle for his life and tried to throw himself out of the window, but we got him."

Another soldier was quoted at the inquest on Patrick Beales whose body was found buried in a cellar. Mrs. Roseanna Knowles, at whose house some soldiers were billeted described the conversation: "One of them said: 'There was a good deal of our men killed and a good deal of the others. . . I only pitied the poor fellow (Beales) . . . and the woman who was fainting. . . I pitied him from my heart though I had to shoot him. He had made tea for me. . . When they brought him (Beales) downstairs, he had not the heart to shoot him (Beales) straight, and that they told him (Beales) to go up again, and at the foot of the stairs they shot him —'that they let bang' at the foot of the stairs."

The struggle round "Reilly's Fort" lasted for sixteen hours. The fire of the Volunteers on the British troops was so heavy that it drove back the attackers even when supported by an armoured car, and put some of the Volunteers' rifles out of action. The Volunteers during one retreat of the British troops dashed out and seized the rifles that the soldiers had flung away in their flight. Heavy fire was kept up on the Volunteers by the British creeping along through the tunnelled North King Street houses. Volunteer barricade after barricade in the network was driven in, and the defenders slowly fell back towards the Four Courts. The men in "Reilly's Fort" fought until they fired their last shot, and dashed away in the open under a rain of rifle and machine-gun fire to a Church Street barricade. The Father Mathew Hall was evacuated, and the headquarters removed to the Four Courts. As there were no men to spare from the barricades, Piaras Beaslai and Eamonn Morkan, the Battalion Quartermaster, had to carry all the ammunition and explosives in numerous heavy loads across half a dozen barricades to the new H.Q., while the North King Street battle raged and the whole street at night was lighted by O'Connell Street ablaze and the flashes of rifles and machine-guns. Several times the Volunteers were driven from their barricades by the terrific barrage turned on them. Again and again, they returned and strengthened their positions.

About six o'clock on Saturday evening, Daly told Piaras Beaslai with tears in his eyes that he had received orders from Pearse to surrender.

When he announced it later to his men there were cries of "Fight it out!" Daly answered: "That is what I would like to do, but as a soldier I must obey Pearse's order."

Fifty-eight Volunteers behind a North Brunswick Street barricade under Patrick Holahan, and cut off from the Four Courts and Church Street men, refused to surrender until an order was brought to them signed by Pearse on Sunday morning. Father Augustine, the Franciscan, who with Father Columban, had arranged the Four Courts surrender, negotiated a truce between Holahan and the British until Pearse's order arrived. This truce lasted all night. When Pearse's order came, Holahan marshalled his men, and they were led away under military guard to the Castle. The resistance in the Four Courts area was at an end.[10]

---

[10] This chapter's sources are the accounts of some participants at the various positions mentioned; *Capuchin Annual*, 1942, "The Fourt Courts Area," P. Holahan; *Dublin Brigade Review*, 1939, pp. 13-16; *Limerick's Fighting Story*, pp. 18-27, and sources already given.

CHAPTER XVI

THE BATTLE OF ASHBOURNE

THE battle of Ashbourne, fought on the very eve of the general surrender—under the leadership of Thomas Ashe, Commandant of the Fifth Dublin Battalion (known after the Rising as the Fingal Brigade)—was not only the one clear military success of the insurrectionists, but foreshadowed the flying columns and barrack attacks in the 1920 phase of the struggle for independence. On Friday, April 28, 1916, Ashe with less than fifty men overran North County Dublin, captured four police barracks, and decisively defeated the R.I.C. with heavy casualties in a stand-up fight. The capture of Ashbourne Barracks and the accompanying action at Rath Cross near-by crowned a bold sweep through the counties of Meath and Dublin by the Fingal Volunteers: three police barracks —Garristown, Donabate, and Swords—were seized almost without a shot or a blow, and a large quantity of arms and ammunition taken. Thomas Ashe, after his release from prison in 1917 summed it all up in the quip: " I was a rich man once! I owned twenty motor cars, about a hundred rifles, and some ninety prisoners." Their enemies, as in the case of the Dublin positions, had the most exaggerated estimates of the actual strength of the Volunteers, and believed that the numbers engaged at Ashbourne numbered 400 men.[1]

The actual strength of the Volunteers was about forty-eight men, all equipped with bicycles; about twenty other members of the Fingal force had been sent to reinforce the G.P.O. garrison, and most of them later took part in the fight at the Mendicity Institute which they joined on Tuesday. The Press reports, as well as the R.I.C. estimates, however, mostly credited Ashe with at least 300 Volunteers, a rumour which the overthrow of the R.I.C. at Ashbourne seemed to confirm.

---

[1] *The Revolution in Ireland*, Alison Philips, p. 103. " The Volunteers numbered some 400, and the police . . . were forced to surrender."

The preliminary preparations for the Rising had been in progress for several weeks before. Frank Lawless, senior, Battalion Q.M., was in charge of these preparations. On Good Friday, he visited Kimmage camp and obtained twenty-six single-barrelled shotguns, buckshot, medical supplies, and sixty lbs. of gelignite. By an error a figure had been rubbed off the requisition form, which entitled him to receive 160 lbs.; a mistake which had serious consequences because the demolitions planned for North County Dublin could not be fully carried out: the attempt at 2.30 p.m. on Easter Monday to wreck the railway lines at Rogerstown Bridge was only partially successful, although a second attempt later on Tuesday-Wednesday threw the " loyalists " of Skerries into a panic, rumours of a Volunteer invasion of the town spread, and wild police and military signals of distress brought a destroyer with 200 soldiers who built up powerful barricades to keep out Thomas Ashe and his fabled hundreds.

Messages which reached Connolly and Clarke at headquarters from North County Dublin led them to believe that the railway demolitions had been successfully carried out. Clarke was very perturbed when a Volunteer dispatch carrier later told him of the true state of affairs. Connolly, however, said in his last dispatch on April 28:

" The men of North County Dublin are in the field, have occupied all the police barracks in the district, destroyed all the telegraph system on the Great Northern Railway up to Dundalk, and are operating against the trains of the Midland and Great Western."[2]

When the countermanding order appeared on Sunday morning, Ashe sent Joseph Lawless to Connolly at Liberty Hall for instructions as to the action to be taken in North County Dublin. Already there had been a strong muster of the Battalion at Swords in spite of MacNeill's order and the Volunteers remained at Saucerstown —the farm of Frank Lawless, senior—until official orders arrived from Connolly, that " everything was off for the present, but hold yourself in readiness to act at any moment." The Battalion then

---

[2] Attacks were made on the Midland and Great Western Railway on Monday and Tuesday; attempts were made first to dominate the bridges at Cabra and North Circular Road, and later to blow them up; a culvert near Liffey Junction was partly damaged, the permanent way at Blanchardstown was blown up, and a cattle train derailed; a locomotive was also set in motion and thrown across the line near Liffey Junction.

dispersed, and Ashe returned to Lusk with his friend, Dr. Richard
Hayes, who earlier in the year had been Commandant of the Battalion, but whose work now was to attend to the medical side of
the campaign which Ashe and he were hourly expecting.

They had not long to wait.   Early on Monday morning, Frank
Lawless received the order in Pearse's handwriting: STRIKE AT
ONE O'CLOCK TO-DAY.   The message was sent at once to Thomas
Ashe, who busied himself with the dispatch of the reinforcements
to Dublin, and then turned to operating of the plans already laid
down for Fingal.   There was some delay in regathering the Volunteers who had, as elsewhere, gone home bewildered and disappointed after the hint of conflict in higher councils.

Richard Mulcahy arrived from Baldoyle on Tuesday with two
other Volunteers, and acted thenceforth as Chief-of-Staff to Ashe.
All accounts agree that he was the driving force of the Ashbourne
fight, which was fought out on the lines he proposed.

Ashbourne R.I.C. Barracks lay on the main road from Dublin
to Slane.   From Thursday night, April 27, Sergeant Tuohy, who
was in charge with three constables, feared an immediate attack
from the insurgent force which, he learned, had encamped in the
Garristown area, captured the local barracks, erected the Tricolour
over it, and occupied the post office.   Since Wednesday, in fact,
Ashe's men had been on the move.   They had divided into four
sections under Charles Weston, Joseph Lawless, N. Rooney, and
Jim Lawless, twelve men to each section; one as rear guard, one
with Ashe and his staff—the main body—one as advance guard,
and the fourth which looked after supplies and camp sites.   According to Tuohy's information the successful Republicans bivouacked
at Baldwinstown Bridge, and then proceeded in the early morning
to Boranstown, a townland one and a half miles from Ashbourne.
Their scouts were active in all directions, destroying telegraph and
telephone communications and menacing the railways, with great
thoroughness, even sawing down the telegraph poles.   About five
o'clock on Friday morning, Tuohy got in touch with his district
headquarters at Dunshaughlin and was informed that some fifty
police under Inspector Gray were on the way from Slane, and
were expected to reach Ashbourne at noon the same day.[3]   Some
hours later, the Ashbourne garrison was reinforced by District-

[3] *Saturday Herald*, Dublin, May 6, 1916.   *See* also *Gaelic American*,
September 23, 1916, for Volunteer officer's account, quoted later in this
chapter.

Inspector McCormack, two sergeants, and five constables from Dunshaughlin, all fully armed.

The barracks was prepared hastily to withstand a siege. The defence force was parading outside the barracks at 11 a.m. when the Volunteers—who were on their way to destroy the railway line at Batterstown—captured two constables on patrol and discovered through their scouts that Ashbourne was being prepared for siege. They sent word to Ashe, and took up their positions to attack before the defence preparations could be completed. The Volunteer outposts suddenly appeared at Rath Cross, some 300 yards away from the barracks, mainly cyclist scouts. They dismounted, unslung their rifles, and began sniping operations. Soon the barracks was encircled by small parties posted in the fields bordering the railway line, and volley after volley was directed against the bullet-proof screened windows. The police defence was embarrassed by a fierce fire kept up, in particular, by one party sheltered by a hedge in front of the station: well-directed fire was concentrated on the windows, and the police replied only at long intervals, and that with danger and difficulty, to the incessant volleying kept up by this section of the attackers until 12.30 when one of the attackers advanced into the open and hurled a bomb which burst with a terrific report in front of the building in a huge cloud of earth and dust, falling short by only a few yards. Bomb attack now alternated with the volleys until there was a short lull in the attack.

Even as the lull ended, a more terrifying and menacing sound reached the police above the sound of the resumed sniping: a deadly series of volleys from the direction of Rath Cross told the besieged all too plainly that a heavy attack had been opened on the expected R.I.C. reinforcements arriving from Slane. In fact, the main body of Volunteers, some hundred yards away from the barracks, were now engaging the relief force.

A young Volunteer officer, in charge of one of the Volunteer sections who fought through it all and later escaped through the British military cordons into Dublin,[4] gave this account of how he led his section into action:

[4] *Gaelic American*, September 23, 1916, " Graphic Story of Ashbourne," told " by a young Volunteer officer." The first part of this article describes a journey to the General Post Office, an interview with Tom Clarke and Connolly, and the return to Fingal. It was from this officer that Clarke learned the state of Fingal. News of demolitions, attacks on railways, etc., came from the same source.

" We proceeded to Garristown where we captured the police barracks without a fight, imprisoned the Peelers, and took over their notebooks. We then took what money was in the Post Office, leaving a receipt for it in the name of the Republic, and smashing the telegraph installation. Afterwards, having posted guards on all the roads, we took command of the village for the night. The following day we marched to Newbarn by a roundabout route, where we camped for the night. Friday morning we breakfasted and marched on Rath Cross police station [Ashbourne] which is near Ashbourne. I was in charge of the advance party, and on reaching the cross-roads found a party of thirty-five Peelers standing in front of the barracks, and partly behind what I surmised was meant to be a barricade, but which merely consisted of a couple of barrels and a ladder. We opened fire on them and they retreated into the barracks."

Sometime before the reinforcements arrived, and the fight at Rath Cross began, Thomas Ashe approached the barracks, waving a white flag and demanded the surrender of the police. According to the Press accounts of the time, already quoted, Ashe was accompanied by Sergeant Brady of Dunboyne, then a prisoner, who, Ashe informed Inspector McCormack, would be freed with the entire body of the R.I.C. on condition that the barracks was surrendered with all arms. The police, according to the Volunteer accounts, were inclined to agree to these conditions, as their position in the absence of the expected reinforcements was very critical. This was Ashe's second appearance before the barracks with a demand for surrender. Colonel J. Lawless who watched Ashe, soon after the attack opened, make his first demand for surrender was impressed by his coolness mixed with a certain flamboyance as he called out for the place and arms to be handed over in the name of the Irish Republic. He stood calmly in the open with a disregard for danger that was inspired by something of the same spirit which led Connolly to defy danger to preserve morale. Even the prompt volley with which the R.I.C. met Ashe's first appearance left him quite unmoved. The Volunteers nearest to him rushed forward and dragged him protesting to safety while others returned the fire, and vigorously kept up the attack.

The most critical, indeed the turning point of the fight then came with the arrival of the relief force, fifty strong, in ten motor cars under County-Inspector Gray at Rath Cross. It was noon and the section under Charles Weston immediately attacked the cars. Ashe, Lawless and many of the participants later recalled that they were thrown off their balance by the arrival of the R.I.C. They were conscious mainly of their vulnerable position between the barracks and the powerful police force which swept up to Rath Cross at the very point when the Ashbourne garrison was on the point of surrender. The situation was saved by the desperate attack opened at once on the police cars by the Weston section which deceived the police as to the strength of the Volunteers. Moreover, Richard Mulcahy perceived that the police position at Rath Cross was very vulnerable, and at once outlined a plan of attack, which Ashe adopted with enthusiasm, and thereby regained a sure grip on the situation. Gone was the hesitation and momentary dismay that coincided with Gray's arrival, and the consequent resumption of the struggle for the barracks.[5]

Five hours later, a constable arrived at the barracks to inform the garrison that the relief force was defeated, and had surrendered at Rath Cross with the loss of a County Inspector, a District Inspector, two sergeants, and four constables.

The fight had been a long and desperate one in the Rath Cross area, where two by-roads converge on the main road. The ditches there were seven feet high, topped by thick and close hedges. The Volunteers took cover on all sides of Rath Cross while their outposts extended halfway up Hammondtown hill on both sides. This hill is beyond the Slane side of the cross-roads. It was a few minutes after noon when Gray gave the order to dismount as the cars reached the ascent of the hill. He was in the leading car, and intended to march his men to the rescue of Ashbourne Barracks. He was unaware of the Volunteers in wait, some fifteen yards ahead. A fusillade was opened which enfiladed the police cars from both sides of the main road, while snipers on the Ballymoden road, part of which gives a clear view of Hammondtown hill, fired volley after volley into the surprised R.I.C. Inspector

---

[5] *An Cosantóir*, November, 1946, "Thomas Ashe," Colonel J. V. Lawless. *See* also articles by the same writer, *An Cosantóir*, Vol. I, Nos. 24 and 25, 1941; *An t-Oglách*, Vol. V, N.S. No. 4, July 31, 1926. The *Gaelic American* writer notes that Gray's hesitation and overestimate of the Volunteer strength at that point lost the fight for the R.I.C. A bold dash forward to join the R.I.C. in Ashbourne Barracks might then have demoralised the Volunteers. Mulcahy, realising this, at once urged the Volunteers to concentrate their fire on Gray's force, and saved the day. Mulcahy's plan, in brief, was to pin down the R.I.C. in the most unfavourable spot until they were forced to surrender.

Gray received several severe and ultimately fatal wounds; Sergeant Shanagher of Navan was shot through the heart as he stepped from the same car. He fell dead into a channel of water near the Cross and was found there afterwards in a sitting position, still wearing his helmet. After the first shots, the police dashed from the cars and sheltered behind and, in some cases, underneath them. A demand for surrender was refused. Some of the constabulary retreated into a double ditch and fired wildly towards their mainly invisible assailants. Two commercial travellers—John Hogan and J. J. Carroll—driving along the main road in a car were killed by the enfilading fire which caught them, too, as the attack began. One of them had a British Military Service card in his pocket showing that he had registered at Birkenhead that January, doubt-less expecting battles in Flanders rather than bullets on a holiday jaunt along the Meath roads.

Some Volunteers attached to Dublin Battalions failed to join their units in time and on their way towards the city heard the sounds of the Ashbourne fighting. Guided by the sound of heavy firing they made their way to Ashe's position as the nearest scene of action, and gave up their attempt to reach the city for the moment. Their impression was of an expanse of green fields and high hedges with rifle fire on every side.

The police in their rude cover of cars and ditches were gradually surrounded by the snipers who closed in steadily on their cramped, and out-manœuvred enemies. Police casualties mounted as the hard-fought and stubborn duel went on, hour after hour. District-Inspector Smyth was twice wounded. He tried with a sergeant and some constables to gain the rear of his assailants, but when he reached the ditch he thought should be the rear, the snipers' circle of hidden fire still baffled him. Sniping, casualty, sniping, casualty, sniping, casualty—on and on it went, until the police were worn down. Sergeant Young of Kilmoon was shot dead, and the toll of wounded R.I.C. men mounted and mounted among the ditches and fields and the fortress of cars. Long after the Volun-teer snipers had located him, one constable beneath one of the cars bore a charmed life, and blazed back at them.

Suddenly the attackers appeared on a ridge which commanded the R.I.C. position and opened a terrific and conclusive fire on cars and hedges. District-Inspector Smyth was killed by a shot through the head. The police ammunition was at last exhausted, and their nerve broken. They threw down their rifles and raised their hands over their heads, shouting: " We surrender. We surrender. Remember we are Irishmen, too." Their rifles and ammunition were seized. Ashe addressed them from a high bank near the cross-roads, telling them they were free to go, adding a warning that they must not be found in arms against the Irish Republic again. Colonel Lawless, who listened to the speech, noticed that the R.I.C. men seemed thankful to Ashe, and on their faces, especially on that of the only R.I.C. officer who had not been wounded, something which indicated that a revolutionary and devastating revelation had suddenly stunned the force which had held Ireland in its hand and under its eye for over fifty years without effective challenge.

The Volunteer casualties were stated at the time to be two killed, and five wounded; the R.I.C. eight killed and fourteen wounded. Colonel Lawless gives the police casualties as eleven killed, and between thirty and forty wounded, adding that ten more were stated to have died later of wounds. The Volunteer casualties he estimates as: one killed in action, John Crenigan;[6] one died of wounds, Tom Rafferty; and four seriously wounded, Matthew Kelly (bullet through forearm); N. Rooney (bullet splinter in eye); Walsh (bullet wound in fingers); J. Rafferty (bullet wound in scalp).

Contemporary descriptions give a grim account of the aftermath on Ashbourne fields. District-Inspector Smyth's dead body was found, a bullet through his brain, stretched in a double ditch halfway up Hammondtown hill, his brains scattered all over the ground. In the centre of the road lay the dead constables, Hickey, Gormler, and McHale. Sergeant Young lay dead at the back of a cottage near Rath Cross. Wounded constables weltered in agony in bloody pools through the fields and on the roads. One of the Volunteers saved the life of a wounded constable, a fine young man with red hair, who was slowly bleeding to death. The Volunteer, who had some medical knowledge, saw the case was one of life or death, applied a tourniquet and stopped the bleeding. A dying R.I.C. man, with four fatal wounds, asked the Volunteer who dressed them, whether he would recover, and through pity

---

[6] *Catholic Bulletin*, September, 1916, has an account of John Crenigan, p. 524. It states he belonged to Roganstown, Swords, worked in the Dublin Tramways Company, and as a member of Swords Company, Irish Volunteers, was killed at Ashbourne, aged 21. His brother, aged 16, was also in the Rising and was sentenced to a year's imprisonment.

P

was told he would. The dying man smiled, asked for whiskey, drank some, and said: " Is it any harm for a dying man to have a drink? It's a pity we are fighting each other." He closed his eyes and died. Less tragic was the fate of the constable captured during the battle who was blandly told that the war was over for him. When he agreed, he was politely asked, according to his own statement in court later, to retire to a field within sight and stay peacefully behind a ditch until hostilities were over.

After the Ashbourne fighting ended, two of the Dublin Volunteers who had joined the Ashe contingent said good-bye to the Fingal fighters, and set off again towards the city. On the way they met a detachment of British troops, Lancers, on the way to Ashbourne. Posing as farm labourers, the Volunteers talked to two of the Lancers, asking for news of Dublin, and answering vaguely the soldiers' questions. Suddenly one Lancer said cheerfully: " Chum, you've dropped your sugar stick!" Both Volunteers kept their faces with remarkable coolness as they looked down and saw one of them had in fact dropped a stick of gelignite. Picking it up and thanking the soldiers, they went off, grateful for their escape and, unaware of the impending surrender, or that Hussars and Lancers in force were concentrating on Ashbourne, continued their journey towards their comrades in Dublin.

The Fingal Volunteers marched in high spirits and cheering for the Republic to their camp at Newbarn near Kilsallaghan where they remained until their surrender to the British forces two days later. The camp was an empty farmhouse behind strong walls and outhouses, and surrounded by a belt of high beech trees. They were aware of the arrival of Lancers in the area, and in high fettle after their first victory looked forward eagerly to a second. Then came the crushing news of the complete surrender of the Dublin fighters. On the morning of May 1 in the early hours, news reached the camp of the Dublin surrender and Pearse's order to lay down arms and cease fighting in Dublin City and County. Ashe read Pearse's order and recognised the handwriting which he knew very well. It was handed to him by a police sergeant, and a detective-officer in plain clothes, who arrived carrying a white flag. The officer noticed that Ashe was astonished and not at all in the mood to lay down arms. The devastation, the heavy fighting, and the hopeless position in Dublin were then not realised outside the centre of the city, and if the Commandants of some of the city positions had been slow to accept defeat, even more so was Ashe after the great successes of the Fingal Volunteers. The officer thereupon offered Ashe a safe conduct by car to Kilmainham to consult with Pearse himself. Ashe accepted the offer as he was so bewildered that he was very glad of an opportunity to think out the new situation thoroughly. It was agreed that Richard Mulcahy should go by car to Arbour Hill prison, and the police sergeant was left behind as a hostage. Mulcahy returned an hour and a half later after an interview with Pearse which impressed him deeply, as Pearse, for a defeated insurgent leader in the shadow of execution, seemed to him to wear a look " of the most sublime peace and the most sublime hope."[7] Mulcahy confirmed the authenticity of Pearse's order, the surrender was arranged, the Fingal Volunteers headed by Ashe marched into Swords under Lancer escort, and were then conveyed in motor lorries to Richmond Barracks.

---

[7] Mulcahy later gave this description of the interview at a Michael Collins' commemoration at Beal na Blath, Co. Cork, August 21, 1932, reported *Cork Examiner*, August 22, 1932: " When Pearse sat in his cell in Arbour Hill it was my privilege, four days before his execution, to stand in his cell with him to ask him was it true that surrender had been ordered, and whether the men of Fingal, who had given an excellent account of themselves during the week, could do any more good by holding out any longer?"

CHAPTER XVII

THE RISING IN THE COUNTRY

CONFUSION, broken plans, divided counsels, and inaction prevailed outside Dublin with a few exceptions, as in Galway, Louth, and Wexford. The countermanding order, the failure of the arms landing, the poverty of armament, uncertain communications, the very limited training of many of the country Volunteers, all combined against any widespread attempt at a general insurrection. Much agony of mind was endured by the country Commandants and the rank and file alike as soon as it was known that Dublin was in arms. Many unjust and unmerited reproaches were afterwards thrown upon even such men as Austin Stack, Terence MacSwiney, Monteith, Colivet, and the rest. There is much significance in the findings of the 1917 inquiry, carried out by the I.R.B., which exonerated the Cork Commandants, and the I.R.A. inquiry in 1918 which stated that no charge could be sustained against Kerry.[1] Nor indeed, as the facts reveal, was the case for Tipperary, Limerick, the North, and other Volunteer centres, less strong: on Easter Sunday the mobilisation was effective, on Easter Monday, MacNeill's order had created chaos, doubt, division, because his word prevailed against that of the Military Council. Moreover, the *Aud* was gone.

Nor was it the failure of the arms landing and MacNeill's countermand alone that checked the impulse towards insurrection outside Dublin. The circumstances in Dublin and in the country were radically different. Dublin communications were better, it was easier to concentrate forces there, and the Dublin Volunteers were far better drilled and armed. Little attention had been given by the country fighters to guerrilla tactics. The Dublin plan, however, as Pearse's last dispatch declared, was only part of a combined plan for a simultaneous revolt of the whole country.

---

[1] Quoted, *Rebel Cork's Fighting Story*, p. 20, Florence O'Donoghue; *An Phoblacht*, September 13, 1930, P. Cahill. Cork and Limerick were also cleared. Their officers replied sharply to an implied censure for the surrender of arms.

In 1922 a statement of Cathal Brugha's set out the Dublin and general plan:

" Connolly it was who prepared the plan for the defence of Dublin. Strong positions between the city and the various military barracks that almost surround it were to be seized by the Volunteers. The one in the city itself (Ship Street) was to be dominated by the seizure of certain strong buildings in its vicinity. A human chain was to link up such strongholds with the others. There was to be an open chain from the Liffey to Clontarf and Fairview and up to Phibsboro', over this space a mobile force was to be concentrated. The defence was to be carried out by the Volunteers and the Citizen Army acting together. The successful holding of the city for a certain time was based on the assumption that at least 1,500 would participate. Arrangements were made in various parts of the country to rise simultaneously."[2]

Or in more precise terms, according to those in touch with Connolly at the time, the Dublin plan of operations is best described as a line drawn through the 1916 positions—from Boland's Mill to the South Dublin Union, including the General Post Office, College of Surgeons, Four Courts, Jacobs' factory, the Mendicity Institution, and other outposts in its circle, with a line left open for retreat to Cabra and Phibsboro to the country. The defence was originally planned for operation by, at least, 2,000 active Volunteers and Citizen Army men, with the expectation of speedy aid from 1,000 more sympathisers. These defences were to be held in strength at various positions with light connecting files. As Brugha pointed out, within this line no British barracks were situated,—with the exception of Ship Street, which was held with a weak garrison of military police in the main.

The task set the provinces was that the Volunteers, armed with the rifles and supplies from the *Aud* on the Kerry coast, and their existing resources gathered since 1913, were to attack and keep the British troops from concentrating on the capital. Encircling tactics were to be used to isolate the British garrison at Enniskillen, troops moving from the Curragh were to be harassed as well as the artillery headquarters at Athlone. Whenever circumstances became favourable, reinforcements were to be sent to Dublin. Attacks on railway lines and demolition of bridges at crucial points were mapped out. The general direction was given from Dublin, and the country

---

[2] *Poblacht na h-Eireann*, Easter No., April 20, 1922.

Volunteer leaders were left to work out for themselves details for their own areas.

The Cork Volunteer leaders awoke from the confusion of Easter Eve with the guns of the British command dominating the town from the hills. Their situation is best sketched in the words of Miss Mary MacSwiney:

" The first hint of a hitch was the visit of Mr. J. J. O'Connell to Cork on Good Friday. He brought word from MacNeill that all ' the manœuvres ' for the following Sunday were to be cancelled. MacNeill—who had only been fully informed of the details of the plans for Easter Week on Holy Thursday or the day before—had received private information that Dublin Castle was ' in possession of the facts about the expected shipload of arms, and was only waiting for a favourable opportunity to strike '."[3]

After a conference between the three leaders, Thomas MacCurtain, Terence MacSwiney and Seán O'Sullivan, with O'Connell at MacSwiney's house, the Cork leaders realised the division in the Dublin leadership and that MacNeill had not been fully in the confidence of the fighting men. They asked O'Connell to withdraw while they discussed the matter, and then decided that they would adhere to their original orders to march out to meet the Kerry men who were to hand over to them a quota of arms and equipment. A second dispatch came at six o'clock on Saturday morning from MacNeill ordering them to proceed according to their original instructions as it was then impossible to cancel the plans. This came with a covering note from Seán MacDermott which stated that the Dublin leaders were united and that MacNeill was completely with them at last. Almost immediately came the news of the destruction of the *Aud*. The orders to the Cork leaders were to march their men out towards Kerry to receive their quota of arms, but beyond that no definite instructions had been given. The loss of the *Aud* at once nonplussed them. On Easter Sunday, however, Seán O'Sullivan marched one Volunteer contingent out of the city. MacCurtain was about to follow with a second when a special messenger arrived from Dublin with MacNeill's countermanding order. As the previous Dublin message had assured the Cork men that there was a united leadership in Dublin the city Volunteers were at once recalled, and the county units ordered to disperse.

---

[3] *Poblacht na h-Eireann*, Easter No., April, 1922.

What happened on Easter Monday was described to the American Commission on Conditions in Ireland by Miss Mac-Swiney in December, 1920:

"An order followed on Monday signed by Pádraic Pearse and John MacDermott that they were to rise, that the orders were to be kept to. By the time these orders reached the outlying districts it was too late. Cork was not in the Easter Rising. The fact that it was not was a lasting source of grief to my brother.[4] Many of the people thought they should have gone out, even though they were certain to fail. There were some people, I am not sure how many, who accused them of cowardice or funk at the last moment. That charge was not justified, and I do not think it will ever be made again. But the situation in Cork made it impossible for them to rise. Cork is built in a valley. The order to rise did not reach the Commandants until Monday evening. By the time they could have got their men together every hill in Cork was mounted by a huge field gun, the largest piece of artillery they could get. Cork is built in a valley. The British military barracks are on the highest hill in the district. By Tuesday night they had a huge gun planted on every hill around the city. They could have shelled the city in an hour until there was nothing left of it. The Volunteer commanders in Cork knew that. They did not want to order the men out to what was absolutely certain slaughter. They realised that Dublin was only a first battle in the war, and for the time they had to remain inactive.

"I can speak of personal knowledge of the very, very great reluctance with which they came to that decision. I can tell you what very few people in Ireland knew of that time or even now, that as late as Thursday evening at 7 o'clock they had made plans to get out of the city into the country districts where they could have fought. Cork is not like Dublin, which is suitable for street fighting. Cork could not have street fighting. It would have been shelled from the hills within an hour. By Thursday evening they were trying to call the Volunteers out of the city, and as late as Thursday evening at 7 o'clock I had orders to get in a fresh supply of first aid material in case they were able to manage it. They

[4] Towards the end of his hunger-strike, Terence MacSwiney wrote to Cathal Brugha: " The pain of Easter Week is properly dead at last." Quoted, A Trinity of Martyrs, " Sceilg," p. 7.

were not able to manage it, but I can testify to the grave reluctance with which they finally gave it up."[5]

The Cork Volunteers remained mobilised until the news of the Dublin surrender reached them. More light on Cork conditions at the time is given by an unnamed correspondent of Devoy's— in fact Miss MacSwiney herself—quoted in *Documents Relative to the Sinn Féin Movement*, p. 17. The letter was written in June, 1916. "We want American friends to understand what happened and take Cork as a fairly typical example: Cork men were out as arranged for manœuvres on Easter Sunday; county was regularly linked up, men in trim for anything. Orders came while they were out cancelling all arrangements. Weather was atrocious and as nothing was to be gained by staying out all night in the open, men disappointed, returned to their districts Sunday night. Some men did not get home until Tuesday morning. Meanwhile, the two chief officers had been making a tour of inspection all through country by automobile. Only commander returned to Cork Monday night. Monday afternoon he got news from Dublin that the Rising was to commence there at noon and an order signed by Pearse for Cork to join in. It was late Monday evening before other two staff officers got word. Mobilisation was out of question that night and by Tuesday morning city was surrounded on all sides. The men could not have got out if they had had munitions in tons and guns in hundreds, which they had not. It seemed to us here that Dublin had made criminal mistake. We have since learned that it was ' Come out and fight or be disarmed' Tuesday morning. But we did not know at that time.

"We still think that Inner Circle were not justified in keeping MacNeill in dark so long. I cannot go into that now. Provinces wished not to be left out of affair but there certainly was regrettable disregard of provincial conditions on part of Dublin. Dublin was well supplied with arms, munitions, provinces not; Dublin had been told that without arms, etc., we could do nothing. I have only written that much to explain why so few counties were ' out '."

The writer, who was described a month later in Devoy's letter to de Lacy as a woman writing on behalf of the men, expressed a mood prevalent among the Volunteers outside Dublin: that the leaders in Dublin were obsessed by military textbooks and thinking

---

[5] American Commission on Conditions in Ireland, pp. 215-19.

too much on the lines of a regular army without any real appreciation of tactics suitable to the conditions outside the capital. Patrick Cahill, after 1916, expressed similar criticisms, and urged on a reorganisation of the Kerry Volunteers in sections rather than in battalions.

In Cork, through the intervention of the Lord Mayor and Dr. Cohalan, Bishop of Cork, an agreement was reached, by which the Cork Volunteers handed over their arms to the Lord Mayor for safe keeping. These arms were handed over, according to Miss MacSwiney's statement to the American Commission, after a promise by Colonel East, the British Commander in Cork, to the Lord Mayor and Dr. Cohalan that if the arms were handed over as a guarantee that the Volunteers were not bent on insurrection, these arms would not be seized, nor the leaders arrested. As soon as the arms were handed over and locked up in his offices, the military after several demands and threats obtained them, and arrests began, which were followed by releases after protests from the Lord Mayor and the Bishop, and rearrests all over again as soon as the news reached Maxwell. This situation, with slight variations, was to recur in Limerick.

During the military swoop in County Cork after the Rising, a party of R.I.C., led by Head Constable Rowe, on the night of May 1, surrounded Bawnard House, Castlelyons, about four miles from Fermoy, the home of the Kent family, who had been prominent in the Land League struggle. Thomas, David, Richard and William Kent lived there with their mother. They were all prominent members of the Volunteers, and the house contained rifles, revolvers and shotguns. A pitched battle followed, which lasted three hours. Military reinforcements were sent for, and the Kents were arrested. Richard Kent was mortally wounded in an attempt to escape after the fight. Mrs. Kent loaded the guns and handed them to her sons during the fray; she was over eighty years of age. The Kents refused to surrender until their last shot was fired and the farmhouse a wreck. Head Constable Rowe was killed and several of the police badly wounded. David Kent owed his life to the severe wounds he received. Thomas Kent was court-martialled and executed on May 9. William Kent was acquitted, and David Kent's death sentence commuted to five years' penal servitude.

In Limerick, which was a pivotal point for the insurrection plans, no movement was made by the Volunteers, in spite of the plans which Colivet, Clancy and the rest of the Volunteer leaders had drawn up with great thoroughness at short notice. On Easter Saturday morning the *Cork Examiner* published the news of the discovery of a collapsible boat on Banna Strand. Before Seán Fitzgibbon left for Dublin the same day, Colivet arranged for him to send a code message as to whether the Rising was to take place or not. On Sunday afternoon the code message arrived that the insurrection was off. In the meantime, Colivet had learned of Casement's arrest, and of the arrests of Austin Stack and Con Collins in Tralee, from Lieutenant Whelan, whom he had sent to Tralee as soon as he heard of the collapsible boat seizure. As no message reached Limerick from Dublin headquarters on Saturday, although Colivet had sent up two special messengers—Captain Forde and Lieutenant Gubbins—he sent out orders cancelling all arrangements in his command for the time being, with the warning that further orders would follow.

On Sunday morning, The O'Rahilly arrived with written instructions from Eoin MacNeill, " Volunteers completely deceived. All orders for to-morrow, Sunday, cancelled." From The O'Rahilly Colivet also heard of the serious differences at Dublin headquarters and the arrest of Hobson. Colivet at once sent final orders cancelling arrangements for the outside units of his command, and arranged to take the City Battalion to Killonan to camp out there in the usual way as if nothing had happened. This decision was taken after consultation with his staff. Lieutenant Gubbins returned from Dublin with two lorries sent by Seán MacDermott in response to Colivet's request for them transmitted by Seán Fitzgibbon. The O'Rahilly also confirmed the news which had reached Limerick on Saturday night that the German arms ship was lost, and the arms gone.

On Holy Thursday very definite hints had been given to the City Battalion at a parade addressed by Commandant Colivet that a fight was near, and orders to parade on Easter Sunday morning, fully armed and equipped, with two days rations. These orders were also issued to those Volunteers who had previously been exempted from public parades, while all Volunteers unable to parade on Sunday had been asked to hand over their arms to their Company officers. First-aid equipment had been distributed. On Easter Sunday morning 130 Volunteers paraded for the march to

Killonan. These were all from the City Battalion which, at full strength, never exceeded 200 men. The weather was wet and chilly. As it was clear that the insurrection had been at least postponed, forty or fifty Volunteers returned to the city. On Sunday afternoon, Colivet received Fitzgibbon's code message that the Rising was " off." Late on Sunday night, Captain Forde arrived from Dublin with a message from Pearse cancelling all arrangements with a warning added to be ready for further orders.

On Easter Monday morning, Lieutenant Whelan returned from a second visit to Tralee where he had met Captain Monteith who told him that no men were coming from Germany, that the aid in arms and munitions sent from there was gone, that " the Germans were out for cheap Irish blood," and that the best thing the Volunteers in the South could do was to try and bluff through. (This conversation with Monteith took place on Easter Sunday.) Between 1.30 and 2 p.m. a message from Pearse was handed to Colivet by Miss Agnes and Miss Laura Daly. This was the second message which reached Colivet from the Dalys. On Saturday night he had heard from them that " everything was all right," including MacNeill. Pearse's message read : " Dublin Brigade goes into action to-day. Carry out your orders." Colivet immediately summoned a meeting of all available Volunteer officers. It was decided that as the orders to Limerick were based on the arrival of the arms ship, the orders could not be carried out. There were, in fact, only seventy-six of the City Battalion left in Killonan camp, and the outlying units had been demobilised. There was a unanimous decision that nothing could be done. The Volunteers were marched back to Limerick and dismissed. They returned to their homes with their arms, very much on the alert, as they were prepared for a possible British attempt to disarm them.

Colivet, Clancy, and the remaining officers of the Limerick command, were deeply disturbed and distressed by their helplessness while the Dublin fight was in progress. They discussed whether some officers might go to Dublin. Father Hennessy, O.S.A., their chaplain, however, told them their place was in Limerick to take charge in such a crisis. On Tuesday, April 25, Colivet called a final meeting of his staff, the Board of Management, and all officers who had been concerned in the previous discussions. After a full and long discussion a vote was taken, and it was decided by a majority of ten to six that nothing could be done. Without the arms ship's cargo, the plans arranged could obviously not be carried out. The Limerick Volunteers, with the exception of some units, were not well armed. Nor was there any chance to bring even 100 Volunteers to Dublin to help the fighters there. The minority vote showed the deep disappointment at the situation rather than any real conviction that action was then possible. The improvised plans were useless in the new circumstances.

The British commander, Sir Anthony Weldon, sent a demand for the surrender of their arms to the Volunteers through the Mayor of Limerick, James Quinn. This demand was refused by the Volunteers and was repeated several times. Colivet sent a reply on one occasion that the Limerick Volunteers would be delighted to give the British commander an opportunity of seizing the arms, if he gave them an hour's start they would march out of Limerick, and he could follow and take them—if he could. The Mayor, with great diplomacy, suppressed this offer. When Colivet reminded Weldon of it later, the British commander said indignantly that it was the first he had ever heard of it and he certainly would have accepted it! Sir Anthony Weldon, in fact, was a strong anti-Carsonite. He contented himself with a parade of force through the city, three regiments of infantry, a regiment of cavalry, and an artillery brigade with eighteen guns. No arrests were made until pressure was exerted on Weldon from Dublin. At last, faced with the seizure of their arms, the Limerick Volunteers, to avert bloodshed, decided that the arms should be handed over to the Mayor, with the proviso that each Volunteer should hand over his arms to Colivet, who would then surrender them to the Mayor as guardian of the peace and security of the city. Weldon and other British officers were present during this ceremony. One officer attempted to take some of the arms. The surrender of arms stopped until he laid them aside. Weldon blandly ignored this byplay, although some of his officers groaned and swelled with rage. In due course, the British, as in Cork, took over the arms from the Mayor. The Limerick Volunteers, however, preserved a quantity of arms they had dumped. There was a swoop on the Volunteers and their officers within a few days but they were all released and not deported.[6]

---

[6] This account of Limerick during the Rising is based on a statement of M. P. Colivet to the writer, a version of Colivet's dispatch, published in *Banba*, September, 1922, and *Limerick's Fighting Story*.

The narratives of Monteith and Stack best tell the story of Kerry in the Rising.[7] Austin Stack's tale of events repeats the picture of confusion, broken plans, and divided counsels. His difficulties with the arms landing have already been described in a previous chapter. His story, in general, confirms Monteith's picture of the Kerry Volunteers, full of enthusiasm, almost leaderless, almost unarmed, and cut off from Dublin.

Under Stack's command, as Monteith found it, there were some 300 Volunteers armed with a medley of 200 rifles, Howth single loader Mausers, a few Lee Enfield magazine rifles, and, for the rest, shotguns, and mainly Martini Enfield carbines. The rifle ammunition available, moreover, was suitable for the magazine rifles but liable to jam in the carbines. Some of the Volunteers marched in forty miles from Dingle, armed with walking sticks.

Monteith's landing with Casement and Bailey on Banna Strand on Good Friday morning was the first jar to the Kerry plans for the Rising. It was a tragic hour as Casement brooded outside MacKenna's Fort, looking away over the bay where he and his companions had battled in the light boat after their exit from the submarine. He waited for Monteith's return, weak from the effects of a recent attack of malaria, and a drug, but happy in the sunshine. From neighbouring houses friendly eyes watched the stranger in wonder. A step across the sands, a whispered word, and there was shelter in those houses. One word, " Casement!" and his pursuers would have searched the Kerry sands and hills in vain in spite of prowling spies and bewildered friends. But Casement had come with another purpose. He buried his papers in the sands of MacKenna's Fort, among them probably a copy of his treaty with the Germans. Meanwhile, Monteith succeeded among the lanes of Tralee, and in due course, Stack heard.

Con Collins—a close friend of Seán MacDermott—had arrived from Dublin on Thursday night, and stayed in Stack's lodgings. On Good Friday morning, after some delay, they both interviewed Monteith. Stack heard from Monteith, Casement's opinion of the German help, of the presence of the *Aud* in the bay, the details of the arms, machine-guns, and munitions on the ship, that field guns, crews, and German officers were not coming. Monteith also inquired about the non-appearance of the pilot boat to meet the

[7] Monteith, *Casement's Last Adventure*; Stack, *Kerry Champion*, August 31-September 21, 1929; also published in abridged form in *Silver Jubilee 1916 Souvenir* (*Kerryman*, Tralee, 1941).

submarine, and Stack explained that the ship and submarine had not been expected till Sunday night.

Stack then made every effort to locate Casement. Unfortunately, Monteith and Bailey were necessarily somewhat vague as to where they had landed. It was six miles from Tralee, and Stack mistook the description of MacKenna's Fort for Ballymacquin Castle, between Ardfert and Ballyheigue. More unfortunately still, one, MacCarthy, had located the collapsible boat and informed the police, who were even then scouring the sands to find the men who had obviously landed from a submarine. Monteith could give only a very general picture of the spot: it was somewhere near the coast beyond Ardfert, beyond that they could tell him little. Collins, Stack and Bailey left for Ardfert by motor car, and after a few miles found themselves on a high point commanding a view of the Bay from Ballyheigue. Guided by Bailey, Stack made for Banna, but met the collapsible boat as it was driven past on a cart under the escort of one policeman. Stack noticed other policemen busily searching the sandhills. Bailey told Stack that the boat was the one from which they had landed. They went steadily towards the police while Stack pondered how to keep those police busy until he could send help to Casement. The police approached and questioned the three men. Collins gave his true name and said he was a civil servant on holiday from Dublin; Bailey said his name was David Mulcahy, and he also was on holiday from Dublin. They turned the car when the police sergeant had finished his questions. The driver mended a puncture and drove off slowly in the opposite direction from where Casement was still resting, unsuspecting his danger. The police were suspicious of Stack and one constable followed on his bicycle. This was just what Stack wanted. He drove slowly to the house of a farmer named Lawlor whose two sons were sympathetic. After some delay, Stack found one of the sons, and sent him to find Casement and take him to a safe hiding place. There was one problem very much on Stack's mind: his explicit instructions from Dublin that " there should be not as much as a single shot fired until general hostilities had begun on Easter Sunday. I knew that the Executive in Dublin (P. H. Pearse had conveyed the order to me) were very strong on this point, for had there been anything like an outbreak, no matter how small, it was likely to lead to an attempt on the part of the British Government to have a general round-up of Volunteer leaders."

As they left Lawlor's the police who had trailed the car again questioned the party. Stack was very amiable with the police whom he was delighted to see turning their attention to him rather than to the sandhills of Banna Strand. He said that he was showing his friends the scenery around Ballyheigue and Kerry Head. While he talked away to the sergeant, Stack noticed another constable enter the post office nearby and concluded that he was telephoning Tralee when this constable rushed out and demanded information about the party's future movements. Stack, still very suave, looked thoughtful, said he had changed his mind, would not go round Kerry Head, but would show his friends the beauties of Ballybunion. Trailed still, the car drove off in Ballybunion direction. At Causeway, the car was again held up by the police. Three constables ordered Collins and Bailey on to the road, and searched them. A Browning pistol was found on Collins. When Stack was asked if he had any firearms, he pulled out an automatic pistol and said: " Yes, I have this, but will not give it up to anybody." Collins and Bailey were taken into the police barracks. Stack waited in the car for ten minutes. He then jumped out with his gun in his hand. Entering the barracks, he ostentatiously put his gun into the pocket of his overcoat, and as ostentatiously kept a firm grip on the gun. He asked how long he was to be kept waiting for his friends. To his surprise, this bluff succeeded. The sergeant said respectfully: " They will be with you in a minute, sir." Collins demanded the return of his gun, and again the sergeant handed it over without argument. A few minutes later the car was on its way back towards Tralee. Bailey was handed over to a local Volunteer officer at Killahan to save him from arrest. As Stack was driven into Tralee, he understood that the police were on the alert. A plain-clothes detective, one George Neazor—who was later shot in a stand-up fight at Rathkeale during the Black and Tan war—shadowed Collins and Stack from the car for which he was evidently on the watch. He called to their lodgings, but Stack refused to answer some questions he asked. Collins went away to visit friends. Stack left for a Volunteer meeting at the Rink where several officers from the Kerry battalions were waiting Stack's final orders for Sunday. The secret of the Rising and the plans were known only to Stack, Patrick Cahill, and a few others. Michael Flynn, a Gaelic League organiser, arrived with a message from Collins that he had been arrested, and wished to see Stack

at the police station. A cycle scout next arrived from Ardfert and
informed Stack that the local police had brought in a prisoner
which Stack knew at once must be Casement. Stack then told
the meeting that the Rising was fixed for Sunday, that the arms
were to be landed on Monday morning early, that he had definite
orders not to allow a shot to be fired.   Stack took the meeting
fully into his confidence after he had informed it of Casement's
arrest, and one of the officers pressed strongly for an attempt to
rescue Casement. When the news of the imminent arms landing
and Rising was given by Stack, and his strict orders to avoid a
conflict, the meeting reluctantly agreed to give up the project of
freeing Casement. Casement himself about the same time was taking precautions to avoid any attempt at a rescue.

Stack made arrangements to inform Dublin of Casement's arrest
and walked down to the police barracks into the artless trap set
for him. He was a solicitor's clerk and thought his visit to Collins
was a business one. His successful bluffing of the police earlier
in the day had thrown him off his guard. According to the police
evidence at his trial, he asked his captors if they were serious in
arresting him.

There was considerable panic in the barracks for the next few
hours. Bodies of police were drafted in from outlying districts.
It was learned later that Casement and his escort were due to
arrive in Tralee about the time Stack was arrested. Collins and
he spent the night in captivity, and heard next day that Casement
had been removed about 9 or 10 o'clock in the morning. The police
did not seem sure as yet of Casement's identity, and tried to trick
Stack into confirming their suspicions.   He was visited twice
during the night by the Head Constable in search of clues. On
the first occasion, a dark hint was dropped that a very interesting
captive was upstairs. Stack merely said: "Who are you speaking
about, some tramp?" On the second visit, the head constable was
very confidential, the prisoner *was* Casement, and he had asked
about Stack. Stack smiled, and said that if the prisoner were
Casement he could not have asked for Stack whom he did not know
and could not even have heard of.

Casement met the Dominican, Father Ryan, at the barracks after
he had asked for a priest. He told Father Ryan to keep his identity
secret until he had been taken out of Tralee so as to avoid any
attempt at rescue, and that he had come to Ireland to stop the

impending rebellion. Casement's main purpose in sending for Father Ryan was to convey a warning to Dublin and to the local Volunteers. The police also tried to discover from Father Ryan whether their prisoner was Casement, and he declined to answer the question.[8]

After the arrest of Casement, Stack and Collins, Easter Week passed quietly in Kerry. At Firies near Killarney two policemen were shot and seriously wounded while posting up the proclamation of martial law. Formidable reinforcements of military and police were rushed into the county. Monteith escaped capture. The Volunteers gradually dispersed.

Here and there through the country a Volunteer in desperation struck a blow. Michael O'Callaghan of Tipperary Town, dropped two policemen dead with quick revolver shots as they came to arrest him after a Volunteer council of war where lack of arms and news bent the Tipperary fighters to acquiescence in inactivity even while Seán Treacy was scouting through the county after rumours and chances of battle until he saw a white flag over the heads of Volunteer officers driving from Cork, and heard from them that all was over. Tipperary in general was bewildered by the clash of order and counter-order, there was no co-ordinated movement there, although several Volunteer companies mobilised until news of the Dublin surrender reached them. The resources and arms of the Tipperary Volunteers were then very limited, and their arms were few.

Typical of the dilemma that faced the Volunteer Commandants in country areas is the experience of Commandant Liam Manahan, Galtee Battalion, Limerick Brigade, whose visit to Dublin on Holy Thursday has already been referred to. On Holy Saturday he issued orders for Sunday manoeuvres at Galbally, but altered company routes and concentration points to avoid any clash with military raiding parties. Some of his officers protested against any parade with arms because it was difficult to collect them from dumps and exposed the weapons to the risk of capture. Since the publication in the *Cork Examiner* of the news about arrests in Tralee and the mysterious boat on Banna Strand there was a spirit of uneasiness abroad. The MacNeill letter and countermand in the *Sunday Independent* intensified this feeling: it semed a hint

---

[8] Casement's request to Father Ryan is quoted in a letter from Father Ryan himself to Mr. Gavan Duffy. *Roger Casement*, Parmiter, p. 272.

Q

that something dangerous had been afoot, and that there was indeed " a very critical position." All the companies of the Galtee Battalion were already moving off when MacNeill's message appeared. At 11.30 Manahan received a message from one of his men which had been brought into Mitchelstown by The O'Rahilly: MacNeill's order as Chief-of-Staff cancelling all movements of Volunteers for that day. Manahan decided to go ahead with some show of manœuvres until some more definite news reached him. He was hampered by a great need of dispatch riders, and the few he had were badly overworked. He warned several companies which were badly armed to route march in their own areas until further orders, and carried out the manœuvres with companies from Galbally, Kilross, Tipperary, Ballylanders, Mitchelstown and some other units. At 7 p.m. the MacNeill order was confirmed from Cork, Limerick and Tipperary. Some officers of the various units pointed out to Manahan the weariness of the men, the bad weather in which long night marches would dishearten their followers, but above all the urgency of safe disposal of the arms before morning. No other orders reached them, and the battalion was dismissed company by company.

After midnight on Monday, Manahan, then at Ardpatrick, was roused by a Volunteer captain who informed him of rumours from Kilmallock of fighting in Dublin. A tour of various local Volunteer centres the following morning was made by Manahan to collect as many dispatch riders as he could, and to be ready for definite news and orders. He held his dispatch riders all day. Dublin remained shut off in a fog of rumour and silence. The dispatch riders stood-to all night. On Wednesday two of them were sent to Limerick to inquire into the position and Manahan tried to get in touch with Cork. All his messengers reported demobilisation everywhere. At last at 9.30 p.m. Manahan utterly bewildered and baffled allowed his dispatch riders to go home. Two dispatch riders from Galbally brought back a stranger with them at the request of the local officers.

This stranger who arrived about 10 o'clock was Seán Treacy, a young man unknown to Manahan who was much impressed by his evident sincerity. Treacy was wearing knickerbockers and carrying a huge revolver. He was then about twenty years old. He was on a mission of inquiry from Pierce McCann, County Commandant, Tipperary, with no definite orders or information.

Treacy merely said that there was still fighting going on in Dublin; that the County Commandant and other officers were eager to do something and wanted to get in touch with Limerick; that a section in Tipperary were keen on action, and if the Galtee Battalion mobilised would fall in with it.

Some of the officers present were critical of Treacy's arguments but Manahan was moved by his earnestness, and as he himself still hoped for definite orders, ordered remobilisation. Most of the dispatch riders had gone home; a messenger sent to a local unit for riders was misunderstood, and the company mobilised—and waited in vain. At midnight, by great efforts, the dispatch riders were gathered to get in touch with the dispersed units, and by 6 a.m. on Thursday the Ballylanders Company was on the march with Galbally Company moving in to join it. Arrangements were made to cut communications and dismantle telegraph and telephone wires, and assemble arms and ammunition. Dispatch riders next reported great difficulty in gathering the men and bringing them to posts before daylight. Officers were confused and losing confidence as uncertainty, lack of clear directions and all sorts of rumours spread. There was a hitch about getting in touch with the better-armed units, and this was serious indeed as many units had only shotguns and others practically no arms at all. What was really conclusive was the definite news that Cork had demobilised and Limerick had decided not to move. As daylight drew nearer, Manahan's mobilisation and plans for seizing went from bad to worse. He decided that action without support from the better organised Brigade areas could only be a flash in the pan; action without any plan or order would only cause blank despair and demoralisation.

Seán Treacy was at the end of the Company, extended towards Galbally and closing in, found the Company marching away to dump its arms and ammunition. Treacy expressed his disappointment in terms that moved Manahan in spite of the weight of his own responsibilities. Treacy tried to get a few men to go with him to Tipperary and Limerick Junction to blow up bridges. His first proposal for an attack on Ballylanders Barracks was then impracticable. As Treacy continued his journey he appreciated that the reports of general inaction and collapse which had reached Ballylanders were only too true, and that the Rising in the South was already over.

In Galway, Liam Mellows, after a brave start and the mobilisation of some 1,500 Volunteers, faced the same experience of dis-
integration as he watched his forces fade away.   Yet Mellows
before that had certainly given his enemies more than a run for
their money.   He captured barracks, was one of the last leaders
to disband, while even on Easter Monday his mobilisation was successful.   Mellows had left Dublin on Holy Thursday in a " do
or die " mood.   He told a friend that his men were very badly
armed with less than 100 guns among them all.   He had in fact 30
rifles and 70 shotguns.   He made no secret of his belief that he was
certainly going away on the most hazardous expedition of his life.
Yet this expedition was one after his own heart.   He had been
arrested and deported in March, and the officer in charge of the
party that put him aboard ship had said abruptly :

" You Irish are a bloody ungrateful pack after all we have tried
to do for you.   Do you know what I'd do with you?   I'd give you
your bloody little potato patch of a country, and let you all go to
Hell ! "

" Thanks very much," said Liam.   " That's all we want ! "

He escaped from the area in England in which he had been
ordered to reside, spent a short time in Connolly's house in Belfast,
and made his way to Pearse at St. Enda's disguised as a priest where
he remained until he was driven off on a motor cycle combination
and reached the West late on Holy Thursday night.   Mellows had
been very friendly with Pearse since the occasion shortly before his
arrest when he had heard Pearse criticised as one of the leaders
likely to precipitate a premature Rising, and had gone to Pearse and
boldly taxed him with it.   Pearse's arguments, whatever they were,
won him over, and Mellows was given the task of leading the
Galway fight.

After his escape to America in the autumn of 1916, Mellows
wrote in the *Gaelic American* that the capture of the arms ship had
dealt the greatest blow to the insurrection in the West where 3,000
rifles were to have been distributed, if the gun-running had been
successful, on Easter Monday " by which time the entire county
would have been in our hands.   And there was a Galway man ready
to shoulder every one of the 3,000 rifles, as well as the rifles that
would have been captured from the police." He criticised
MacNeill's countermand because it " resulted in great numbers of
men becoming disheartened—good and brave men who were pre-

pared to do all required of them on the Sunday night. Worse than all, through this order of MacNeill's the ' element of surprise ' upon which the plan of campaign depended, and which was a dead certanty on Easter Sunday, was lost. The police never suspected that anything was intended for that night. They went about their duties as usual. That they had no suspicions, received no warnings, and were quite unprepared for the Rising on Easter Sunday, speaks volumes for the integrity, discipline and earnest patriotism of the Volunteers. At least 1,000 men and hundreds of women in County Galway, as well as the men in the other parts of the country knew the date and hour from Easter Saturday, and some several days earlier; yet nothing leaked out. As to the projected plans . . . they were carefully prepared months ahead. . . The ' element of surprise ' lacking, these plans could not be put into operation. When the news reached the West that ' Dublin was going out,' the police became alive to the situation and were on the alert. Their first act was to abandon nearly all the smaller barracks, and concentrate themselves in the towns of Galway, Gort, Loughrea and Ballinasloe."[9]

Mellows received Pearse's orders for insurrection late on Easter Monday evening. He mobilised, as his own and the British accounts show, at least 1,000 men throughout the county. He set up his headquarters at Killineen some miles from Craughwell on the road to Oranmore. When one of his dispatch riders was captured he set out to intercept the police near Galway. He failed in this as the prisoner was taken to Limerick. He proceeded to Clarinbridge and Oranmore, captured six policemen after rushing the barracks, and had a sharp shooting match with a police sergeant who escaped and barricaded himself in a house. Mellows then fell back on Athenry. He was the last man to leave Oranmore. There had been an unsuccessful attempt to blow up a bridge when news was received that the military were approaching from Galway. Mellows told his men to retreat outside the village, some on horseback, some in charge of the stores on carts, armed mainly with shotguns and revolvers (where they were armed), and with a few magazine rifles. He remained in Oranmore until his men were safely

---

[9] Quoted *Wolfe Tone Annual* (1946). This also contains the account of the Rising, and an appreciation of Mellows by Father Feeney, who accompanied him, and who received Pearse's order for Mellows on Easter Monday.

away. As he walked down the village street he saw some twenty-five R.I.C. men, the advance guard of the Galway police and military reinforcements, marching in. He hid behind a tree and fired on them with his automatic pistol, and set off, the constabulary a-fusillading with great enthusiasm. Mellows and his men could hear the firing going on when they had marched three miles onwards, but there was no attempt to pursue them. Two miles outside Athenry another Volunteer contingent met Mellows's force. They proceeded to Athenry and camped on a model farm there. It was obvious that the combined forces were all very badly armed and crudely trained. The Town Hall was occupied for a short time. Telegraph wires were cut and foodstuffs commandeered. No attack was made on the barracks. Next morning Mellows marched to Moyode Castle, two and a half miles east of the town. The R.I.C. estimate of the Volunteer numbers at this stage for the whole county was 1,000. Mellows knew by this time that neither Cork nor Limerick had risen. On Thursday night, a council of war was held, after reports of a coming military attack reached the Castle. Some of the officers were for disbanding, and Mellows was aware that these were in the majority. It was agreed that the officers would remain, and the men left free to go home or stay as they chose. Two hundred men left.[10]

On Thursday night a messenger arrived with a story that " something like half the British Army and all the big guns England could command were coming to crush the rebels in Galway who had about two digpikes, 80 shotguns, 40 rifles, some revolvers, miniature rifles, and some harmless bombs." Liam told this fellow that we came out to fight and not to run away, and the fellow looked at him and asked him what age he was. Liam said 24 years. Then the scaremonger shook his head in a very wise fashion, and said: " Very young, very young, entirely."

The officers, however, were more and more in favour of disbanding. Mellows handed over his command and told them to do what they liked. They changed their minds and insisted that Mellows again resume command. An hour later Mellows sent out twelve motor cars full of Volunteers on scouting expeditions, with the warning that if they were not back in two hours, it would

---

[10] See " Liam Mellows in Galway," *Poblacht*, December 3-31, 1927; *Sinn Féin*, April 26, 1924, Prionsias O h-Eidhin.

be concluded that they had all been captured or shot.   They scouted round in various directions and returned with the news that they could not find the enemy anywhere.

On Friday, learning of the presence of some 900 soldiers in the neighbourhood, Mellows offered them the choice of disbandment or a retreat to Clare.   He sent many of the married men home.   His force now numbered 500 men.   They agreed on a retreat in order with the cry: " We will stick together."

Liam marshalled his column in order; the main body, prisoners on carts, about thirty motor cars, the rear guard with Mellows, Ailbhe Ó Monachain, Prionsias Ó h-Eidhin, and other officers.   His men were held together by his will, good humour, and enthusiasm.   Mellows's " fight to a finish " was partly a bluff to keep up their morale, and partly a sincere belief that the fight could not fizzle out so early.   He was somewhat embarrassed by the very largeness of his force.   He thought on guerrilla lines as did Ailbhe Ó Monachain, and they believed that they could harass the British forces and hold them at bay for a considerable time with smaller numbers.   Soon grave news was to reach them which would compel the disbanding that Mellows already knew was inevitable, although he was gratified that County Galway which had seen no insurrection for more than a century had given a good account of itself, and that he had met with wide support among the people: food, information, and a spirit that in happier circumstances would have blazed into a formidable insurrection throughout the West.

At Lime Park, Father Tom Fahey, who was very friendly to the Volunteers and Irish-Ireland in his sympathies, overtook the column, and informed Mellows and the officers that he had serious information to give them.   A conference was called in an old and empty house.   Father Fahey then gave them the news he had received that Dublin—or rather the Volunteer positions there— was in flames, that there had been no general Rising in the country, that some 600 marines and as many soldiers were marching on Mellows's force, and would overtake it in about two hours.

In Ailbhe Ó Monachain's recollection the conference was a long and general discussion among the officers in which Father Fahey only intervened to give what information he had, and to express his own opinion that in the circumstances the Volunteers could only disperse and " hide their arms for another day."[11] Mellows sat on the floor, with his back to the wall, and listened to officer after officer give his opinion that as there was no doubt that Father Fahey's information was correct, it would be merely rashness and not bravery to face more than twice their own number of well-armed troops with shotguns and a few rifles. Mellows fell asleep during the long debate. There was a general demand that before deciding finally, the Captain, as they all called him, should be asked what he had to say. Then Liam woke up, apologised for falling asleep, and said that he still thought they had come out to fight. It was better in his opinion to die fighting even against odds than to be shot like rabbits running over the country. .He had had no sleep for three nights. If the men decided to disband, he would stay where he was and fight it out with the soldiers whenever they came.

In the end the officers decided that the force must disband, and the men were informed. There was no stampede. Many wept. Liam Mellows chatted with them and shook hands with each man before he left. He had kept the Tricolour flying as long as he could, and knew at heart that he could hold out no longer as the British forces were closing in, that his ill-armed force could do no more, and that his men must make their way to safety before the net closed in around them. Ailbhe Ó Monachain as Volunteer organiser, would naturally remain with him. He saw Prionsias Ó h-Eidhin was still in the house as the last of the motor cars yet remained at the door, and came across to shake hands and say good-bye to him. He was much moved when Prionsias Ó h-Eidhin said he had decided to stay with him. Mellows clasped his hand warmly, looked into his eyes, and said with great feeling: " God bless you!" Then, although he said nothing of it until long afterwards, he remembered Prionsias Ó h-Eidhin had a wife and family, and changed his plan. He said that it would be better to fight in the open rather than wait for whatever soldiers might find them and a hot reception in the house. Mellows called out to the driver of the car at the door to wait as it was moving away. The three men were driven as far as the high road where they walked away to face many months of wandering and narrow escape from arrest and capture.

There was a serious move by the Volunteers in County Wex-

---

[11] Statement of Ailbhe O Monachain to the writer.

ford when 600 Volunteers led by Robert Brennan, Seamus Doyle, J. R. Etchingham, Michael de Lacy, and Seamus Rafter seized Enniscorthy and established their headquarters there. The town was occupied on Thursday although the Volunteers had been mobilised as soon as a verbal order to rise reached them two days before from Dublin. Enniscorthy was taken by a surprise attack. Sentries were posted, cars and food commandeered, and houses searched for arms. The police barracks was held by a district inspector and five constables, a local bank by a sergeant and a constable. There was no serious and decisive clash between the police and the Volunteers beyond a few exchanges of shots between them without any casualties. The police fired at the Volunteer posts on Vinegar Hill and a castle overlooking the town, and the Volunteer sentries fired back. Railway communications were cut, and Volunteer parties entered Gorey and Ferns. The British dispatched a crude armoured train with a 15-pounder gun, and a force of 1,100 infantry and 70 cavalry against Enniscorthy. The military force arrived first and the Volunteers retired to their positions at Vinegar Hill outside the town. News of the surrender in Dublin arrived before hostilities began, and Pearse's order was brought to the Volunteer leaders by a messenger whom they trusted. They declined to believe the message and suspected it was a ruse. The messenger insisted that it was genuine. A message was sent to Colonel F. A. French in Wexford, who was both commander of the British forces there and a Wexford man, asking for two Volunteer officers, Seamus Doyle and J. R. Etchingham, to be given a safe conduct to Pearse to receive from him personally the command to surrender as they had gone out on his orders, and would take them from no one else. The offer was accepted, and Doyle and Etchingham were taken by car to Dublin under military escort. After a three hours' journey they entered the capital over which a thick pall of dark smoke hung. They saw the deserted streets and heard shots now and then which seemed to make the silence deeper by contrast. In Stephen's Green there was a dead horse and an overturned tramcar. At the Royal Hospital, Kilmainham, a crowd of staff officers surrounded them and brought them by car again to Pearse in Arbour Hill prison.[12]

---

[12] *Irish Press*, May 3, 1932, "With Pearse in Arbour Hill," Séamus Doyle.

Pearse was lying on a mattress covered by a greatcoat in his cell, " the first President of the Irish Republic . . . physically exhausted but spiritually exultant. His uniform was complete except for the Sam Browne belt which they had taken from him. The Dublin Brigade, he said, had done splendidly—' five days and nights of almost continuous fighting.' Amongst the dead were The O'Rahilly and Captain Tom Wafer (an Enniscorthy man), and dealing with the surrender, he told us that one impelling factor was that the British were shooting the people in the streets. ' I saw them myself,' he added with that quiet air of finality so familiar to those who knew him. ' No,' he was not aware that we in Wexford were out."

Then Pearse wrote the surrender order for the Wexford men, whispered to them to hide their arms in safe places, " for they will be needed later," and Etchingham and Doyle " said farewell to him with something of the sorrowful reverence with which one takes the last leave of a dead parent."

On Easter Monday County Louth Volunteers mobilised and entered the North Dublin area. One section marched towards Dundalk through Castlebellingham where some R.I.C. men were arrested ; one constable was shot apparently accidentally, and at the same time a British officer was severely wounded when cars on the main road were stopped and seized. Some of the Louth Volunteers then proceeded to Dublin, and took part in the G.P.O. fighting.

There were also mobilisations of the Volunteers in Clare, Kilkenny and Ulster which caused the R.I.C. and military much anxiety, although no action took place. On Tuesday a British flying column of 300 men were dispatched to Dungannon where all postal, telephonic, and telegraphic business was prohibited. Over 300 Irish Volunteers were arrested in Ulster where the MacNeill countermand had been very effective.[13]

The lessons of the 1916 Rising burned deeply into the hearts and minds of the Volunteers as was proved less than two years later in many an area where force of circumstances had broken or thwarted any move during Easter Week.

---

[13] See *A History of the Irish Rebellion of* 1916, Wells and Marlowe, ch. X; *Irish Times* 1916 *Handbook; Portrait of a Rebel Father*, ch. XXI; *Easter Fires*, (Dublin, 1943), Dr. J. Ryan and Seán MacEntee, for further accounts of the Rising outside Dublin.

CHAPTER XVIII

PEARSE ORDERS THE SURRENDER

On Saturday morning the headquarters in Moore Street were completely isolated. The noise of the Four Courts' area fighting could be heard, and the rattle of machine-guns and the duels of the snipers away in the city. British barricades covered the Parnell Street end of Moore Street where there was an artillery post, and other barricades covered laneways off Moore Street. In O'Connell Street the great buildings blazed and the flames in the Post Office were slowly dying down. The Volunteers sat in the Moore Street rooms or walked through the tunnelled walls. George Plunkett heard a British soldier crying and moaning somewhere out in the street. He went out and carried in the wounded man. He was taken upstairs and put into a bed in one of the rooms. He moaned restlessly, and would not be still. Pearse came in and the soldier asked one of the Cumann na mBan, Miss Julia Grenan, to be allowed to speak to him. Pearse in his grey-green uniform had some strange fascination for the wounded man. "I want to speak to the big man," said the soldier again and again. "That's Pearse," he was told. "Yes, I know," said the soldier, "I want him." Pearse heard the conversation, and came across quietly and gently to the bedside. "I want you to put your arms round me, and lift me," said the soldier, gasping in pain. Pearse did so at once, and asked the man what else he could do. "That's all I want," said the man, and fell asleep in a few minutes.

All through the night the Volunteers had tunnelled through the Moore Street houses towards Parnell Street. A party of fifty men went rifles in hand through the narrow openings in the walls and down stairways, glancing at the crudely barricaded doors and seeing nothing in the street outside but the cobbles over which a dark stillness seemed to brood. On and on they went until they reached a warehouse yard opening on the end of Moore Street. Away beyond a half-tumbled wall they saw a British barricade and khaki sentries and machine-gun nest. In twos and threes the Volunteers

gathered and more and more of the party stole up silently. A halt
was called and the men were told that at a word they were to
charge into the open and attack the barricade.   They were to fire
point-blank, create a diversion in which the rest of the garrison
might make a dash across Parnell Street to Williams & Woods or
perhaps escape to the north of the city.   Tom Clarke arrived and
looked at the barricade critically.   He shook his head and walked
back through the tunnelled walls.   Other officers came on the
scene, and ordered the men to retire and rest, saying the attack had
been postponed until dark.

Dr. Jim Ryan heard of the plan in the headquarters room and
was concerned for the wounded.   Connolly's stretcher had been
too big for the openings in the walls.   He had been removed on a
sheet, uncomplaining as he was jolted in the painful journey.   Dr.
Ryan asked Seán MacDermott whether the wounded could not be
removed to hospital, and offered to go to the nearest British post,
Red Cross flag in hand.   MacDermott laughed and told him he was
an innocent to be so trusting, but as for the wounded, something
must be done.   Later Dr. Ryan was called to Connolly who
said he wanted to be prepared for a journey to the Castle, that
Pearse already there had sent for him.   Pearse was seeking terms.
Connolly thought that the leaders would all be shot but the rest
set free.   Dr. Ryan doubted this version of the peace terms, but
later Tom Clarke and Joseph Plunkett told him the same thing in
almost the same words.

Shortly before William Pearse came out of the headquarters
room and told the writer: " Connolly has been asked out to negotiate.   They have decided to go to save the men from slaughter, for
slaughter it is."   He shook his head sadly, and then sighed with
relief at the thought that the men might be saved.   A few snipers'
rifles sounded every now and then away in the distance. The Volunteers sat along the floors, on beds, around tables, too tired in many
cases to eat or sleep.   They are tired of boring walls, barricading
windows, hearing rumours of fire in the block, waiting to be called
out on the charge that will never come.   " Say nothing yet," says
William Pearse, " as it may not come to anything."   He returns
and asks for a safety razor for his brother.   Pearse arrives.   He
looks firm and sad and cannot speak.   His brother gives him the
razor.   In the headquarters room, Connolly stares in front of him.
Plunkett is calm.   There are tears in MacDermott's eyes. Winifred
Carney is weeping, pale and quiet.

Dr. Ryan has another conversation with Seán MacDermott. He hears the story which has already spread through some of the groups of waiting Volunteers: out of that burning house across the street, with three corpses lying in front, three men dashed, a white flag in each man's hand. Pearse was watching as they dashed out and saw them shot dead, and the scene angered and grieved him deeply. This incident impressed the other leaders, too, as they discussed the question of surrender. Clarke, according to a story current in Moore Street, wanted still to fight to a finish, and hoist a white flag only as the last shot was fired and spent. Connolly protested that he could endure the men being shot, but that he would not have them burned alive. Another story had Tom Clarke going away quietly when the decision was taken with the dark intention of shooting himself, and then telling a friend who hastened after him that he might well do so but must refuse to give the British the satisfaction of saying he was ever afraid of them, free or a prisoner.

When the decision had been taken to negotiate, there was a meeting of the leaders around Connolly's bedside in 16 Moore Street. Tom Clarke, Joseph Plunkett, Seán MacDermott, Patrick and William Pearse were there. Three wounded Volunteers lay on the floor. In a bed the wounded British soldier whom Pearse had soothed slept. Winifred Carney, Julia Grenan and Elizabeth O'Farrell attended to the injured men. The meeting began some time after noon, and was conducted in low tones around Connolly's bed. At 12.45 Seán MacDermott asked Miss O'Farrell to improvise some white flags. One of these MacDermott hung out of the window of the room. Miss Grenan wept when Miss O'Farrell was chosen to carry a message to the nearest British post: it seemed certain death to go into the street where men had been shot down before their eyes. But Connolly roused himself and spoke reassuringly. Miss O'Farrell stepped out into the street waving the white flag high above her head. Her message from Pearse was a verbal one: " The Commandant-General of the Irish Republican Army wishes to treat with the Commander of the British Forces in Ireland." As Miss O'Farrell went towards the Parnell Street barricade all firing stopped. On her way she saw The O'Rahilly's hat and revolver at the corner of a lane. When she reached the post she gave the officer in charge her message. He asked how many women were with the rebels, learned there were three, and advised her to go back and bring the other two with her, then changed his mind, and said her story had better be told personally to headquarters. Miss O'Farrell was led through the barrier to the British headquarters at 70 Parnell Street, where she was interviewed by a very truculent and panicky colonel who snorted when the Irish Republican Army was mentioned, saying she must mean the Sinn Féiners, snorted even more when Miss O'Farrell insisted that Irish Republican Army was the right name and a very good one, roared out in alarm that she was a spy when she contradicted his statement that Pearse was wounded and should forthwith be forwarded on a stretcher. He ordered her to be taken away and searched, and her Red Cross badge cut off her armlet and apron. The result of the search proved to the Colonel that Miss O'Farrell could not be a dangerous person or a spy. He calmed down and sent her as a prisoner to Tom Clarke's shop in Parnell Street, a few doors away. After an hour, General Lowe, who was in charge of the O'Connell Street area operations, came to interview her there. He was courteous and paternal and listened quietly to the message. He refused to treat with Pearse except on the basis of an unconditional surrender and Connolly must follow on a stretcher. Failing this, hostilities would begin in half an hour. It was 2.30 p.m. when Miss O'Farrell reached Moore Street, and as she passed Sackville Lane again she saw The O'Rahilly's corpse lying a few yards up the laneway, his feet against a stone stairway in front of a house, his head towards the street.

After the second visit by Miss O'Farrell to General Lowe with a query, she finally at 3.30 accompanied Pearse to General Lowe at the Parnell Street post where Pearse handed his sword to the General. General Lowe said that he would allow the other Commandants to surrender separately, and suggested that Miss O'Farrell should be detained until the following morning so that she could bring Pearse's order to surrender to the Commandants at the other positions. Pearse asked her if she would agree to this, and said that he personally would like her to do so. When she consented, Pearse shook her warmly by the hand, and without a word took his place in a car with General Lowe's son, and was driven away to interview Sir John Maxwell at the British Military headquarters.

Pearse, after this interview, wrote out the order for surrender on behalf of the members of the Provisional Government, which read:

"In order to prevent the further slaughter of Dublin citizens, and in the hope of saving the lives of our followers now surrounded and hopelessly outnumbered, the members of the Provisional Government present at Headquarters have agreed to an unconditional surrender, and the Commandants of the various districts in the City and Country will order their commands to lay down arms.

> P. H. PEARSE,
> 29th April, 1916,
> 3.45 p.m."

Connolly was taken to a room in the Castle Hospital. His statement ran:

"I agree to these conditions for the men only under my own command in the Moore Street district and for the men in the Stephen's Green Command." The word "only" was added in Connolly's own handwriting. On Sunday morning Connolly, at General Lowe's request, assured Father Aloysius and Father Augustine, the Franciscans, who were visiting the various Volunteer positions to conclude the surrender, that his signature was genuine. Connolly said: "Yes—to prevent needless slaughter," adding that he spoke only for his own men.

Pearse's interview with Maxwell was brief. Maxwell's biographer states that General Lowe transmitted Pearse's first demand for negotiations to Maxwell "who replied that the only terms that could be considered were 'unconditional surrender,' although the British Government might exercise clemency to the rank and file and that the treatment of these would depend on their method of surrender." After General Lowe brought Pearse to Maxwell: "The interview was short and stern. The malignant seemed suddenly stunned by the thought of what he had brought on his followers, and unhesitatingly yielded to the demand to write and sign notices ordering the 'commanders' to surrender unconditionally."[1]

The men in Moore Street were marshalled by their officers, and

---

[1] *Maxwell*, Arthur, p. 250. Miss O'Farrell's account of the surrender is given, *Catholic Bulletin*, April-May, 1917, and in *An t-Eireannach*, Feabhra 15-29, 1936—two chapters of "Cú Uladh's" *Bliadhain na h-Aiséirighe*, a complete history of the Rising in Irish based upon original statements of the participants, translations of documents, and covering all the Volunteer positions in Dublin and the country.

told to be ready to march out soon. The news of the surrender spread. Down the cheeks of some tears ran. Others in a passion muttered threats, sullen and angry eyed. Others sprang up and splintered the butts of their rifles against the floors and walls, and hurled bolts, magazines and ammunition down stairways, snarling. The destruction was checked, and small groups discussed the news. Two Volunteers were asked to go through the rooms and ask every man whether he had taken anything from the houses that did not belong to him and, if so, to leave it behind, as the British would be only too glad to call them looters. Most of the Volunteers laughed at the question, a few were angry, one worried man had taken a cheap comb with a tinsel back as a souvenir for his wife. The worried man agreed to restore the comb to the mantelpiece. There was a principle at stake, he said, those so-and-sos must not get a chance to call them thieves. " You'll see another Rising in six months' time," said one.

At last the officers called the men together and they marched through the ruined walls, company by company, to a warehouse. Seán MacDermott read Pearse's letter to them, sombre, with a hint of tears in his eyes although his look was calm, clear, intense. Then MacDermott spoke with a touch of pride and passion in his voice, as he looked at the weary and haggard ranks in front of him who had listened in silence to the unconditional surrender order. He spoke simply, directed that food should be served out to the men, and telling them to take one good meal as they might not be too well fed for some time where they were going. Again he explained the position :

" The only terms the British military authorities would listen to were an unconditional surrender. We surrendered not to save you but to save the city and the people of this city from destruction. You would have fought on. No matter, I am proud of you. You made a great fight. It was not your fault that you have not won the Republic. You were outclassed, that is all. They had the men, the munitions, the force. But this week of Easter will be remembered, and your work will tell some day."

Then out into Moore Street marched the Volunteers, less than 200 of them, sleepless, weary, hungry, defeated, yet with a curious pride and sense of freedom stirring in them all. Moore Street was strewn with debris, with waxen bodies in green and in khaki uniforms, with huddled and ragged forms of civilians with red gashes in their foreheads, and the same waxen look as the dead British soldiers and Volunteers scattered in the gutters or lying across the footpaths. Final instructions were given. They were to march to the Parnell Monument and lay down their arms. There was some misunderstanding that an order for the liberation of the prisoners held by the Volunteers meant that they themselves would soon be free. A few cheered the words " then you are free." An angry hiss from the Volunteer ranks drowned the cheer: they were defiant even in defeat and would thank no one for freedom. William Pearse and Joseph Plunkett headed the march with waving white flags as if they were banners of victory. At the rear still other white flags flew. " Suddenly from out a side street," runs a description quoted by Maxwell's biographer, " marched out the first detachment of the rebels. Down the street they came in fours, arms at the slope, marching like trained soldiers . . . halted, laid down arms, and stepped back to the pavement. The arms were of various kinds, but all were very formidable weapons."

The Rising was over, one of the most arresting and indubitable examples in all history of the triumph of failure.

R

APPENDIX I.

PEARSE'S COURT-MARTIAL AND LAST SPEECH

PEARSE, Tom Clarke, and MacDonagh were tried by court-martial at Richmond Barracks on the morning of May 2, and at the same time, in another small room on the opposite side of the passage, Eamonn Duggan, Joseph MacGuinness, and Piaras Beaslai were also tried. On the previous day, Monday, May 1, they had all received written copies of the charges against them of " rebellion with the intent of assisting the enemy." All the prisoners had been identified by the political detectives of the Dublin police, the notorious " G men," who had descended on the prisoners like a flock of malignant birds of prey. Their victims were lined up against the wall of the gymnasium, and later packed in parties of forty in separate rooms of the barracks, mostly unfurnished except for stinking slop-pails.

While the prisoners waited in the gymnasium, Beaslai had conversations with his friends among the hundred chosen victims of the " G men." Joseph Plunkett was there, obviously very ill. Another Volunteer noticed that Plunkett's neck was tightly bandaged, the traces of an operation he had undergone in a nursing home before the Rising. Plunkett was in good spirits in spite of this. Beaslai found Tom Clarke convinced that the Rising would have a very good effect on the morale of the country. MacDermott quietly described the scenes in the Post Office and Moore Street, and how the surrender came about.

There was a preliminary investigation for all the accused prisoners, where British officers and soldiers, held during the fight by the Volunteers, gave evidence of identification and of bearing arms against those charged. Some of these witnesses were vindictive; others generous, many refusing to recognise and identify, while the R.A.M.C. officer said briefly he knew nothing about combatants, his job had been to care for British and Volunteer wounded impartially, and he had done that. Some of the " G men " themselves openly offered chances to Volunteers they knew to escape, or hustled them out of sight of their more officious colleagues.

After the serving of the charges on the prisoners on Monday, the regular courts-martial took place from the Tuesday on. Piaras Beaslai has described the procedure,[1] and, as the sole survivor of those who were tried at the same time as Pearse, Clarke and MacDonagh, his account is particularly valuable. (It casts grave doubt, moreover, on the alleged speech afterwards attributed to Thomas MacDonagh, in which the words, " you have sentenced me to death " occur. The sentence, as will be seen from Beaslai's account, was communicated

---

[1] In a written statement to the writer. Also in *Indiu*, November 22, 1946.

to those tried and found guilty in their cells later, and no formal sentence was passed at the actual trial.)

Each prisoner's case was taken separately in succession. The small room was suffocating with the crowd of witnesses, detectives, guards, three officers of the court martial, and the prosecutor. There was no officer for the defence, and no opportunity to call witnesses for the defence. The attitude of the officers of the court-martial towards the prisoners, however, was exceedingly courteous. Two military witnesses identified the prisoner as one who had taken part in the insurrection to their own knowledge, and then the "G men" gave evidence as to his political character, his activities and the length of these in seditious organisations. The prisoner was asked whether he had any statement to make in his defence, and, after this had been heard, his trial was over. No very accurate record was made of the proceedings except the long-hand notes of the officers conducting the trial—a labour which added to the tedium of the ordeal.

The terms of the charge, "assisting the enemy," compelled those accused to put up a defence. The six prisoners, Clarke, Pearse, MacDonagh, Beaslai, Duggan and MacGuinness, were brought back to the gymnasium after their trials, and were able to converse freely. MacDonagh chatted gaily and told them all that the Germans had landed in England, and very shortly the British Empire would be finished. Beaslai, who noted that MacDonagh could not then have had the slightest idea that he was going to be shot the very next morning, concluded later that MacDonagh had heard some rumour of the German bombardment of Yarmouth and Lowestoft on Easter Tuesday. Pearse sat on the floor, deep in his own thoughts, so full of them that he noticed nothing around him. He spoke only once, a complaint about something he had asked for and had not got.[2]

The six men remained in Richmond Barracks until evening when they were removed to Kilmainham. Beaslai did not expect that the judgment of the court would be announced until a week or so. On Wednesday morning he was awakened by the sound of rifle-fire at dawn. He thought it was probably shots fired by some Volunteer snipers in the city who had not surrendered, and fell asleep again. An hour later he learned that he had heard the firing party executing Pearse, Clarke, and MacDonagh. When an officer entered his cell and told him: "You have been sentenced to three years penal servitude. . . you are lucky," he understood.

---

[2] Pearse received a brief acknowledgment from Maxwell to a letter he wrote the same day: " I shall be grateful if you see that the three statements on business affairs (two with regard to my financial affairs and one with regard to the publication of some unpublished books of mine) and also the four poems which I handed to one of the soldiers on duty at Arbour Hill Detention Barracks this morning, are duly handed to my mother. . . . I shall also be grateful if you see that the sum of £7 odd (a £5 Bank of England note and two gold sovereigns with some loose change) which were taken from me at headquarters, Irish Command, on Saturday, be handed to my mother or sister, as also the personal effects taken from me on same occasion, and the watch and whistle taken from me later at Arbour Hill." This property was returned to Mrs. Pearse, who gave the watch mentioned, a wristlet watch with luminous dial, to the writer.

S

Pearse, however, had no illusions. There is a story that Joseph Plunkett, meeting Pearse in Richmond Barracks that Tuesday, said: "I suppose this means twenty years?" Pearse is supposed to have replied, with a gesture of his hand round his neck, "No, it means *this*!" As it is certain that none of the Provisional Government expected anything but death after the surrender negotiations, as the statements of Clarke, MacDermott, and Plunkett himself to Dr. James Ryan prove, the story bears all the marks of a fable, but it reflects Pearse's mood. It is certain that he had neither the hope nor the wish to survive.

This is as certain as it is also certain that he made every effort to save his colleagues and followers at the sole cost of his own life, though he must have realised that this hope was a slender one. The British authorities withheld all letters of his which expressed his final views of the insurrection, and it was not until August, 1946, that the text of his court-martial speech was discovered and published in *Indiu* and the *Irish Press*.

The summary Pearse wrote of his speech was as follows:

" I desire in the first place to repeat what I have already said in letters to General Sir John Maxwell and to Brigadier-General Lowe. My object in agreeing to an unconditional surrender was to prevent the further slaughter of the civilian population of Dublin and to save the lives of our gallant fellows who, having made for six days a stand unparalleled in military history, were now surrounded and (in the case of those under the immediate command of headquarters) without food. I fully understand now, as then, that my own life is forfeit to British law, and I shall die very cheerfully if I can think that the British Government, as it has already shown itself strong, will now show itself magnanimous enough to accept my single life in forfeiture and to give a general amnesty to the brave men and boys who have fought at my bidding. In the second place I wish to be understood that any admissions I make here are to be taken as involving myself alone. They do not involve and must not be used against anyone who acted with me, not even those who may have set their names to documents with me. (The Court assented to this.)

" I admit that I was Commandant-General Commanding-in-Chief of the forces of the Irish Republic which have been acting against you for the past week, and that I was President of the Provisional Government. I stand over all my acts and words done or spoken, in these capacities. When I was a child of ten I went down on my bare knees by my bedside one night and promised God that I should devote my life to an effort to free my country. I have kept that promise. First among all earthly things, as a boy and as a man I have worked for Irish freedom. I have helped to organise, to arm, to train, and to discipline my fellow countrymen to the sole end that, when the time came, they might fight for Irish freedom. The time, as it seemed to me, did come and we went into the fight. I am glad we did, we seem to have lost, we have not lost. To refuse to fight would have been to lose, to fight is to win, we have kept faith with the past, and handed a tradition to the future.

" I repudiate the assertion of the prosecutor that I sought to aid and abet England's enemy. Germany is no more to me than England is. I asked and accepted German aid in the shape of arms and an expeditionary force, we neither asked for nor accepted German gold, nor had any traffic with Germany but what I state; my aim was to win Irish freedom; we struck the first blow ourselves but I should have been glad of an ally's aid.

" I assume that I am speaking to Englishmen, who value their own freedom and who profess to be fighting for the freedom of Belgium and Serbia. Believe that we too love freedom and desire it. To us it is more desirable than anything in the world. If you strike us down now we shall rise again and renew the fight. You cannot conquer Ireland; you cannot extinguish the Irish passion for freedom; if our deed has not been sufficient to win freedom then our children will win it by a better deed."

APPENDIX II

THREE SPEECHES OF CONNOLLY'S

THE *Irish Worker,* September 5, 1914, published a speech of Connolly's delivered at a meeting in Beresford Place, Dublin, on Sunday, August 30, 1914. It shows his mood on the war's outbreak in the following passages:

" . . . After Grey and Asquith had plunged England into war there arose a clamour for Redmond, and Redmond, without consulting you the people of Ireland, pledged us to war with as kindly, gracious a nation as God ever put the breath of life into—what happened then? Redmond, when they shouted for him, might have sat still and let them shout, then before another sun rose have got a measure greater than Grattan ever dreamed of. Redmond, as spokesman of the majority of the Irish people, might have risen and said: 'I and my colleagues will go to Ireland and consult the Irish nation. . . . We have waited and now Germany has come, and we will start our own Parliament. Stop us if you can.' Help would have come from all sides. Why the R.I.C. would have acted as a guard of honour. . . . Whether my speech is pro-German or pro-Irish, I don't know. . . . The Irish workers hold themselves ready to bargain with whoever can make a bargain. . . . If you are itching for a rifle, itching for a fight, have a country of your own; better to fight for our country than for the robber empire. If ever you shoulder a rifle let it be for Ireland. Conscription or no conscription, they shall never get me or mine. You have been told you are not strong, that you have no rifles. Revolutions do not start with rifles; start first and get your rifles after. Our curse is our belief in our weakness. We are not weak, we are strong. Make up your mind to strike before your opportunity goes."

Frank Robbins, *Irishman,* Dublin, May 19, 1928, has recorded his memory of Connolly's last public speech at the concert held in Liberty Hall on Easter Sunday evening. He dealt specifically with the secret session of the House of Commons which had been announced for the next week, and took for granted that the Irish question would be discussed as well as the question of peace with Germany. He said Ireland must be represented at the peace negotiations, and ended with a declaration that the Citizen Army would stand to arms until the Irish claim was heard.

Even while Connolly was speaking the printing press of the *Workers' Republic* was working at the best imitation of top speed the rickety and antiquated machine could make towards its total of 2,500 copies of the Republican Proclamation, which three men, Christopher Brady, Michael Molloy and Liam O'Brien, compositors, finally finished late on Sunday night, after considerable difficulties with shortage of type, mixed founts, and missing and battered letters which had to be contrived with much labour and ingenuity. The setting-up operation had to be repeated owing to mixed and meagre type.

Thomas MacDonagh handed the MS. of the Proclamation to Christopher Brady an hour before noon on Easter Sunday after Connolly in uniform had introduced the three men to him in the Liberty Hall machine room. MacDonagh shook hands with each, and after they had read the Proclamation in turn, said to them: "Do it if you wish, but if not we won't be the worse friends." The three men said that they were proud to have the honour of setting up such an historic document. (*Irish Press*, April 24, 1934, "The Three Printers of the Proclamation," Nellie Gifford-Donnelly.)

William Partridge with a Citizen Army guard was in charge.

Connolly's daughter, Nora Connolly O'Brien, gives in her books, *The Unbroken Tradition* and *Portrait of a Rebel Father*, the text of the statement Connolly gave her in Dublin Castle at their last interview before his execution. This speech to his court-martial reads:

To the Field General Court-martial, held at Dublin Castle, on May 9th, 1916.

(Evidence mainly went to establish the fact that the accused, James Connolly, was in command at the General Post Office, and was also Commandant-General of the Dublin Division. Two of the witnesses, moreover, strove to bring in alleged instances of wantonly risking the lives of prisoners. The court held that these charges were *irrelevant*, and could not be placed against the prisoner.)

"I do not wish to make any defence except against charges of wanton cruelty to prisoners. These trifling allegations that have been made, if they record facts that really happened, deal only with the almost unavoidable incidents of a hurried uprising against long established authority, and nowhere show evidence of set purpose to wantonly injure unarmed persons.

"We went out to break the connection between this country and the British Empire, and to establish an Irish Republic. We believe that the call we then issued to the people of Ireland was a nobler call, in a holier cause, than any call issued to them during this war, having any connection with the war. We succeeded in proving that Irishmen are ready to die endeavouring to win for Ireland those national rights which the British Government has been asking them to die to win for Belgium. As long as that remains the case, the cause of Irish freedom is safe.

"Believing that the British Government has no right in Ireland, never had any right in Ireland, and never can have any right in Ireland, the presence, in any one generation of Irishmen, of even a respectable minority, ready to die to affirm that truth, makes that Government forever a usurpation and a crime against human progress.

"I personally thank God that I have lived to see the day when thousands of Irish men and boys, and hundreds of Irish women and girls, were ready to affirm that truth, and to attest it with their lives if need be.

JAMES CONNOLLY, Commandant-General,
Dublin Division,
Army of the Irish Republic."

APPENDIX III

THE EXECUTIONS

SIR FRANCIS VANE denounced the executions of "the so-called rebel leaders" as being "carried out in the most brutally stupid manner. The execution of three of the senior chiefs would have been adequate for justice, instead of fourteen, one or two a day, over a fortnight, culminating by Connolly, a badly wounded man, taken out, tied to a chair, for he could not stand, and shot like a dog." (*Agin the Government*, p. 271.)

George Bernard Shaw, before the last of the executions, wrote in the *Daily News*, May 10, 1916:

". . . an Irishman resorting to arms to achieve the independence of his country is only doing what Englishmen will do, if it be their misfortune to be invaded and conquered by the Germans in the course of the present war. Further, such an Irishman is as much in order, morally, in accepting assistance from the Germans, as England is in accepting the assistance of Russia in her struggle with Germany. The fact that he knows his enemies will not respect his rights if they catch him, and that he must therefore fight with a rope around his neck, increases his risk, but adds in the same measure to his glory in the eyes of his compatriots, and of the disinterested admirers of patriotism throughout the world. . . . The shot Irishmen will now take their places beside Emmet and the Manchester Martyrs in Ireland, and beside the heroes of Poland and Serbia in Europe; and nothing in heaven or earth can prevent it."

Dr. O'Dwyer, Bishop of Limerick, in an exchange of letters with Sir John Maxwell told him bluntly: "You took care that no plea for mercy should interpose on behalf of the poor young fellows who surrendered to you in Dublin. The first information that we got of their fate was the announcement that they had been shot in cold blood. Personally, I regard your action with horror, and I believe it has outraged the conscience of the country." In a speech, when the freedom of Limerick City was conferred on him in September, 1916, Bishop O'Dwyer asked: "Was I to condemn them, even if their rebellion was not justifiable theologically? Was I to join that gang of renegades who were throwing dirt on Pearse and MacDonagh and Colbert and the other brave fellows whom Maxwell had mercilessly put to death? Was I to join in the condemnation of the men and women, too, who, without trial, were deported by thousands? The British Government and their friends ring the changes on the hopelessness of the Rising and the folly of a couple of thousand badly armed Volunteers attempting to overthrow the British power in Ireland. There is something in it, and even, from the point of view of our country's freedom, there is wisdom in the admonition:

> Bide your time, your worst transgression
> Were to strike and strike in vain;
> He whose hand would smite oppression
> Must not need to strike again.

The Irish Volunteers were too few for the enterprise, but that is, perhaps, the worst that can be said against them. Rebellion, to be lawful, must be the act of the nation as a whole, but, while that is true, see the case of the Irish Volunteers against England. The very Government against which they rose, and which killed them so mercilessly, has proclaimed its own condemnation. What is that ghost of Home Rule which they keep safe in lavender on the Statute Book but a confession of the wrong of England's rule in Ireland? . . . Sinn Féin is, in my judgment, the true principle, and alliance with English politicians is like the alliance of the lamb with the wolf."

Those executed were:

P. H. Pearse, Tom Clarke, Thomas MacDonagh—May 3; Joseph Plunkett, Edward Daly, William Pearse, Michael O'Hanrahan—May 4; John MacBride—May 5; Eamonn Ceannt, Michael Mallin, Con Colbert, Seán Heuston—May 8; James Connolly, Seán MacDermott—May 12.

Thomas Kent was shot in Cork, May 9. Roger Casement was hanged at Pentonville Prison, London, August 3.

There were 97 death sentences commuted to penal servitude for various terms, from three years to life. There were 160 courts-martial and 122 sentenced. Apart from these, several thousand men and women were deported to various British prisons and internment camps. All these were released at different dates up to Christmas, 1916. Those sentenced to penal servitude were released under a general amnesty in the summer of 1917.

APPENDIX IV

John Adams, Thomas Allen, Andrew Byrne, James Byrne, Joseph Byrne, Frank Burke, Seán Connolly, James Corcoran, Harry Coyle, John Costello, John Cromean, John Crinigan, Philip Clarke, Charles Garrigan, Charles Darcy, Peter Darcy, Brendan Donelan, Patrick Doyle, John Dwan, Edward Ennis, Patrick Farrell, James Fox, George Geoghegan, Seán Howard, John Hurley, John Healy, John Kealy, Gerard Keogh, John Kelly, Con Keating, Richard Kent, Peadar Macken, Francis Macken, Peter Manning, Richard Murphy, D. Murphy, Michael Malone, Charles Monaghan, D. Murray, J. McCormack, William McDowell, The O'Rahilly, J. O'Reilly, Richard O'Reilly, Thomas O'Reilly, Richard O'Carroll, Patrick O'Flanagan, John O'Grady, J. Owens, James Quinn, Thomas Rafferty, Frederick Ryan, George Reynolds, Domhnall Sheehan, Patrick Shortis, John Traynor, Edward Walsh, Philip Walsh, Patrick Whelan, Thomas Wafer, Peter Wilson.

This list is incomplete.   The number of insurgent wounded exceeded 100. It was at least 120 but definite figures are not available.

APPENDIX V

THE POSITION IN THE WEST

UP to Friday night the news that reached the County Galway Volunteers of the events in Dublin was cheering.   Mellows and his men heard the guns booming in Galway Bay, and were under the impression that the warships were sealed up in the bay by the activities of German submarines.   No shell from the warships—or warship—fell nearer than five miles away.   Mellows could feel that he had achieved his objective as his one object was to pin down the British forces in the West and prevent them from concentrating on the Dublin fighters.   Poorly armed as his forces were, the Galway Volunteer leaders had no hope of doing anything else.

The isolation of the Volunteer areas from each other prevented the fighters in the various areas from knowing the real position until after the Rising.   Mellows and his officers knew of Casement and the capture of the *Aud* but hoped that the Volunteers throughout the country had risen. Outside the larger towns the Volunteers ruled County Galway and, for a week, some 600 square miles of country from Galway City to Ballinasloe, and from Tuam to Gort, were free from British control.

When the Volunteers left Moyode Castle they marched to Lime Park where Father Thomas Fahey, who had visited them at the castle, and heard their confessions there, overtook them in company with Father Martin O'Farrell. Father O'Farrell had news of the movements of the British troops in Ballinasloe and Athlone. Father Fahey, who had cycled to Galway City on Friday, heard reports there that Dublin was in flames and that the Volunteers could not hold out any longer. Mellows went on to Tullira Castle where a final halt was called. (Lime Park is close to the Clare border; Tullira Castle was a former residence of Mr. Edward Martyn, dramatist, and President of the Sinn Féin organisation, 1905-8.) About 2 a.m. on Saturday morning, Father Fahey urged Mellows to disband the men because it was folly to remain in the castle where they would be surrounded by British troops almost immediately. Mellows replied, according to Father Fahey's later account of the talk to Ailbhe Ó Monacháin, that he would not disband, that death would be their ultimate fate at the hands of the British anyway, and that it was better to die fighting. Father Fahey then suggested that the matter should be put before the officers, to which Mellows consented. A meeting of the officers, fourteen in all, was held in one of the rooms of the castle. Father Fahey gave his views to the meeting, stating also Mellows's views, and adding that he himself regarded further stay in the castle as sheer throwing away of their lives. Twelve officers voted for immediate disbandment, Mellows and Ó Monacháin against. Ó Monacháin supported Mellows but urged that he thought it better for the better armed section of the force to keep together, take to the open country, and carry on a guerrilla fight. This advice was not accepted by the majority of the officers.

Father Fahey then asked Mellows to communicate the decision of the meeting to the men. The general feeling of the meeting was that with Dublin in flames—as the Galway reports stated—with the greater part of the Volunteers in the South inactive in the Rising, and with the undoubted approach of strong British forces from the North and elsewhere it would be merely slaughter to venture the weak Volunteer force in the West against them. Mellows refused, and said that he had asked the men to follow him, that they had followed him, and that he could never endure to disband them. Father Fahey then went out personally, informed the Volunteers what the meeting had decided, advised them to break up as quietly as possible, and to stick to their arms as they would need them again.

One difficulty against disbanding urged by Mellows to Father Fahey was that the six R.I.C. prisoners might identify the men. Father Fahey thereupon spoke to the R.I.C. men, who consulted among themselves, and then stated that they would give no information, a promise which they afterwards kept. Mellows told Father Fahey that, to give the prisoners their proper meals, he had sometimes gone without his own. One R.I.C. prisoner fell ill during the Rising, was left behind on the road with the advice to find some house to rest in, recovered, and overtook the column again, and his place as a prisoner of war.

There were only sixty rifles (thirty-six service magazine rifles, and the remainder single shot Martini Enfields) in the whole force, with fifteen rounds for each rifle; four miniature rifles; 350 shotguns of all sorts; about twelve revolvers; many pikes, newly forged, and pitchforks.

The countermanding order reached one Volunteer company on Sunday evening as they were taking up positions to attack a police barracks. Early on Tuesday morning, Gort and Oranmore barracks were attacked; the first was evacuated, the second held out until the arrival of help from Galway. On Wednesday, fifteen Volunteers from Castlegarr were attacked by nine lorry loads of R.I.C. and military at Carnmore Cross under Captain Bodkin. The Volunteers were armed only with shotguns but answered the attack. The British withdrew as Volunteers from Claregalway rushed up. One R.I.C. man named Whelan was killed. "The man who fired the fatal shot," says the *Irish Times Handbook*, p. 39, "was seen to be carrying a gun of antique pattern, and it is believed that he was shot in the back while getting over a stone wall." There were, in fact, no Volunteer casualties. The Volunteer who fired the shot was, in fact, so disturbed that until he had been packed off to confession, and his companions had pointed out to him that in wars men get shot, and he might be shot himself "to-morrow as the policeman had been shot to-day," his peace of mind could not be restored.

On Thursday, Kinvara R.I.C. barracks was attacked. A flying column in motor cars from Moynode pursued a party of R.I.C. back to Athenry.

APPENDIX VI

THE RISING AND ULSTER

PRACTICALLY nothing has been published on the events in Ulster during the Rising with the exception of Nora Connolly O'Brien's short references to events in Belfast and County Tyrone in her *Portrait of a Rebel Father*, and two detailed articles by "Cú Uladh" in *An t-Eireannach*, Bealtaine 16-23, 1936. According to "Cú Uladh's" information, based on his own first-hand knowledge of the North, and the statements of active Ulster Republicans, no Rising was contemplated in Belfast or even in Ulster itself. The Ulstermen were to go to Galway and join up with Liam Mellows. On the Wednesday before Easter guns were sent from Belfast to Tyrone. About 100 Volunteers left Belfast for Dungannon and Coalisland on Good Friday and the following day, armed with some sixty rifles of various makes. A Volunteer mobilisation on Easter Sunday in Tyrone amounted to no more than 120 men, including the Belfast contingents just mentioned, and the Tyrone men had only fifteen rifles. The orders to proceed to Connacht fell through, and the Belfast contingents went home on the evening train. The arms were left in Tyrone. MacNeill's countermand was late in reaching the North but was even more effective than elsewhere. During the week there were several minor attempts to remobilise the Ulster men but without avail. Arrangements were made to cross Loch Neagh by boat, and certain boatmen agreed to bring the Volunteers across at any time, day or night, when required. The activities of the British column in Dungannon, and the successful raiding for arms and ammunition in Tyrone were heavy blows to the Volunteer plans in the North, even if the fear of Volunteer action was an anxiety to the British forces which were held there until the failure of the efforts for a general revolt became clear. Some Belfast Volunteers eventually started for Dublin and arrived just as the surrender was announced, including Cathal O'Shannon, who was arrested on his return to Belfast.

APPENDIX VII

THE CONNOLLY KIDNAPPING

JOSEPH PLUNKETT told his sister, Mrs. Gertrude Dillon, in January, 1916, that Connolly had been decoyed into a taxi and driven to a house outside Dublin. Plunkett, Pearse, MacDermott were also in the car. They informed Connolly at once of their plans for insurrection, and insisted he must discuss their differences once and for all. The discussions lasted three nights and the Rising plans, based on Plunkett's scheme, were adopted in outline. Connolly, at first angry, became so enthusiastic that his captors could hardly persuade him to leave. A Volunteer on duty at the house informed the writer that no attempt to detain Connolly was made. The house was near Chapelizod. Connolly sent a message to his wife during his absence. He is quoted as saying: "I have been beaten on my own ground." Plunkett said that he never talked so much and had never been so tired in all his life and had never enjoyed anything so much as this three nights' wordy duel with Connolly. Connolly, on his part, no longer held as he had snapped at Seán McGarry, "Rossa was prepared to fight England *at peace*. You fellows won't fight her *at war*."

INDEX.

A.

Abbey Theatre, 3.
Act of Union, 2.
Afghans, 24.
Agnew, Arthur, Kimmage garrison, 134.
Albert, Father, O.F.M.Cap., 163.
Aloysius, Father, O.F.M.Cap., 255.
Ancient Order of Hibernians, 8.
Arbour Hill, 249.
Arms landing, 1916, 36, 79, 89, 101-114, 237.
Arthur, Sir George, biographer of Maxwell, 208, 209, 210, 255.
Ashling, code word used by Joseph Plunkett, 45, 46.
Ashbourne, battle of, 218-227.
Ashe, Thomas (1882-1917), Commandant of Fifth Dublin Battalion, leader of Ashbourne fight, sentenced to penal servitude for life, released under 1917 amnesty, died after forcible feeding during his hunger strike at Mountjoy Jail, September 25, 1917, 189, 218, 220-7.
Asquith, H. H., Prime Minister, later Lord Oxford and Asquith, 59.
Athenry, 245.
Athlone, 1, 100, 229.
Aud, the, German arms ship, 15, 28, 36, 66, 69, 70, 77, 79, 93, 97, 101-14, 230, 235, 236, 237, 241, 244. See also Casement, Arms landing, Spindler.
Augustine, Father, O.F.M.Cap., 217, 255.

B.

Bachelor's Walk shooting, 5.
Bailey, Daniel Julien, 93, 101, 238, 239.
Balfe, Dick, Mendicity garrison, 159, 161.
Ballykissane, 110, 112-14.
Banba, 4, 41, 68, 150, 192, 236.
Banse, Herr, 29.
Barrett, Mrs., City Hall garrison, 118.
Beales, Patrick, North King Street victim, 216.
Beaslai, Piaras, 203, 216.
Belfast, 4.
Belvederian, The, 150.
Bernstorff, Count von, German Ambassador to U.S.A., 21, 23, 24, 25.

Bethmann-Hollweg, von, German Chancellor, 41.
Birrell, Augustine, Chief Secretary, 1-6, 98.
Blunt, Wilfrid Scawen, 21.
Boland, Michael, G.P.O. garrison, 142, 143.
Boland's Mills, 148, 170, 187-192.
Bowen-Colthurst, Captain, 72, 167-70, 180.
Boxer Rising, in China, 1900, 12.
Brady, Sergeant, R.I.C., 222.
Brady, Christopher, compositor, 262.
Breen, Father Joe, Tralee, 108, 109.
Breen, Captain Liam, G.P.O. garrison, 153.
Brennan, James, Mendicity garrison, 159.
Brennan, Miss Lily, 173.
Brennan, Michael, Clare, 87.
Brennan, Patrick, Clare, 88.
Brennan, Robert, Enniscorthy, 249.
Brennan, Whitmore, J., 124, 131, 151.
Broadstone Station attack, 206-7.
Brosnan, Tadhg, 110.
Brugha, Cathal (1874-1922), later Minister of Defence, Dáil Eireann, killed in Civil War, July 5, 1922, 172, 173, 176; character of, 180; saves South Dublin Union from capture, 182-5; on the Rising plans—his own copy of which was burned at his request after 1916, 229.
Bryce, James, later Lord, 31.
Bullitt-Grabisch, Frau Dr. Agatha, 29.
Bülow, von, 25.
Burke, J. J., 53, 56, 57.
"Byon," the, 164.
Byrne, L. P. (Andrew E. Malone), 70.

C.

Cahill, Patrick, Tralee (d. 1947), 38, 78, 79, 239.
Callender, Ignatius, 158.
Capuchin Annual, the, 70, 97, 146, 160, 163, 205.
Carney, Winifred, Connolly's secretary, 124, 147, 150, 151, 155, 252, 253.
Carson, Lord, 5.
Casement, Roger (1864-1916), 2, 12, 14-29, 31-46, 66, 76, 93, 94, 101, 103, 104, 105, 106, 110, 114,

234, 237, 238, 240, 241 ; career, 12 ; views on insurrection, 37–8 ; and Pearse, 34 ; and Clarke, 7, 17, 34 ; "Findlay affair," 33 ; John Devoy on, 17–18 ; execution under Act of Edward III, August 3, 1916, 264.

Ceannt, Mrs. Aine, 96.

Ceannt, Eamonn (1881–1916), executed May 8, 1916, 6, 47, 51, 57, 95, 96, 98, 149 ; views on Rising, 95 ; defence of South Dublin Union, 172–186 ; clash with Michael Mallin, 51 ; character, 51 ; and House of Commons secret session, 96.

Chalmers, Lieutenant, 124, 125.

Chesterton, G. K., 208.

Childers, Erskine, 5.

Christensen, Evind Adler, Casement's Norwegian servant, 17, 18, 33, 35.

Christian, William, 195.

Citizen Army, Irish :

Connolly on, 58 ; at Stephen's Green, 120–2, 167 ; at City Hall, 118–23 ; attack on Dublin Castle, 117 ; and Connolly kidnapping, 49, 51–2.

Clan na Gael, Irish-American revolutionary organisation, founded 1867, affiliated to I.R.B., 6, 17, 23, 24, 34, 35, 36, 37, 39, 102, 103, 104, 105, 107.

Clancy, George, Vice-Commandant, Limerick Brigade, 86, 234, 235.

Clancy, Peadar, Dublin, later Vice-Commandant, Dublin Brigade ; murdered, November, 1920, 211.

Clarke, Austin, 126.

Clarke, Joseph, 195, 197, 200.

Clarke, Liam, G.P.O. garrison, 132.

Clarke, Thomas J. (1857–1916), First signatory of the Republican Proclamation ; emigrated to the United States in 1881, returned to Ireland in 1883 on Clan na Gael mission, and sentenced to penal servitude for life the same year. Went to America on his release in 1899, and remained there until his return to Dublin, 1907, 6–8, 9, 10, 12, 13, 17, 21, 25, 47, 52, 59, 63, 97, 124, 129, 135, 136, 139, 154, 221, 252, 253 ; his prison life, 7 ; and Casement, 7, 17, 34 ; and Monteith, 12 ; and Connolly, 57 ; execution, May 3, 1916.

Coade, a youth shot by Colthurst, 168.

Cockran, Burke, 23.

Cohalan, Dr., Bishop of Cork, 233.

Colbert, Con, Marrowbone Lane garrison, executed May 8, 1916, 54, 174, 175.

Colivet, M. P., Commandant, Limerick Brigade, 82, 83, 85–8, 233–6 ; interview with Pearse, Holy Week, 1916, 85–6 ; plans for the Rising, 86–88 ; and Easter Week, Limerick, 233–6 ; and I.R.A. 1918 Inquiry, 228, footnote.

College of Surgeons, 122, 136.

Collins, Michael (1890 – 1922), Chairman, Provisional Government and Commander in Chief, 1922. Returned from London, January, 1916, for the Rising. From 1917 was one of the guiding spirits of the I.R.A., Sinn Fein, and I.R.B. A reward of £10,000 was offered for his capture. Killed in an ambush in West Cork, 1922, 79, 112, 124, 125.

Colum, Padraic, poet, dramatist, and critic ; close friend of Thomas MacDonagh, 19, 20, 33.

Columban, Father, O.F.M.Cap., 217.

Columcille Hall, Blackhall Place, 203.

Connolly, James (1869–1916), b. Co. Monaghan, Socialist propagandist, trade union organiser, and Labour Leader. Executed May 12, 1916, 4, 16, 26, 76–78, 81, 91, 118, 124, 125, 129, 130, 131, 134, 135, 139, 141, 143, 145, 146–9, 154, 155–7, 189, 219, 221, 229, 252, 253, 254, 255 ; and MacNeill, 26, 62–3, 91 ; kidnapping of, 47–63 ; and German aid, 14, 16, 49, 149 ; and "Castle Document," 70 ; prepares plans for the Rising, 11, 77, 229 ; Pearse's tribute to, 145 ; and surrender, 252–5 ; part in Rising, 124, 125, 130, 131, 134–5, 141, 143, 145–9, 154 ; last statement and execution, 262–3.

Connolly, Seán, 117–19.

Comhar, An, 94, 116.

Cosantóir, An, 39, 73, 166, 173, 223.

Cosgrave, William, later President, Executive Council, Irish Free State, 180, 183.

Cotton, Alfred, Volunteer organiser,

acting Vice-Commandant of the Tralee Battalion, 79-81, 109.
Coyle, Eithne, 150.
Crampton, J. Walker, 201.
Crenigan, John, 225 and footnote.
Crofts, Gerald, 133.
Cumann na mBan, women's auxiliary force, affiliated to Irish Volunteers, 133, 150-1, 158, 171, 175, 251.
"Cu Uladh," 255, 267-8.
Curry, Dr. C. E., 32, 33.

D.

Daly, Agnes, Limerick, 235.
Daly, Dennis, 79, 112, 113.
Daly, Edward (1891–1916), Four Courts leader, executed May 4, 1916, 203–17.
Daly, John, famous Limerick Fenian, 9.
Daly, Liam, Kimmage garrison, 134, 135, 154.
Daly, Miss M., 114.
Daly, P., 205.
Dark Invader, 106.
Davy's public-house, Portobello, 77, 119, 120.
De Coeur, Bob, Citizen Army, 120.
De Lacy, L., 17, 18, 33.
De Lacey, M., 249.
Delahunt's, Camden Street, 165.
De Valera, Eamon, b. October 14, 1882, New York. Adjutant, Dublin Brigade and Volunteer leader, 1916 ; sentenced to death, commuted to penal servitude for life ; released under general amnesty, wins East Clare election, President of Sinn Féin and Irish Volunteers, 1917 ; deported to Lincoln Jail, 1918 from which he escaped in February, 1919, elected President of Dáil Eireann, and begins his American tour the same year ; returns to Ireland, December 1920 ; opposes 1921 Treaty and participates in Civil War, 1922-3 ; enters Dáil Eireann, after foundation o, Fianna Fáil, 1927 ; in power, 1932-47, 95, 148, 170, 187–9, 190, 191, 193.
Devoy, John, Fenian and Clan na Gael leader, 6, 12, 17, 18, 19, 21, 23, 24, 26, 28, 29, 33, 35, 36, 37, 39, 44, 102–3, 104, 105, 112 ; and Casement, 17–18, 33–4, 35–6 ; and the Rising, 6, 17, 24, 25, 39, 102–3, 105–7 ; opinion of the Germans, 17, 18.

Dillon, Mrs Gertrude, 114, 268.
Donabate, 218.
Donnelly, Mary, 150.
Donnelly, Simon, 187, 188, 189, 190, 191, 197 footnote.
Doyle, Sir Arthur Conan, 19.
Doyle, James, Clanwilliam House garrison, 196, 201, 202.
Doyle, Joseph, Citizen Army, 77.
Doyle, Alderman P. S., 183.
Dublin Castle, attack on, 115–17 ; Connolly's objections to capture of, 117.
Dublin Mansion House, plan to seize in 1914, 59.
Dublin Metropolitan Police, 117, 125, 131, 133, 153.
Duggan, Eamonn, Volunteer officer, later signatory of 1921 Treaty, 258–59.
Duffy, George Gavan, 38, 39.
Dundalk, 149.
Dungannon, 250, 267–8.

E.

Easter Eve, 76–100.
Easter Fires, pamphlet, Dr. J. Ryan and Seán MacEntee, 250.
Emmet, Robert, 1, 143.
Ennis, 87.
Ennis, Peter, Liberty Hall, 140.
Enniscorthy, 249.
Enniskillen, 229.
Etchingham, John R., 249.
Evening Mail Office, Dublin, 118.

F.

Fahey, Father T., 247, 248, 266.
Father Mathew Hall, 206, 216.
Feeney, Father, 245.
Fenit Pier, 36, 78, 80, 110.
Ferns, 249.
Findlay, Mansfeldt de Cardonnell, British Minister to Norway in 1914, 33, 34, 35.
Fitzgerald, Desmond (d. 1947), later Free State Minister of Defence, 133.
Fitzgibbon, Seán (d. April 21, 1948), 83, 84, 85, 94, 96, 115, 117, 234-5.
Flynn, Michael, Gaelic League organiser, 239.
Flynn, Maurice, pilot, 109.
Forward, Glasgow, 60.
Four Courts, the, 136, 153, 155, 159, 160, 166, 203–17.
Fox, R. M., 150.
French, Colonel F. A., Wexford, 249.
Frey, Captain von, 37.
Friend, General L. B., G.O.C. in

Ireland, 1913–16, 4, 67, 71, 72, 74.

G.

Galway, the Rising in County, 244–48, 265–7.
Gerrard, James, 41.
Gifford, Grace (Mrs. Joseph Plunkett), 73.
Gifford-Donnelly, Mrs. Nellie, 262.
Gilbert, Sir John, 156.
Gillie, D. R., 15.
Good, Joe, Kimmage garrison, 135.
Gorey, 249.
Gormler, Constable, R.I.C., 225.
Gort, 245.
" G.R's," the, 194.
Grace, James, Northumberland Road garrison, 195–8.
Grattan, Henry, 43, 157.
Gray, Inspector, R.I.C., 220–23 and footnote.
Green Flag, in 1916, 76, 126, 154, 189, 190.
Grenan, Julia, 150, 251, 253.
Grey, Sir Edward, later Lord, 34.
Griffith, Arthur (1872–1922), founder of Sinn Fein, first President, Irish Free State, 59, 94, 119.
Guinness's Brewery, shootings in, 162.

H.

Hayes, Dr. R., 220.
Healy, T. M., 169.
Hennessy, Father, O.S.A., 235.
Heuston, Seán, executed May 8, 1916; leader of Mendicity garrison, 109, 155–163, 207.
Hibernian Rifles, independent Volunteer corps, associated with American Alliance, A.O.H., 135.
Hickey, Christopher, North King Street victim, 212–14.
Hickey, Thomas, North King Street victim, 212–14.
Hickey, Constable, R.I.C., 225.
Higgins, John, medical student and writer, engaged in ambulance work during the Rising, d. 1917, 127 footnote.
Hirsch, Gilbert, American journalist, 30.
Hitler, 24.
Hobson, Bulmer, secretary of Irish Volunteers and editor, Irish Freedom, 7, 20, 21, 22, 25, 26, 37, 65, 83, 88–92, 93, 116; his statement of Casement-MacNeill policy, 21–2; opposition to 1916 insurrection, 21, 76; Palm Sunday,

1916, speech, 76; kidnapping of, 93; and Pearse, 25, 42, 76, 91, 92; and Connolly, 26; and Casement, 20-2; and Devoy, 21,
Holohan, Garry, 205–7.
Holohan, Patrick, 160, 205.
Hopkins and Hopkins corner, 133 143.
Howth gun-running, 5.

I.

Igel, Wolff von, 24, 28, 106.
Imperial Hotel, Dublin, 1916, 143, 156.
Indiu, 258, 260.
International law, and insurgents, 149–50.
Innistooskert, 109–10.
Irish Council Bill, 7.
Irish Freedom, 9, 20, 21.
Irish Independent, 38, 46.
Irish Life, 122, 127, 171, 201.
Irish Press, 210, 249, 260.
Irish Republican Brotherhood, secret revolutionary body, founded by James Stephens in 1858 to win independence by armed uprising, and affiliated with Clan na Gael, 1, 6, 7, 10, 61, 102, 116, 228; constitution and aims, 8, 9, and footnote, 61. See also Military Council.
Irish Republic, Macardle, 46, 73 footnote.
Irish Review, 19–21.
Irish Times 1916 Handbook, 140, 169, 212, 250, 267.
Irish Times, 192; paper store burned, 133.
Irish Volunteers, founded November, 1913, by Eoin MacNeill, at instigation of I.R.B., after Sir Edward Carson had started the Ulster Volunteers in North-East Ulster. The Irish Volunteers were known after the Rising as the Irish Republican Army, or I.R.A., passim.
Irish Worker, 146.

J.

Jacobs' Factory, 148, 164–171, 191.
James's Street, 173–8, 182.
Joy, Maurice, New York, 20.
Joyce, Major John V., 172, 173, footnote, 176.
Joyce, James, Citizen Army, 77.

K.

Kain, Tom, Citizen Army (d. 1948), 117–18.

Keating, Con, 79, 112, 113.
"Kelly's Fort," 134; 143.
Kelly, Fergus, 138.
Kelly, Michael, Citizen Army, 77.
Kelly, Alderman Tom, 74.
Kenny, John, New York, 25.
Kent, Mrs., Castlelyons, 233.
Kent, David, Castlelyons, 233.
Kent, Thomas, Castlelyons, executed May 9, 1916, 233.
Kent, William, Castlelyons, 233.
Keogh, Nurse, 178–9.
Kerry Champion, 38, 82, 237.
Kerryman, 81, 88, 237.
Kilmainham, 249.

L.

Larkin, Jim (1876–1947), 13, 136.
Larne gun-running, 4, 5, 15.
Lawless, Frank (d. 1922), Q.M. Fifth Dublin Battalion, 219-20.
Lawless, Jim, 220.
Lawless, Joseph, 219, 220, 223 footnote, 225.
Lawless, Peadar, North King Street victim, 215.
Leader, The, Dublin, 96.
Lenin, 14, 15, 17, 56.
Lennon, M. J., 4, 150, 192.
Le Roux, Louis N., 8, 22, 41, 73, 93.
Liberty Hall, Dublin, 4, 16, 56, 65, 71, 72, 74, 76, 77, 94, 96, 97, 99, 124, 130, 134, 140, 210.
Liffey Junction, 219.
Liebknecht, Karl, 30.
Limerick, 78, 79, 82, 83, 84–8, 112, 135, 233–6, 243.
Lime Park, 247.
Linenhall barracks, burning of, 148, 207–8.
Little, P. J., 70, 71.
Loch Neagh, 268.
Logue, Cardinal, 73.
Lloyd George, 208.
Looters, 10, 137, 138, 207.
Louth, 228, 250.
Lowe, Brigadier-General W. H. M., commander of Curragh forces and in charge of O'Connell Street area operations, 254, 255.
Lynch, Diarmuid, 153.
Lyons, George A., 49, 50, 53, footnote, 54, 61, 188, 192.

M.

MacAmhlaoibh, R., 149, 150.
Macardle, Dorothy, 46, 73.
MacBride, Major John (1865–1916), leader of Irish Brigade in Boer war, executed May 5, 1916, 158, 164, 166, 167.

McCann, John, 163.
McCann, Pierce, Tipperary Volunteer leader, T.D., East Tipperary, 1918, d. Gloucester Jail, March, 1919, 242.
McCartney, James, North King Street victim, 215–16.
McCarthy, John, 238.
MacCarthy, Justin, 40.
McCormack, R., Citizen Army, 77, 78, 120.
McCormack, District-Inspector, R.I.C., 221, 222.
McCullough, Denis, 8, 52, 53, 54.
MacCurtáin, Tomás (1882–1920), Lord Mayor of Cork and Volunteer leader, murdered by Black and Tans, March 19, 1920, 27, 230.
MacDermott, Seán (Seán MacDiarmada), 1884–1916, 6, 8, 9, 10, 48, 49, 50, 52, 53, 57, 63, 79, 81, 92, 93, 94, 112, 124, 129, 138, 147, 154, 252, 256, career, 8; and "Castle Document," 75; in the Rising, 124, 129, 138, 139, 147, 150, 154; and the surrender, 252, 256.
MacDonagh, Donagh, 39, 40, 73, 166.
MacDonagh, Thomas (1878-1916), colleague of Pearse at St. Enda's College, English lecturer, U.C.D., poet, Volunteer leader, 6, 11, 47, 89, 91, 92, 93, 94, 96, 97, 98, 120, 129, 135, 164–7, 170–1, 191, 205; Easter Eve statement, 96–7; leadership at Jacobs', 164–7; 170–1; alleged last speech, 258; courtmartial and execution, 259.
MacEntee, Seán, 250.
McGarrity, Joseph, Clan na Gael leader, 18, 107.
McGarry, Seán, Volunteer officer and editor Rossa Souvenir, 57, 59, 135.
McGee, Castleconnell, 88.
McGinn, Michael, 53.
McGooey, John, 45.
MacGowan, Seamus, Citizen Army, 140.
McGreevy, Thomas, 126, 127.
McGuinness, Joseph, later T. D., Longford, 204.
MacHale, Constable, R.I.C., 225.
McInerney, Thomas (d. 1922), 112, 113.
Macken, Peadar, 191.
MacKenna, Stephen, 51, 126–7.
McManus, Arthur, 60.

MacNeill, Eoin (1867–1944), Ulsterman, b. Glenarm, Co. Antrim,
one of the founders of the Gaelic
League in 1893, Professor of
early Irish history, U.C.D.,
founder and Chief of Staff, Irish
Volunteers, 1913, first Minister
of Education, Irish Free State,
21, 22, 26, 37, 49, 62–3, 64, 65,
66, 68, 83, 84, 85, 89, 90, 91, 92,
93, 94, 95, 96, 97, 102, 111, 113,
115–17, 119, 130, 145, 268;
policy on insurrection, 21–2,
62–3, 111; and Easter Eve,
89–96, 115–19; and Maxwell,
119; and "Castle Document,"
64–5; Pearse and, 42–3, 90–2, 145.
MacNeill, James, 65.
MacSwiney, Mary, 27, 230, 231,
232.
MacSwiney, Terence (1879–1920),
Volunteer leader and Lord Mayor
of Cork; died in Brixton Prison,
October 25, 1920, after 74 days
on hunger-strike, 27, 230, 231.
Madden, D. S., Waterford, 109.
Magazine, Phoenix Park, 136, 174,
205–6.
Malcolm, James, pseudonym of
Joseph Plunkett, 39, 46.
Malone, Michael, Northumberland
Road garrison, 187, 193, 194,
196, 197.
Maloney, Dr. W. J., 15, 38, 42, 45.
Mallin, Michael, Citizen Army
leader, silk weaver, executed May
8, 1916, 167, 171; clash with
I.R.B. Military Council, 51–2;
in the Rising, 121–2.
Manahan, Liam, Galtee Battalion,
88–9, 241–43.
Marie, L., 205.
Marrowbone Lane distillery, 174,
175, 176, 181.
Markievicz, Constance (1868-1928),
52, 120–1.
Martin, Eamonn, 205, 206, 207.
Martyn, Edward, 266.
Maxwell, Sir John (1860–1928),
110, 162, 263–4; views on Rising,
110, 208–9; methods, 208, 209,
210, 263, 264; Bishop O'Dwyer
on, 264; Sir Francis Vane on,
162, 263; his libels on insurgents,
200; on North King Street
shootings, 162, 212; interview
with Pearse, 255.
Maxwell, Lady, 208.
Mellows, Barney, brother of Liam
Mellows, 205.

Mellows, Liam, Fianna and Volunteer leader, one of the organisers
of de Valera's American tour,
1919–20, T.D., Meath, Director
of Purchases, I.R.A., opposed
1921 Treaty, fought in Four
Courts under Rory O'Connor,
executed "as a reprisal," by
Free State Government, December 8, 1922, 10, 64, 149, 244–48,
265–67; and "Castle Document,"
64; as leader of Galway Rising,
149, 244–48, 265–67.
Mendicity Institution, 155–63.
Metropole Hotel, Dublin, 141.
Military Council, I.R.B., 6, 14, 15,
37, 39, 41, 47, 48, 50–4, 57, 58,
61–3, 64, 67, 70, 84, 91, 93, 96,
102, 108.
Molloy, Michael, compositor, 262
Molony, Helena, 61, 118.
Monaghan, Alfred, see Ailbhe
O Monachain.
Monaghan, Charles, 112, 113, 265.
Monk's bakery, 211.
Monteith, Robert, 12, 13, 16, 21,
32, 33, 36, 37, 38, 46, 79, 88, 93,
101, 235, 237, 238.
Moore lane, 154, 254.
Moore Street, 153, 154, 251–7.
Morkan, Eamonn, 216.
Mount Brown, 173, 176.
Mount Street bridge, 182, 193–202.
Mulcahy, Richard, Volunteer leader,
later Free State Minister of
Defence, 1922, and leader of Fine
Gael party, 220, 223, 227; at
Ashbourne, 220–3; Arbour Hill
interview with Pearse, 227.
Murphy, Richard, 196, 201.
Murphy, Seamus, 174.
Murphy, William Martin, 156.
Moyode Castle, 246, 266.

N.

Nadolny, Captain, 44, 45.
Nathan, Sir Matthew, Under Secre-
tary, 98, 99, 115.
Neazor, George, R.I.C., 239.
Nevinson, H. W., 12.
New Ireland, 70.
New Statesman, 71.
Nicholls, Harry, 120.
North King Street shootings, 162,
211–16; Maxwell on, 162, 212;
eye-witness accounts of, 212–16;
casualties, British and civilian,
212.

O.

Oates, Colonel, 181.

Oath of Allegiance, 40.
O Briain, Professor Liam, 94, 115-19.
O'Brien, Dr. C. M., 201.
O'Brien, Kathleen, Clonmel, 109.
O'Brien, Liam, compositor, 262.
O'Brien, William, Dublin, 59, 60.
O'Brien, William Smith, 1, 2, 195.
O'Callaghan, Denis, 206.
O'Callaghan, Michael, Tipperary, 241.
O'Casey, Seán, 59.
O'Connell, J. J. (d. 1944), 22, 65, 88, 90, 91, 230.
O'Connor, John, Kimmage garrison, 135, 138.
O'Connor, Sir James, 69.
O'Connor, Captain Joseph, 187, 188, 190.
O'Connor, Rory (1883-1922), later Director of Engineering, I.R.A.; leader of Four Courts garrison, 1922, executed by Free State Government, 70, 73.
O'Connor, Tommy, I.R.B. courier, 102, 103.
O'Duffy, Eimar, 73.
O'Dwyer, Dr., Bishop of Limerick, 68-9, 72, 263-4.
O'Farrell, Elizabeth, 150, 253-4.
O'Farrell, Father Martin, 266.
O'Grady, John, 170.
O'Hanrahan, Michael (1877-1917), writer, Gaelic Leaguer, Volunteer officer, executed May 4, 1916, 264.
O h-Eidhin, Prionsias, 246, 247, 248.
O'Hegarty, P. S., 49, 50.
O'Kelly, Dr. Seamus, 70, 94, 115, 116.
O'Kelly, Seán T., b. 1883, later President of Ireland, ˅9.
O'Leary, Mort., pilot, 1c˅, 110.
O Lochlainn, Colm, 73, 11˅, 113.
O'Mahoney, R.A.M.C., 147, 258.
O'Neill, John, 78.
O'Neill, Owen Roe, 20.
O'Rahilly, The (1875-1916), 57, 93, 94, 95, 124, 137, 139, 149, 125, 153, 234, 254.
O'Reilly, John Boyle, 40.
O'Reilly, M. W., 146.
O'Shannon, Cathal, 61, 63, 268.
O'Shea, P. N. T., Castlegregory, 109.

P.

Parliamentary Party, Irish, 2, 3, 4, 7.
Partridge, W., 78, 79.
Pearse, P. H. (1879-1916), 6, 7, 10, 11, 21, 25, 34, 42-3, 47, 49, 57, 59, 62, 64-5, 76, 79, 80, 82-3, 84, 85, 86, 89, 90-3, 94, 96, 97, 108, 111, 113, 116, 124, 126, 127, 129, 130, 132, 135, 139, 142, 143, 144, 145, 146, 148, 149, 150, 151, 153, 154, 155, 156; and Germany, 42-3, 260-1; and Connolly, 48-9, 51-2, 59, 145; and I.R.B., 11; visit to U.S.A. early in 1914, 25; and Casement, 21, 34; and "Castle Document," 64-5; and Rising plans, 79, 80, 82-3; courtmartial and last speech, 258-61.
Pearse, William (1881-1916), 142, 143.
Pilsudski, Joseph, 15.
Playfair, Magazine Fort caretaker's son shot, 205.
Plough and Stars flag, 156.
Plunkett, George, 73, 124, 133, 172-3.
Plunkett, Jack, 73.
Plunkett, Joseph, poet, member of Military Council, and signatory of Proclamation, executed May 4, 1916, 6, 11, 67-73, 75, 98, 124, 129, 146, 151-2, 258; and "Castle Document," 67-73, 75, 98; journey to Germany, 39, 41; final message to Casement, 45-6; Connolly's opinion of, 51; on surrender terms, 252, 260.
Plunkett, Philomena, 102, 103.
Price, Major Ivor H., 72, 115, 117.

Q.

Quinn, John, 23.
Quinn's Nursing Home, Miss, 73.

R.

Rafferty, Tom, Ashbourne, 225.
Rafter, Seamus, Wexford, 249.
Redmond, John E. (1856-1918), leader of Irish Parliamentary Party, 5.
Reidy, James, New York, 8, 105.
"Reilly's Fort," 211, 216.
Reis's, 135.
Reynolds, George, Clanwilliam House garrison, 187, 193, 196, 198, 200, 201, 202.
Reynolds, John J., 162, 212.
Rintelen, Captain von, 106.
Robbins, Frank, Citizen Army, 77, 78, 120, 121, 261.
Robinson, Seamus, 133.
Roe's distillery, 174, 175.

Ronan, William, 196, 201, 202.
Rooney, N., Ashbourne, 220, 225
Rossa, Jeremiah O'Donovan (1831–1915), 57, 58.
Rossborough, Major, 180.
Rowe, Head Constable, R.I.C., 233.
Russell, Seán, 141.
Ryan, Father F. M., O.P., 240, 241.
Ryan, Dr. James, 146, 147, 250, 252.

S.

"Sceilg," 173, 231.
Sears, David, 173, 182, 183, 185.
Shanagher, Sergeant, R.I.C., 224.
Shaw, George Bernard, 263.
Shelbourne Hotel, 77, 121, 122, 170.
Shiubhlaigh, Máire Nic (Mrs. Eamonn Price), 171.
Shortis, Patrick (1894–1916), 153.
Simon Commission Report, 169.
Smyth, District-Inspector, R.I.C., 224.
Socialist, Edinburgh, 60.
South Dublin Union, 96, 136, 149, 172–86, 207.
Spindler, Karl, 28, 29, 43, 44, 101, 104, 105, 110.
Sheehy-Skeffington, Francis (1878–1916), 70, 71, 167-70.
Sheehy-Skeffington, Mrs. H., 168, 169.
Stack, Austin (1880–1929) son of William Moore Stack, Kerry Fenian leader, later honorary secretary, Sinn Fein, T.D., Kerry, leader of many hunger-strikes, Minister of Home Affairs, Dáil Eireann, sentenced to penal servitude for life, 1916, 38, 39, 79–82, 101-14, 237–38 ; and Kerry landing, 79–81, 108-10, 237–38 ; his own statement on Easter Week in Kerry, 38, 237–40.
Staines, Liam, 161.
Staines, Michael, 125, 146.
Stephen's Green, 77, 78, 120, 121, 122.
Stephenson, P. J., 155, 159.
Swords, 134, 218.

T.

Taylor, Lieutenant-Colonel H., 211–12.
Telephone Exchange, Dublin, 174.
Thornton, Frank, 124, 133.

Tipperary, 88, 241, 242.
Tivoli Theatre, 140.
Tobin, James, 59.
Torch, The, 51, 53.
Traynor, Oscar, 141.
Treacy, Seán (1895–1920), 242–3.
Tricolour, 126, 154, 185.
Tullira Castle, 266.
Tuohy, Sergeant, R.I.C., 220.
Tyrone, 250, 267, 268.

U.

Ulster, Rising and, 79, 267–8.

V.

Valentia, 112.
Vane, Sir Francis, 162, 172, 179–81, 263.
Vinegar Hill, 249.

W.

Wafer, Captain Tom, 135, 141.
Walpole, Harry, 147.
Walsh, James, 196, 201, 202.
Walsh, Tom, 196, 201, 202.
Walsh, J. J., 135.
Walsh, Dr. William, Archbishop of Dublin (1841-1921), 62, 65, 67, 68, 69, 73, 135.
Waterville, 112.
Watkins brewery, 174, 175.
Wedel, Count Georg von, 34
Weldon, Sir Anthony, 236.
Weston, Charles, 220, 223.
Wexford, 149, 248–50.
Whelan, Constable, R.I.C., 267.
Wicklow, 149.
Williams and Woods factory, 153.
Wilson, Peter, Swords, 162.
Wimborne, Lord, 7, 98–9.
Wolfe Tone Annual, 159, 245.
Woodenbridge, Redmond's speech at, 59.
Workers' Republic, 48, 49, 54, 55, 56, 70, 71, 76.

Y.

Young, Sergeant, R.I.C., 224.

Z.

Zeppelins, 6.
Zimmermann, German Foreign Minister, and Casement, 28, 29.
Zulus, 24.

PRINTED BY CAHILL AND CO., LTD., PARKGATE PRINTING WORKS, DUBLIN.

GREAT WESTERN RAILWAY

RIVER T

Glasnev
Cemetery

Phoenix Park

Cross q
J

Artillery &
used here

Viceregal
Lodge

Marlboro
Barracks

Richmond Asylu

North Dublin
Union

Police Barracks

Royal Military
Hospital

Richm
Hospi

Magazine Fort

Military
H.Q
Parkgate

MAIN ROAD

Royal
Barracks

North Kin

RIVER T

CABRA

Mendicity
Institution

Islandbridge
Barracks

Kingsbridge
Station

Steevens Hospital

Christ
C

RIVER LIFFEY

GREAT SOUTHERN & WESTERN RAILWAY

Kilmainham

Royal Hospital

JAMES'S STREET

Guinness's Brewery

RIVER CAMAC

Richmond
Barracks

MOUNT BROWN

South Dublin
Union

The Coombe
Hospital

St

Rialto

Dolphin's Barn

SOUTH CIRCULAR ROAD

GRAND CANAL

We

Map of
DUBLIN
Easter 1916

Mount Jerome
Cemetery